# THE FIRST NEW LEFT

THE FIRST NEW LEFT

# THE FIRST NEW LEFT
## British Intellectuals After Stalin

MICHAEL KENNY

LAWRENCE & WISHART
LONDON

LAWRENCE & WISHART LIMITED
144a Old South Lambeth Road
London SW8 1XX

First Published 1995 by Lawrence & Wishart
© Michael Kenny
ISBN 0 85315 797 9

Designed and typeset by Jan Brown Designs
Printed and bound by Biddles Ltd, Guildford and King's Lynn

# Contents

*For*
*Alf and Maureen Kenny*

# Acknowledgements

I began my research into the New Left as a postgraduate student in the Department of Politics at Manchester University, finished my doctorate on this subject whilst a Lecturer in Politics at the Queen's University, Belfast, and have now completed this study as a Lecturer in Politics at Sheffield University. *En route*, I have received a considerable amount of help from different sources and am grateful for this opportunity to acknowledge some intellectual debts.

I conducted interviews and corresponded with a number of former participants and contemporary commentators whose recollections helped me tremendously. Sheila Benson, John Rex, Francis Mulhern, Michael Rustin, John Cox, Fred Halliday, Paul Rose and Stuart Hall provided me with a wide range of valuable insights into the life and times of the early New Left, whilst John Saville not only gave me the considerable benefit of his historical wisdom, but also allowed me to use his personal records from this period prior to depositing them with the University of Hull; the reader will find that I have made extensive use of this rich resource in chapter one. I am especially grateful to John for his kindness when I was in Hull.

I have been the grateful beneficiary of help from the staff at the following institutions: the John Rylands Library, Manchester University; the British Library at Bloomsbury; the Modern Records Centre, Warwick University; the Hull University Library; the Central Reference Library, Manchester; the Bodleian Library at Oxford University; the Library at the Queen's University, Belfast; the Sheffield University Library; and the National Museum for Labour History in Manchester.

During my postgraduate studies in Manchester, I was fortunate to have three supervisors: Lewis Minkin and Norman Geras were always wise and encouraging; and David Howell helped me enormously with his unfailing support, high critical standards and acute intellect. Geraint Parry made some valuable observations as one of the examiners for my doctorate, whilst Anthony Arblaster has influenced this project in different ways: first, as a perceptive and benign external examiner; and, latterly, as a colleague who has proved infinitely tolerant in the face of my persistent enquiries about the New Left. In Belfast, Robert Eccleshall, Vincent Geoghegan and Richard English provided encouragement and advice on numerous questions. Since coming to Sheffield, I have learnt much from my new colleagues on matters more or less related to the New Left, and have been helped by them in different ways. I am grateful to James Meadowcroft, Geraint Williams, David Marquand, Patrick Seyd, Ian Kearns, Steve Ludlam and Martin Smith. Andrew Gamble has been connected with this project since he asked me some (overly) perceptive questions as a member of my interview board in Belfast, and, more recently, as the dispenser of thoughtful advice on an earlier draft of parts of this text.

For permission to reproduce excerpts from their contemporary correspondence, I would like to thank Stuart Hall, John Saville and John Rex. And for permission to reprint the photograph on the front cover, I am grateful to Roger Mayne. Finally, my thanks go to Matt Seaton (formerly of Lawrence and Wishart) for his encouragement, and Sally Davison for her editorial skill, critical faculties and enthusiasm. The responsibility for any inaccuracies or errors is mine alone.

Michael Kenny
January 1995

# Introduction

The first wave of the British New Left, which rose and fell between 1956 and 1962, is an important, if unusual, chapter in the history of socialism in the post-war period. This distinctive intellectual and political current emerged in an exciting period, characterised by profound political and social change. In different ways the New Left influenced the ideas of mainstream politicians as well as broader sections of the labour movement. Its thinkers were often prescient in their sensitivity to future developments in British political life.

The influence of the New Left is perhaps surprising since it emerged outside the main political parties and disintegrated within six years; but the early New Left continually crops up in the literature on modern British politics and political thought. This is partly because of the number of significant political and intellectual figures who passed through this movement. The involvement of the late Edward Thompson and Raymond Williams, as well as, among others, Stuart Hall, Perry Anderson, John Rex, Peter Worsley, John Saville, Charles Taylor, Raphael Samuel, Jean McCrindle and Michael Barratt Brown, has generated much interest in this formation.[1] The influence of the New Left is also reflected in the number of references to it in historical reflections on the post-war Labour Party. It figures too in histories of academic disciplines and intellectual fields as diverse as cultural studies, sociology, political theory, political economy and international relations.[2] Despite these citations, no coherent, full-length study of this formation has been published.[3]

This first wave of the New Left is remarkable for the number of intellectuals, politicians, critics and artists who participated within it or came into contact with its activities and ideas. Returning to the early New Left fills a number of gaps in relation to the intellectual and political development of some of Britain's most significant radical thinkers in the

1

post-war period. Indeed, three of the New Left's key intellectuals – Stuart Hall, Edward Thompson and Raymond Williams – produced some of their most important work at this time, though this period in their intellectual careers has generally been underplayed. Unfortunately, the critical assessment of their ideas, and those of other influential intellectual critics, has been patchy: there is a dearth of serious analysis of the historical, political and biographical dimensions of their, and others', intellectual development. Hopefully, this study will contribute, in a small way, to the re-evaluation of the ideas and influence of some of Britain's leading intellectual radicals.

Despite the many references to it, this movement has suffered from a number of misconceptions which have obscured understanding of its specificity and originality. The contemporary commentator is faced with the disturbingly wide range of judgements which have been made about the early New Left, not only by former participants, but also by later academic interpreters. It has, on different occasions, been presented as a radical voice within the labour movement,[4] a failed precursor of the later New Left,[5] a 'talking shop' of little political significance,[6] and a marginal and utopian intellectual current.[7] Nearly all of these judgements have been made on an *a priori* basis, without consideration of the context, culture and complexity of the movement, nor of the political circumstances which seriously affected its prospects. Many have emerged from perspectives which ascribe a designated role to the New Left – as a revolutionary alternative to Labour, or a 'think-tank' for the Labour leadership, for example – and then criticise it for having failed to perform. For many commentators, therefore, especially those for whom the New Left was a sub-plot in a larger story (of Labour politics, the rise of new social movements,[8] or developments in socialist theory), the movement was too utopian, too revolutionary, too reformist, too heterogenous, and even too clever! When dealing with the New Left's failure (another 'given' in much of its historiography), a litany of explanations has been offered: the New Left failed to find a home in the Labour Party; failed to appropriate the Campaign for Nuclear Disarmament as the vehicle for its political ideas; failed to become sufficiently novel in its political orientation;[9] and failed to generate a serious revolutionary alternative. All of these judgements are underpinned by the assumption that the New Left's political identity can be reduced to one particular strategy or project. They have sustained accounts which, on the whole, have done little justice to the singular political and intellectual make-up of the movement. When the eclecticism of this movement has been observed, this too has been regarded

2

as an *a priori* weakness.[10]

These assessments have been supplemented by generally hostile interpretations of the New Left's intellectual contribution. For Perry Anderson – the nemesis of the first New Left in the minds of some, the ideas of this movement were characterised by moralism, populism and empiricism. The first New Left, in his view, failed to develop a serious or substantial analysis of the political and social worlds it inhabited.[11] In the eyes of some commentators, the movement was hampered by the Marxism of its ex-communist participants; according to others, however, its shift from Marxism resulted in ideological eclecticism and ineffective idealism.[12]

Longstanding assumptions about the relationship between the early and later New Lefts have compounded these interpretations. Perry Anderson's suggestion that a naive and populist first wave was supplanted by a more metropolitan and theoretically potent second is still widely invoked.[13] His own reminiscences, and those of the other main actors in the 'drama' surrounding *New Left Review* from 1960-62 (when Perry Anderson was installed as editor) have been widely influential, but are obviously inconsistent as accounts of this period.[14] No single, uncontested narrative of these events exists, whilst the strained personal atmosphere in which the movement broke up has bequeathed an awkward legacy in which individual reminiscence is frequently bound up with personal accusation. As became clear at a conference held in 1987 to reassess the significance of the early New Left, the heat of these particular controversies may have cooled, yet its former participants are no more likely to agree about the nature and meaning of the movement.[15] For the historian of this movement and its ideas (especially one born after these events), research into the New Left throws up a daunting set of problems.

Certainly, the British New Left is known today in terms of the theoretical project pursued within *New Left Review* since Perry Anderson's editorship began in 1962. For many former participants and commentators, it is clear that a line should be drawn in 1962 when the first New Left was apparently replaced by an entirely different formation.[16] This interpretation has been sustained by the dramatic dispute which began in the mid-1960s between the figureheads of each wave – Edward Thompson and Perry Anderson. In the wake of the profound political and theoretical rupture between these men, it seems obvious that the different New Left generations which each represents were worlds apart.[17] In fact, the neatness of such a division is historically misleading. The relationship between the ideas of these different currents was more complex and interdependent than this reading suggests. My own emphasis on the intellectual project associated with Raymond Williams, which at times was quite distinct from Edward Thompson's politics, undermines the notion of a clear division. Aspects of Raymond Williams' work influenced Perry Anderson, among others, and provided an important thematic bridge between the first and later New Lefts. The notion of a complete break between these groups is a fanciful reconstruction which has suited both antagonists and their supporters.

Despite these intellectual continuities, the first New Left expired as a meaningful political project in 1962. The rapidity of its demise led the late Peter Sedgwick to suggest that it functioned as a milieu rather than a political movement.[18] Whilst true in some respects, such an interpretation threatens to neglect the political dimensions of the early New Left's project, which overlapped with the intellectual ferment it unleashed. Its activists launched a number of political initiatives: alongside its journals, clubs were set up throughout England and Scotland, whilst activists considered themselves part of a movement which pursued national as well as local goals. The first New Left's cerebral character is undeniable, but Sedgwick's notion of a milieu underplays the extent to which the first New Left was always more than a 'talking-shop' for disaffected intellectuals. New Left thinkers and activists always straddled the intellectual and political worlds and tapped into different traditions within both. Much of their creativity and distinctiveness flowed from their attempt to juxtapose creative intellectual practice and engagement with hard political realities. Taking the eclectic nature of the first New Left as a starting point, we can better appreciate the variety of directions in which its thinking pointed, obviating simple interpretations of its meaning and failure.

This judgement is reinforced by a careful consideration of the overlapping contexts which shaped the early New Left. Most immediately, the New Left emerged as a response to the problems facing the dominant traditions of the left in Britain – the reformist social democracy of Labour, which had tried in vain to build a 'new Jerusalem' after the war, and the Marxism-Leninism of the Communist Party. The secret speech delivered by Khruschev to the Twentieth Congress of the Communist Party of the Soviet Union in 1956 began to lay bare the realities of socialism in Eastern Europe; the invasion of Hungary by Soviet forces, later in the same year, subsequently engendered a profound political and ethical crisis for communists around the world. 1956 was also the year of another traumatic and, with hindsight, highly symbolic geo-political event. The failed Anglo-French military expedition to the Suez canal encouraged the realisation that Britain's position in the world was fundamentally different in the post-war world; and that with the relinquishing of formal imperial responsibilities, a new national identity and self-image had yet to be forged.

The New Left also emerged on the cusp of some longer term social and economic changes which have transformed the context of modern British politics: not least the steady erosion of the industrial and manufacturing centres which were predominant in the economy during the previous century; the impact of 'affluence' on different groups within British society; and the tensions generated by the changing relationship between state and economy in post-war Britain. In the 1950s these developments encouraged some of Labour's leading intellectuals to reflect critically on the party's historic mission. The New Left also sought to re-evaluate some of the left's core values and assumptions in the context of the social and economic changes slowly reshaping the political landscape. Above all, the movement's intellectuals sought to address the pluralisation of social identities evident in the modern world, exploring the implications of this process for socialism. The New Left's sensitivity to the diverse interests of different constituencies – school leavers, teachers, immigrant 'communities' and new-town dwellers, for example – merged with an instinctive celebration of grassroots mobilisation within civil society. Whereas previously, these groups had been recognised as 'objects' of concern by the left (if they were noticed at all), for the New Left, their particular interests and experiences had to be unified within a more expansive and diverse coalition – a new 'historical bloc', in Gramscian terms.

The New Left can thus be seen as an early response to a long-term representational crisis which has since brought into being a number of radical social and political campaigns and movements. The difficulties experienced by currents which attempt to survive on the fringes of the British party system, and between the poles of orthodox communism and social democracy, were anticipated by the early New Left's praxis. It was not the first socialist current in Britain to occupy this space; the socialism and new life movement of the late nineteenth century, the guild socialists of the 1920s and several Trotskyite organisations were important antecedents. The first New Left was singular, however, in its anticipation of a more participatory and pluralistic conception of political mobilisation. One of its most important legacies consisted of the experience and analytical insight it gathered for subsequent radical movements, an influence acknowledged by several leading British feminists.[19]

Appreciating these different contexts is central to understanding the troubled and divided political soul of this movement. As will become clear, this was always an eclectic milieu in which different traditions co-existed, often awkwardly; nevertheless, important intellectual and political insights were generated by this movement. The critical judgements offered in most accounts have tended to underplay the distinctive and novel aspects of New Left politics. Like the English working class in Edward Thompson's classic contemporary study, the New Left needs to be rescued from the 'condescension of posterity'.

An unfortunate consequence of the dismissal of the significance of the movement's praxis has been the absence of any serious reflection on the relationship between indigenous British New Left theorising and theoretical developments elsewhere. Perry Anderson's exaggerated picture of the early New Left is largely to blame here; underpinning the editorial policy of *New Left Review* after 1962 was the belief that British socialism was cut adrift from exciting theoretical developments in the Marxist tradition which were occurring elsewhere. In fact, following David Forgacs' suggestion that Gramscian concepts have been, 'central to the theoretical reconstruction of Marxism in Britain at all stages since the late 1950s',[20] it can be argued that the intellectual shifts registered by figures in this milieu played a more significant 'brokerage' role for the dissemination of Gramscian ideas than has generally been recognised. This process was important because it left a number of intellectuals open to particular theoretical influences over subsequent decades. In some ways, these figures were groping towards an indigenous version of the theoretical advances registered elsewhere in these years, a process described by Richard Johnson as a turn towards the experiential and cultural throughout Western Marxism.[21] Under the influence of Raymond Williams, some New Left critics developed a distinctive methodology – drawn from his emphasis upon social totality – for understanding contemporary social processes and political changes. This was, however, always a rudimentary and, with hindsight, unfinished project which few sustained in this particular form once the early New Left dissolved.

The New Left's role as a broker for Gramscian themes is also illuminated by consideration of the unique alliances with cultural practitioners and ideas which the movement forged. This was an unusual moment in the history of the British left when a genuinely diverse set of voices, from the cultural as well as political realm, combined for an intense reassessment of the socialist project. Almost inevitably, the results of the process were uneven and politically problematic. Yet, the impact and nature of this unusual conversation have been submerged beneath the often peremptory judgements of this movement.

My assessment of the first New Left's political ideas is prefaced by a description and assessment of its history as both a political movement and organisation in chapter one. To reconstruct the events of this period, I have drawn upon a range of sources, including the verbal and written accounts of some of the key participants, as well as surviving correspondence and records of the period.[22] In chapter two an important, yet neglected, debate about class and consciousness, based around the ideas of Stuart Hall, is highlighted. This chapter focuses on an important aspect of the New Left's legacy – its impact on the reassessment of the socialist project, a process which has intensified in subsequent decades. In chapter three, Edward Thompson's normative alternative to Stalinism – socialist humanism – is reassessed: problems within this formulation are juxtaposed with analysis of the importance and influence of his ideas. Despite the hegemony of his humanist discourse in the early New Left milieu, it is suggested that socialist humanism was undermined by alternative emphases at the very moment of its conception. In chapter four I turn to Raymond Williams' shifting ideas in this period, which provided the basis for an important and critical body of social and cultural analysis produced by New Left writers. This culminated in a fledgling attempt to develop a cultural politics alongside a theoretical reappraisal of contemporary popular culture. In chapter five the New Left's political analysis is examined. Here I argue that a distinctive contribution to socialist political economy was made by a number of its critics, though their work was debilitated by a persistent tension between the concern for community and the modernist aspects of New Left politics. In chapter six I turn to the international ideas of this movement in the light of its involvement with the contemporary peace movement. Despite the appearance of unanimity on these questions, close examination reveals a number of hidden tensions and differences, not least about national identity: these prefigure the difficulties which the left has encountered with this agenda in subsequent decades. In conclusion, I suggest different analytical contexts in which a movement such as this might be placed in order to shed light on its nature and significance. Above all, assessment of the New Left reveals much about the troubled relationship between intellectuals and political life in Britain.

NOTES

1    See S.Hall, 'Cultural Studies and the Centre', in S.Hall *et al*, *Culture, Media, Language: Working Papers in Cultural Studies 1972-1979*, Hutchinson, London 1980, pp15-47; M.Rustin, *For a Pluralist Socialism*, Verso, London 1985; R.Williams, 'The British Left', *New Left Review*, 30, 1964, pp18-26; E.P.Thompson, 'An Open Letter to Leszek Kolakowski', in *The Poverty of Theory And Other Essays*, Merlin, London 1978, pp303-403; M.MacEwen, *The Greening of a Red*, Pluto, London, 1991; and the contributions collected in R.Archer *et al* (eds), *Out of Apathy: Voices of the New Left Thirty Years On*, Verso, London 1989.

2    See A.J.Davies, *To Build a New Jerusalem: The British Labour Movement from the 1880s to the 1990s*, Michael Joseph, London 1992; K.Jeffrys, *The Labour Party Since 1945*, Macmillan, London 1993; D.Howell, *British Social Democracy: A Study in Development and Decay*, Croom Helm, London 1976; J.Callaghan, *Socialism in Britain Since 1884*, Basil Blackwell, Oxford 1990. For consideration of this movement against a range of different intellectual backgrounds, see A.Davies and P.Saunders, 'Literature, politics and society', in A.Sinfield (ed), *Society and Literature 1945-1970*, Methuen, London pp13-50; L.Jardine and J.Swindells, *What's Left: Women in Culture and the Labour Movement*, Routledge, London 1990; E.Wilson, *Only Halfway to Paradise: women in postwar Britain 1945-1968*, Tavistock, London 1980; Hall, *op cit*; Rustin, *op cit*.

3    A number of theses have been completed on this movement, however: C.Bamford, 'The Early New Left in Britain, 1956-62; the Politics of Commitment', PhD, University of Edinburgh, 1983; G.Hughes, 'The First New Left in Britain', M.A, University of Keele, 1973; D.Holden, 'The First New Left in Britain, 1954-1962', PhD, University of Wisconsin-Madison, 1976; T.Wengraf, 'An essay on the early new left review', M.A, University of Birmingham, 1979.

4    See Davies, Jeffrys and Callaghan, *op cit*.

5    L.Chun, *The British New Left*, Edinburgh University Press, Edinburgh 1994.

6    P.Sedgwick, 'The Two New Lefts', in D.Widgery, *The Left in Britain 1956-1968*, Penguin, Harmondsworth 1976, pp131-55; R.Bellamy, 'Review of *Out of Apathy*', *Capital and Class*, 40, 1990, p189.

7    See R.Kilroy Silk, *Socialism Since Marx*, Allen Lane/Penguin, London 1972, p316.

8    D.Hebdige, *Hiding in the Light*, Comedia, London 1988, pp187-8.

9    N.Young, *An Infantile Disorder? The Crisis and Decline of the New Left*, Routledge and Kegan Paul, London 1977, p148.

10   Young, *op cit*.

11   P.Anderson, *Arguments Within English Marxism*, New Left Books, London 1980.

12   See J.Cameron, 'The New Left in Britain', *The Listener*, 8, 15 and 22 September, 1960; J.Weinstein, 'The left, old and new', *Socialist Revolution*, July/August 1972, p40; Sedgwick, *op cit*.

13   Chun, *op cit*, accepts the later New Left characterisation of this earlier movement rather uncritically, pp62-3.

14   See Thompson, *op cit*; and Anderson, *op cit*.

15   Archer, *et al*, *op cit*.

16   For a more subtle assessment, though, see Williams, *op cit*.

17  See P.Anderson, 'Origins of the Present Crisis', *New Left Review*, 23, 1963, pp26-53; and 'The Myths of Edward Thompson, or Socialism and Pseudo Empiricism', *New Left Review*, 35, 1965, pp2-42; T.Nairn, 'The British Political Elite', *New Left Review*, 23, 1963, pp19-25; and 'The English Working Class', *New Left Review*, 27, 1964, pp43-57.

18  Sedgwick, *op cit*.

19  S.Rowbotham, 'The Women's Movement and Organizing for Socialism', in S.Rowbotham, H.Wainwright and L.Segal, *Beyond the Fragments: Feminism and the Making of Socialism*, Merlin, London 1979, pp21-155, p21.

20  D.Forgacs, 'Gramsci and Marxism in Britain', *New Left Review*, 176, 1989, pp70-88, p70.

21  R.Johnson, 'Culture and the historians' in J.Clarke, C.Critcher and R.Johnson (eds), *Working-Class Culture: Studies in History and Theory*, Hutchinson, London 1980, pp41-71.

22  For a list of my interviewees and correspondents, see my Acknowledgments. I have made greatest use of Lawrence Daly's records, which are kept at the Modern Records Centre at Warwick University, and contain a welter of correspondence and memoranda from his stint on the *New Left Review*'s editorial board; and the hitherto unused collection of letters and documents which John Saville has now deposited at the Labour Archive at Hull University. I consulted the latter before they had been catalogued and have listed items from them according to the titles of the files in which they had been placed. I have benefitted enormously from the insight which these provide into the minds of leading participants in the *New Reasoner* milieu throughout this period.

# CHAPTER ONE

# The Rise and Fall of the First New Left

Sadly, after 1918 this tradition of pluralism, tolerance and of building a movement from the bottom up was largely, but certainly not completely, squeezed between the pincer movement of labourism, concerned above all with electoral politics and the smooth running of a party machine, and Communism which sacrificed personal consideration to the demands of 'the Party'.[1]                                          A.J.Davies, 1992

Then suddenly, from 1956 onwards, there came a crack in the social-political situation that relaxed old allegiances and left conventional parties frozen into postures that ignored these changes. There came Poland, Hungary, Suez, death of Stalin, rise of Africa, the New Left, the teenage phenomenon, the race riots, the teacher strikes, Osborne and the new wave writers, and, for what it is worth, CND...[2]

Colin MacInnes, 1962

Today Molly rang me. Tommy is involved with the new group of young socialists. Molly said she had sat in a corner listening while they talked. She felt as if 'she had gone back a hundred years to her own youth' when she was first in the CP. 'Anna, it was extraordinary! ... Here they are, with no time for the CP, and quite right too, and no time for the Labour Party ..., there are a few hundred of them, scattered up and down Britain, yet they all talk as if Britain will be socialist in about ten years at the latest, and through their efforts of course ... I felt as if they were mad or as if I were mad ... but the point is, Anna, it's just like us, isn't it? Well? And even using that awful jargon we've been making fun of for years and years ... The point is, oughtn't they to be more intelligent that we were, Anna?.'[3]                                          Doris Lessing, 1972

These three extracts provide vastly different interpretations of the first New Left. According to A.J.Davies, the roots of this movement lay in the 'socialism and new life' tradition of writers such as Edward Carpenter and William Morris, which was marginalised in the labour movement in the early years of the twentieth century. In his analysis, the New Left represents an interesting and lively variation of a much older tradition – the articulation of a broader and more creative socialist agenda against the dominant traditions of the British left. Colin MacInnes' somewhat breathless, contemporary commentary suggests that the New Left is best understood as one aspect of a larger political and social sea-change. In the late 1950s, the political map was being redrawn as old certainties were rapidly supplanted by new ideas and trends. The New Left, in his view, constituted an unconventional response by forward-thinking sections of the socialist movement to this fundamental shift. Finally, Doris Lessing's account of this movement, portrayed through the eyes of her fictional character Molly, presents an altogether more cynical view. The New Left was trapped by its history, unable to avoid the mindless optimism and meaningless jargon of the principal organisations on the left: beneath the veneer of novelty and liberation from the past lay the moral and intellectual bankruptcy of previous socialist generations.

Each of these readings reveals something about the significance and meaning of this unconventional political mobilisation, and has been repeated, in different guises, by later critics. Indeed, they have infiltrated nearly all analyses of the New Left, generating interpretations which regard it either as a marginal group concerned with the re-creation of an older political tradition, or as a decisively new force on the British political scene, tapping into the 'new times' of the post-war world, or as an attempt to perpetuate old left ideas and values under the cover of a glossy, new rhetoric.[4]

The first and third of these interpretations have proved most popular with later commentators, especially those who refer to the New Left in the course of their assessments of the labour movement or Labour Party. Juxtaposing the New Left with these traditions encourages critics to regard the movement either as the continuation of an older socialist lineage or as an intellectually orientated aberration. One of the most frequent criticisms emanating from labour movement historians concerns the absence of coherent organisation within this milieu. A.J.Davies, for example, argues that 'in rebelling against Communist Party rigidity, the New Left often went too far the other way and decried the need for any kind of formal organisation';[5] whilst one former participant is even more critical, describing the movement as 'a bunch of amateurs'.[6] This accusation has been supplemented by the belief that the New Left failed because of its ambivalence towards the 'real' centres of political power – the Labour Party or the industrial working class. Whilst some important observations are contained in these arguments, many of the criticisms of the first New Left's organisational abilities have emerged from writers engaged in the practice of labour history, who seem reluctant to develop historical empathy for this different kind of political milieu.

The literature on the first New Left has frequently pointed to its historical antecedents, ranging from *fin-de-siècle* socialists, nineteenth-century anarchists, the Popular Front of the 1930s, the Left Book Club and the Commonwealth Party during the Second World War.[7] These were all important precursors for the New Left. Like these earlier currents, it sought, unsuccessfully, to reform the practice and philosophy of British labourism. Comparison with the guild socialist movement of the inter-war period is especially revealing. As Stuart MacIntyre argues, G.D.H.Cole and likeminded intellectuals attempted to stake out an alternative to Leninism and Labour Party electoralism. They combined theoretical innovation – the development of a 'pluralist school of political theory', utopian speculation and the attempt to redefine socialism within the labour movement, stressing the replacement of the state by co-operative institutions.[8] The parallel with the New Left is striking, and was the product, in part, of the direct influence of figures such as G.D.H.Cole on this later current. Stuart MacIntyre's evaluation of guild socialism seems appropriate for the New Left too:

> The influence of Guild Socialism should be calculated not by its accomplishments, for it failed absolutely to achieve its objects; nor by the membership of its organisation, the National Guilds League, which was never more than a thousand; but by its indirect influence in the wider labour movement. Its warning of the dangers of state socialism caused many to reconsider their assumption that state ownership was synonymous with socialism.[9]

The first New Left undoubtedly rediscovered some important and neglected ideas within the repertoire of the British left, and occupied a similar role to this earlier movement – on the fringes of the Labour Party, but continually challenging its orthodoxies. This comparison also illuminates some absences in the first New Left's thinking. Aspects of the rich heritage of unconventional socialist thought in Britain were 'lost' in the intervening years, resulting in the absence of theoretical attention to the state among this later milieu (discussed in chapter five). This, and other silences – about national identity for instance (discussed in chapter six) – weakened the movement's intellectual project.

The New Left was also inspired by the Left Book Club of the 1930s, a project which fused cultural and political activity and fought to retain its independence from the Labour and Communist Parties. Kevin Morgan notes how 'the Club seems to have fulfilled the sort of political functions in which the Labour Party has traditionally been deficient: disseminating literature, organising educational and cultural activities, public meetings and national rallies'.[10] The tasks of political agitation and education were also important to the first New Left, which reproduced the unusual occupational mix of the Club's participants, observed by John Lewis:

> What was a complete surprise was the awakening of interest among professional people, men of letters, poets, artists, actors and musicians... In addition to the groups organised by actors, poets, writers, artists, and musicians, there were organised groups of journalists, lawyers, architectural students and commercial travellers.[11]

This compares with Raphael Samuel's observation that the 'New Left seems to have appealed to people who wanted to get things done – supply teachers, shocked by the conditions of the secondary modern schools; young architects, eager to see a more generous use of planning powers; reformist trade-union officials, anxious to see decision-making returned to the ranks'.[12] Moreover, the Left Book Club represented aspects of the communist ethos which remained central to the wing of the New Left which congregated around the *New Reasoner* journal, shaping the responses of key individuals like John Saville and Edward Thompson to events in this period. They envisaged the construction of a broad coalition of political and social groups against the establishment, a process in which the left would play a vital leadership role.

Whilst the first New Left was never completely dominated by the past, it was, in many ways, unable to escape the legacy of such movements. But in this study greater emphasis is given to events and ideas after 1956 because the historical conditions in which the New Left operated have often been downplayed, resulting in little analysis of the possibilities and constraints which influenced its organisational efforts. A contextual assessment of its fortunes produces a more cautious judgement about its failure and permits a more systematic and balanced interpretation of its ideas. Simultaneously, a broader perspective on the problems which have beset the left in the post-war period illuminates the novelty and originality of New Left praxis.

This first chapter is concerned with the New Left as a political movement and the organisational dimension of its politics. It will become clear that simplistic characterisations of the 'anarchistic' or 'anti-organisational' beliefs of its devotees are misleading: the story of the New Left as a political movement is more complex, significant and interesting than such arguments suggest. In particular, scant attention has been paid to the possibility that the movement prefigured the shift to a more diverse and countercultural politics akin to the radical currents which emerged in British political life, such as feminism, environmentalism and anti-racism, in the 1970s and 1980s. Its organisational practice is, therefore, central to comprehending this movement's politics. Emerging when the forces of Labour and communism still predominated on the left, it anticipated the declining ability of these institutions to represent an increasingly diversified social and political sphere from the late 1960s onwards. In the account which follows, this movement's attempt to manage the tensions which arose from its particular historical location is critically assessed.

## THE NEW LEFT INTERNATIONALLY

The circumstances in which it was born left indelible marks upon the New Left in Britain. Significantly, it arose as part of a wider international reaction against the polarities of the Cold War and the frustrations of a new generation with both orthodox communism and social democracy. As we shall see, the formation of this current in the British context was disjointed and slow. Once the movement was underway, however, it became one of the most gifted and influential of the first wave of New Left mobilisations internationally. According to Stuart Hall, the New Left label was borrowed:

> from the movement known as the 'nouvelle gauche', an independent tendency in French politics associated with the weekly newspaper *France Observateur* and its editor, Claude Bourdet. Bourdet, a leading figure in the French Resistance, personified the attempt, after the war, to open a 'third way' in European politics, independent of the two dominant left positions of Stalinism and social democracy, 'beyond' the military power blocs of NATO and the Warsaw Pact, and opposed to both the American and Soviet presences in Europe.[13]

Whilst the development and character of the British movement was largely shaped by indigenous political developments, its vibrant eclecticism and political interests were mirrored by and influenced the New Left elsewhere. According to Wini Breines's study of the first wave of the New Left in the United States, this movement, like its British counterpart, was characterised by ideological pluralism, a concern for the concept of community and a commitment to developing a prefigurative conception of politics.[14] Whilst these movements varied widely according to national political culture and party system, the similarities between the first wave of New Left mobilisations in the late 1950s and early 1960s have been neglected. The implications of these similarities for any comparative study of New Left ideas is discussed at greater length in chapter seven.

## THE BIRTH OF THE NEW LEFT IN BRITAIN

The most salient connection between these movements in Western Europe was the crisis for communism which erupted in 1956, the year of Khruschev's secret speech detailing Stalinist atrocities and the Soviet invasion of Hungary. Yet, the impact of these events varied from country to country. According to the recollections of some of the figures who left the party in Britain at this time, the shift from communism to New Left commitment was slow and uneven. Indeed, for many, the party continued to provide a vital context, influencing the responses of many ex-communists to subsequent events and their new political surroundings. These reminiscences highlight some important features of this crisis, which subsequently shaped the internal politics of the New Left.[15] They reveal that little concerted opposition to Stalinist orthodoxy existed within the party prior to 1956, though the events surrounding Stalin's death, increased awareness about human rights abuses in the Eastern bloc (for instance the treatment of Russian Jews) and the suppression of an uprising in Poland, had raised doubts about the official line of the international communist movement before this date. As the key events of the year occurred – Khrushchev's secret speech to the Twentieth Congress of the Communist Party of the Soviet Union in February, and the invasion of Hungary by Soviet forces in November – the absence of an alternative democratic model among the leadership's critics was evident. The first signs of a politically articulate reaction to the shock experienced by many came from party intellectuals: among these, the historians Edward Thompson and John Saville played a central role in responding to events. Together with

Christopher Hill and Eric Hobsbawm, they had developed a more creative interpretation of Marxist ideas under the auspices of the historians' group within the party.[16]

As Thompson's contemporary correspondence reveals, he and Saville reacted swiftly to the news of Khruschev's speech.[17] Contact was made with like-minded members of the party and opinion was tested at different levels of the party. They demanded that an open debate take place within the party's publications about the nature of Stalinism. The main obstacle facing these dissidents was the leadership's refusal to give space to oppositional voices.[18] After a limited amount of correspondence had been published in the party's press in early 1956, only the occasional letter of protest filtered into the columns of *World News*, its official newspaper. These were counterbalanced by arguments for unity from loyalists. Those who opposed the lack of discussion about the serious issues involved in both the Twentieth Congress revelations and the Hungarian uprising were, therefore, driven to the point of voicing their criticisms outside the permitted channels of party discussion. Significantly, they did this with great reluctance. Whilst a group of leading intellectuals (including Christopher Hill, Maurice Dobb and Eric Hobsbawm) published a letter which was critical of the party's leadership in the *New Statesman*, Thompson and Saville declined to break so swiftly with Communist traditions:

> One of the original sins for Communist Party members was to publish criticisms of the Party outside the Party press, and in this context journals such as *Tribune* or the *New Statesman* were no different from any other periodical. We therefore conceived our own independent journal as in no way disruptive of the Party to which we belonged, or, to be more accurate, to which we had dedicated ourselves.[19]

This reluctance to abandon party conventions is central to understanding the nature of the milieu which these ex-communists constructed after 1956. All of these figures had absorbed, in different ways and places, the complex and potent internal culture of the party, described by a number of historians and outlined most graphically by Raphael Samuel's account of the 'lost world' of British communism[20] The virtues of solidarity, self-sacrifice and discipline had been extended into a binding communal ethos by the hostility and marginalisation which individual communists experienced in the Cold War. Breaking from this complex of values and shared experiences, however dissenting individuals were, was a problematic and uneven process which conventional accounts of the formation of the New Left barely touch. The legacy of these events was important for this movement in several ways. First, it bequeathed a number of organisational expectations among ex-communists which came into conflict with the practices of others in this formation. Second, it accounts for the more cohesive nature of the ex-communist milieu within this movement and the apparent consistency of the ideas of key figures such as Thompson throughout this period. As we shall see, this wing of the New Left was more cautious in its ideological revisionism and more resilient in its commitment to the socialist tradition, holding firmly, in the case of Saville and Thompson, to a belief in a libertarian communism which had been displaced by Stalinist apostasy. Third, it helps explain the appearance of a number of ideological divisions between ex-communists and younger members of the movement.

In fact, Thompson and Saville were most concerned to reform the party. They founded a mimeographed discussion journal, *The Reasoner*, which ran for three issues (July, September and November 1956). Its keynote articles focused upon the damage which Stalinism, both as a political philosophy and, critically, as an organisational logic, had done. This latter emphasis led to a full-scale attack on democratic centralism. This had become, in the British situation, too emphatic about centralism and uninterested in democracy.[21] The moral clarity of these issues impelled Thompson and Saville towards the fringes of communist orthodoxy. As the party's disciplinary machinery moved against them, therefore, they presented themselves as defenders of different aspects of communist culture. Appearing first of all before a specially convened sub-committee of the Yorkshire District Committee, they were summoned to a special session prior to the September meeting of the party's political committee in London. Requested to cease publication of *The Reasoner*, they refused and brought out the second edition.[22]

By November 1956, the context in which these dissident views were aired had changed considerably. When it became clear that the Soviet Union had suppressed an uprising in Hungary, with the apparent consent of the leadership of the communist movement internationally, the case for reform burst the bounds of traditional party loyalty. It had become apparent that the Commission on Internal Democracy appointed to report to a special Congress in the following year was unlikely to challenge the party's organisational practices.[23] The leadership of the Communist Party of Great Britain (CPGB) still wished to constrain discussion within the bounds of democratic centralism. In their view, coming to terms with Stalinism meant admitting that mistakes had been made: there were 'spots on ... the sun', as Rajani Palme Dutt famously put it.[24] Yet, for the good of the party, such errors had to be tolerated. Few concessions were made to the outrage many felt at Soviet behaviour in Hungary: the Nagy government was repeatedly denounced as crypto-fascistic and pro-Western. For Thompson and Saville this was too much. The third issue of *The Reasoner* was published and included Thompson's inspired critique of the CPGB's leadership — 'Through the Smoke of Budapest'.[25]

Following the events in Hungary, the opposition movement within the party had broadened considerably. The leadership was no longer able to censor and dilute the disgust felt by many. The editors of *The Reasoner* were suspended, even though they had announced their intention to cease publication altogether, as the journal's fate had become a distraction from more critical events abroad. Both promptly resigned and turned to the production of a new journal based on dissident communist principles.

Two aspects of the crisis within the party proved significant for the New Left's organisational practice. First, Thompson and Saville played a key role as founders of the *New Reasoner*, one of the pillars of the subsequent New Left movement. Both viewed Stalinism as an aberrant strand within the lineage of communism which had become hegemonic in the British party. Neither broke from many of the principles which they had held hitherto, though leaving the party encouraged a sharper critique of Stalinism. Both believed that the communist movement had to be reconstituted, not abandoned. Even as the crisis unfolded in early October, therefore, Saville felt that critical members of the party, especially those in key positions, should stay and fight. In October 1956 he wrote to a member of the staff at the *Daily Worker*, arguing that, 'whatever happens the Party goes on and unless one believes there is really no hope, one should be prepared to accept defeat for the time being and continue to fight in perhaps less spectacular ways...'[26] Stalinist political assumptions, combined with the practice of democratic centralism, had corrupted the communist tradition. Organisational questions were, thus, of primary importance for both men and their ex-communist associates. Encouraging free debate and expression outside the constraints of democratic centralism was imperative, yet this belief remained congruent with the notion that other aspects of communist political culture should be retained. Second, it is clear that no alternative organisational principle was developed by these dissidents, despite the unique conditions in which *The Reasoner* was produced. Saville and Thompson carried the burden of production, finding that resources were few and time often short. As their correspondence attests, *The Reasoner* was produced at great personal and financial cost, requiring them to draw deeply upon communist notions of self-sacrifice and moral outrage.[27] This experience marked them out from others who joined them in the New Left.

Communism was not the only factor which generated divisions within this movement. As Stuart Hall suggests, the different geographical and social locations where this movement's two principal milieux put down their roots were also central:

> The *New Reasoner*'s base was in Yorkshire and the industrial North. Although it had many readers elsewhere, it was organically rooted in a provincial political culture – not just that of the labour movement but also of organizations like the Yorkshire Peace Committee – and was intensely suspicious of 'London'.[28]

As the *New Reasoner* grew, it too established a base of sorts in London – involving Malcolm MacEwen, Doris Lessing and Ralph Miliband – yet the shared experience of ex-communism (its board included Peter Worsley, Kenneth Alexander, Derek Kartun, Randolph Swingler and Alfred Dressler) combined with the 'provincial' location of the grouping to produce a distinctive and cohesive culture, despite the diversity of biographical and intellectual influences which this grouping brought together. The journal championed a lost communist alternative, highlighted sources of dissent in Eastern Europe, explored the radical lineage of British romantic culture (an emphasis partly bequeathed by Thompson's important study of William Morris)[29] and reassessed the moral and intellectual components of the Marxist tradition.

The second international crisis of 1956, Suez, was a more potent source of inspiration for the other wing of the New Left which came into existence shortly after the *New Reasoner*. The Suez expedition, undertaken by the British and French governments against the Nasser regime in Egypt, unleashed a spontaneous revolt against Britain's participation. Significantly, this went beyond the bounds of parliamentary opposition, culminating in the largest political demonstration in Britain since 1945, in Trafalgar Square. The response to Suez was crystallised in the formation of the *Universities and Left Review* and, later, by the New Left Club in London (originally entitled the *ULR* Club). *Universities and Left Review* originated at Oxford University, where its four editors (Stuart Hall, Gabriel Pearson, Raphael Samuel and Charles Taylor) were based. Their original 'constituency' consisted of a diverse and international band of dissidents whom they encountered on the Oxford left, either at G.D.H.Cole's politics seminars or on the fringes of the University's Labour Club. Members of this group first cut their teeth on the club's magazine, *Clarion*, producing, in the summer of 1957, an issue which was altogether too abstract for their more orthodox socialist comrades.[30] In forming *Universities and Left Review* in late 1957, this grouping self-consciously harked back to an earlier publication, the *Left Review*, which had articulated a bold and modernist cultural politics in the 1930s.[31] Like its predecessor, *Universities and Left Review* attempted to reach a wide constituency, beyond the realm of political activists, and to broaden the purchase of socialist analysis. It was, consequently, far less easy to place on the conventional spectrum of socialist politics. Its editorial policy displayed a deliberate eclecticism: the journal juxtaposed heavyweight analysis of contemporary society and thought (including contributions by John Strachey and Ernest Gellner)[32] with writing on cultural questions. As its editors' confidence increased, they utilised its flexible format to develop a distinctive journal with a strong visual content; this characteristic was enhanced by the space it accorded to single photographs and photo-montages.

Both in its form and self-conscious openness to discussion and ideas, *Universities and Left Review* differed markedly from the *New Reasoner*, its more sober counterpart, though both journals noticed and advertised the other from an early stage. Whilst the latter embarked on an ethical and political critique of official communism, *Universities and Left Review* (ULR) seemed to thrive on its nervous eclecticism. But a distinctive project began to emerge within this journal too. Its commitment to a broader and more contemporary socialism, as well as its emphasis on a fresh and realistic analysis of contemporary conditions, provided the guidelines within which its writers worked. As its first editorial suggested:

> What is needed, therefore, is the regeneration of the whole tradition of free, open, critical debate. The socialist tradition ought to be the most fruitful and the most stringent of the intellectual traditions: a tradition of thought and action, alive to the realities of our contemporary world and sensitive to the pressures of the ideals of equality and social justice which have distinguished it in the past. Only in this way, can the socialist

movement draw into its orbit the vigorous, and active minds of the community, and symbolise through itself the intellectual and political ferment of a generation.[33]

The journal increasingly looked to sponsor new political and cultural initiatives. Meetings were held to discuss issues raised in its pages and a range of social and cultural activities were organised. The degree of spontaneity involved in these ventures has been well documented by the New Left's chroniclers. Increasingly, the London Club appealed to young, middle-class Londoners and simultaneously became an attractive venue for more experienced political activists. Whilst a committee was formed to run the Club, the nature of its organisational structure was extremely precarious.[34] Much depended, at least initially, on the enthusiasm and energy of leading activists. Raphael Samuel, for instance, bypassed the more cautious estimates of his fellow editors and Club committee members and set up a New Left coffee house, The Partisan, in premises near to the Club. This venture was indicative of the spirit which animated this burgeoning current. Soon, the increasingly well-attended club meetings were supplemented by the formation of study groups. In *ULR* 2, a series of discussion meetings and a speaking tour by Claude Bourdet were announced for 'provincial readers'. Already, the young turks in the 'golden triangle' of London and Oxbridge had sensed that a sympathetic movement of opinion lay in 'the provinces'. Yet, the ground was prepared for an inevitable clash of traditions and attitudes between the metropolis and outside regions. Some of its leading figures remained firmly committed to recruiting readers and activists outside its cosmopolitan roots,[35] but *ULR*'s purchase lay in its proximity to the novel aspects of contemporary culture and society. As we shall see in subsequent chapters, features of this milieu – its 'modernist' aesthetic preferences and international origins, in particular – shaped its contribution to the New Left's intellectual practice.

Throughout its existence, the pages of *ULR* (especially after its move to London in 1958) were full of announcements. It advertised social activities which connected New Left politics to cultural practice, for instance skiffle and jazz socials at the *ULR* club. As Stuart Hall recalls, the Club 'attracted to its weekly meetings audiences of three and four hundred drawn from across the whole spectrum of the left'.[36] Almost uniquely, those who attended were not recruited to an ulterior project or party, though New Left commitment often overlapped with other political activity. More importantly, the Club provided a space where the theoretical debates and insights of the journal's pages were collectively assessed. An equivalent forum was simply unimaginable in either the Labour or Communist Parties. In this sense, the New Left issued a challenge to the anti-intellectualism of the labour movement, urging the creation of a new, organic bond between the imperatives of left politics and the role of intellectuals and ideas – a rudimentary version, as Stuart Hall notes, of Gramsci's concept of 'organic intellectuals'.[37]

*ULR* generated a diverse and often uncontrollable set of activities, unlike those sponsored by any other political grouping in Britain since the war. Out of the first Aldermaston march (at Easter 1958) was formed the London Schools Left Club, at which an even younger generation was entertained. This resulted in some well-attended meetings, a series of summer schools and a journal, *Perspective*, which ran for two issues. Following the 'riots' of 1958, some members of the Club became involved in local politics in the Notting Hill area of London. This became a longer term involvement with this particular locality for activists such as George Clark.[38] *ULR* was unusual, firstly, in the range of social identities it tried to address (school leavers, teachers and progressive professionals all featured in its imaginary coalition) and, secondly, in the atmosphere which surrounded its politics: hierarchy and bureaucracy were avoided, where possible. No cohesive model of political behaviour and organisation was distilled though conventional patterns of political representation were rejected. In the Club there was developing 'a growing conviction that socialism imposed from above – whether by the halting and timid legislation of a Cabinet, or the ukase of a Party elite – is false socialism'.[39]

Unfortunately, the complexity of this organisational politics has been underplayed by some commentators, leading to one-dimensional assessments of *ULR*. Whilst spontaneity and participation were celebrated, these were seen as sources for the regeneration of a socialist lineage which had run into bureaucratic and conservative sands on the left. Thus, it was perfectly feasible for some in this milieu to regard the diverse activity they had unleashed as merely a source of pressure on the labour movement and Labour Party. For others, this activity was a 'conduit' to a more plural and alternative notion of radical politics. Simultaneously, some in the *New Reasoner* milieu encouraged the novelty, unconventionality and youthful spirit displayed by the *ULR* wing of the movement. A range of attitudes to political mobilisation co-existed within the space occupied by this movement. Whilst some of these differed only marginally from views developed by counterparts elsewhere, others diverged markedly. Increasingly, the journals operated as poles of attraction for differing types of politics and organisation.

## THE MERGER OF THE NEW LEFT, 1959–1961

These tensions were accentuated when the New Left began to cohere as a movement in late 1959. Before this point, problems had emerged for both journals. The strain of work undertaken by a stretched editorial board with scanty resources threatened the future of the *New Reasoner*. Both Saville and Thompson, who remained its primary movers, were exhausted by the volume of their work as well as the stress of editorial dissension.[40] For *ULR*, lack of attention to organisational detail, the desire to avoid even minimal kinds of bureaucratic organisation and the unpredictability of activists' commitment were increasingly debilitating, as was the burden of financing publication. Yet, this wing of the New Left current looked in good health: clubs had appeared in a number of locations outside London; *ULR* activists were involved in the burgeoning peace movement; and the journal itself appeared to have discovered a ready audience, selling, at its height, eight thousand copies.[41] Overall, however, the New Left's activist core was small – two hundred at most, despite the disproportionate influence of its ideas. After two years of intense activity, the prospects of creating a more stable institutional basis for the activities launched around both journals appealed strongly. Merger offered a viable solution to the strains of political activism outside the parties of the left.

As the general election of 1959 approached, *ULR*, in particular, appeared unsure about its political direction. Some within this milieu wished to continue with independent political initiatives, others recognised the importance of supporting Labour's electoral effort. Increasingly, the journal adopted a tone which straddled political realism and utopian aspiration, as well as the interests of older activists and the younger generation. Presciently, The Partisan began to fall apart as a commercial operation. Prefiguring later events, this high-profile New Left institution was rescued, ignominiously, by a friendly private benefactor.[42] The political honeymoon of the burgeoning New Left movement was over: there followed a fateful marriage between the two journals.

The next phase of its life began, therefore, not with the merger of the two journals into the *New Left Review* in 1960 – a conventional watershed within many accounts – but with the negotiations for this union. The idea of merger had been raised as early as the beginning of 1958. It was taken up with greater enthusiasm, however, by both parties towards the end of 1959. In many ways, the period from 1959-61 constitutes the highpoint of New Left activity. Contemporaries talked more certainly of a New Left movement which incorporated some energetic clubs across the country and in Scotland. *New Left Review* proved a success in terms of its sales (9000 readers subscribed in 1960) and the interest which surrounded its appearance. Even the national media began to recognise the New Left as a political phenomenon of more than passing interest.[43] Quite quickly, however, the hopes generated by this movement began to evaporate. *New Left Review* ran into serious financial and organisational difficulties. Many of the clubs began to lose their momentum. Most damaging of all, attempts to institutionalise the movement's diverse activities collapsed under the strain of argument and recrimination. By 1961, many participants recognised that the New Left was going into political reverse. As the battle for the 'soul' of *New Left Review* worsened throughout this and the following year, many activists retreated to their own locality or specialist political activity. Others drifted away from the New Left into rival activities which appeared to hold out greater hopes of success, in particular the Campaign for Nuclear Disarmament and the Labour Party. Some abandoned political involvement completely, disillusioned by the rapidity of the movement's decline.

The story of this rapid disintegration has often been cast in strongly personal terms. Clearly, the clash of personalities and the key role played by leading individuals during this period were of great significance. The New Left's chroniclers have tended, though, to misrepresent the personal dimension of this story: either overstating or underplaying it. Critics who have overemphasised the personal aspect of this crisis have failed to point out the important political themes which underscored and influenced the events which they describe.[44] Those who have explained these events through larger political factors have sometimes neglected the contingency embedded in the options available to the actors in this drama.[45] In fact, the personal dimensions to the conflicts which arose, intertwined with larger political tensions.

It is especially important to consider the events of 1959-61 in the context of long-term factors which militated against the success of the New Left in Britain: the difficulty in mobilising outside the parties of the left; the emphasis it gave to ideological realignment; and the breadth of its political commitments. Interestingly, comparable problems beset a similar movement which emerged in this period and folded far more quickly than the New Left. This comparison suggests that the latter was, in one sense, relatively successful. In the early months of 1957, the Socialist Forum movement emerged out of the crisis engendered by Hungary and Suez. By Spring 1957, twenty local Forum organisations had emerged across the country and in April a national conference was held at Wortley Hall. The Forum movement failed to sustain itself, though it did briefly found a journal.[46] Beset from the beginning by sectarian strife, it rapidly degenerated into an arena for the reassertion of older kinds of Marxism, especially of a Trotskyite variety.[47] Whilst its organisers received an enthusiastic response to their call for the renewal of socialist thought outside the Labour and Communist parties, their own refusal to encourage more critical rethinking, combined with the willingness of sectarian activists to invade this arena, crippled the Forum project. For many, including Thompson and others associated with the *New Reasoner*, this was a salutary experience, reinforcing their commitment to organisational coherence. With hindsight, the collapse of this project illustrates the pressures militating against any political current which tried to function outside the major parties of the left, however favourable the climate of opinion may have appeared for such a venture.

But the experience of the Forum movement did not dissuade the New Left from autonomous activity. As the idea of merging the two New Left journals gained momentum throughout 1959, Thompson and Saville persuaded some of their younger colleagues in London to join them in supporting the candidacy of Lawrence Daly in the general election, under the banner of the Fife Socialist League. This constituted one of the most controversial decisions the New Left ever took. Many of its activists were simultaneously members of the Labour Party: supporting Lawrence Daly was a bold move given the dual political loyalties of many in the New Left. According to Michael Barratt Brown, this step seriously undermined the prospects of New Left influence upon party members.[48] Whatever its merits, supporting Daly was one of a range of activities which were being conducted on a co-operative basis across the movement. The editors of the *New Reasoner* were in increasingly close contact with the slightly overawed young editors of *ULR*. As Saville's and Thompson's correspondence to each other and intimates within their circle reveals, their suspicions of the methods and politics of individuals associated with *ULR* took some time to abate.[49] Nevertheless, the strain imposed by production of the *New Reasoner* impelled this grouping towards merger. As Saville argued in 1959:

> Given, in our view, the necessity of merger or closure within a year we
> have come increasingly to the position that there is much to be said for a
> merger from the beginning of the new dispensation in which the *ULR* are
> involved ie from next Spring when the new journal will be officially
> published commercially. We take this view for a number of reasons, the
> most important being the difficulty of getting a genuine merger after
> publication has begun and the obvious advantages of arguing out the
> basis of the new merged journal.[50]

Not everyone involved accepted the inevitability or desirability of merger.
Clancy Sigal, the American author (of *Weekend in Dinlock*) and journalist, who
was known to both wings of the movement, criticised the idea in letters to
Thompson, anticipating some of the later difficulties which would emerge
for *New Left Review*. The two milieux, he argued, possessed their own
distinctive character and weaknesses and would not combine easily: 'if I may
say so, sometimes the *NR* editors remind me of some of my readers in "The
Observer" who read about a certain new phenomenon and deal with the new
and important problems raised – problems I emphasise for *all* of us – by
pigeon-holing them under Y for Youth'.[51] In a subsequent assessment,
Norman Birnbaum expressed similar reservations.[52] Within the *New Reasoner*
milieu, Ralph Miliband and Mervyn Jones were equally sceptical.[53]

Once the idea of merger was accepted, however, the strategy of the *New
Reasoner* grouping switched to ensuring a structure for the new journal which
would allow them to have a strong input in its production. Throughout this
process, the suspicion with which this group regarded their London
counterparts was marked.[54] But the potential benefits of launching a bi-
monthly journal, into which the efforts and resources of a large pool of
interested parties were poured, were obvious. The journal was formally
launched on 14 December 1959 at a meeting in the St Pancras Town Hall
in London. Stuart Hall was installed as full-time editor, assisted by a full-
time office manager, Janet Hase, and overseen by an editorial board drawn
from across the diverse ideological spectrum of the New Left. In addition to
the editorial members of both original journals, Paddy Whannel, John Rex,
Alasdair MacIntyre, Norman Birnbaum, Michael Barratt Brown, Peter
Worsley, Ralph Miliband and Raymond Williams joined the newly
constituted board of the journal.

Meanwhile, the clubs continued to grow. In venues as disparate as

Manchester, Sheffield, Leeds, Croydon and West Fife, they began to develop an organisational life which was relatively autonomous from the centre, in London. At the height of New Left activity, nearly forty clubs were in existence. Each took root in local conditions and was closely orientated to the political life of its locale. Yet, by the middle of 1959 the demand was raised for a national body to unite and represent these organisations. In September 1959, therefore, the first conference of these assorted clubs was held. At this meeting the range and variety of traditions within the New Left, as well as the different contexts which had spawned these ventures, were immediately apparent. Whilst a standing committee was appointed to oversee the provision of machinery for future integration, the delegates proved unable to reach agreement on a provisional programme for the movement, or, indeed, on the virtue of having such a programme. Suspicions of conventional party life and bureaucratisation still ran deep. Throughout the following year more clubs appeared. *New Left Review* provided a list of these and announcements of local events. Despite these apparent signs of health, by the end of 1960 it was clear that serious difficulties threatened to disrupt the fragile unity of the movement.

Even before the first issue of *New Left Review* had appeared, a series of conflicts had erupted between and within the merging groups. Some within the *New Reasoner* camp felt that the new journal was too influenced by the *ULR* circle.[55] This anxiety loomed large in Thompson's mind in the period leading up to unification. As his correspondence with Saville and Hall in this period reveals, his attempts to develop a working relationship with the new editor and his associates had been assiduous.[56] Two developments, however, concerned him towards the end of 1959. First, the plans for the early editions of *New Left Review* differed markedly from the more serious and heavyweight journal he hoped for. Second, he felt that his own influence was being undermined on the new board and within the journal more generally. His role on the editorial team had, he decided, been futile. Even before the first number of the journal had come out, therefore, he intimated that he wished to resign from the team.[57] In fact, its first issues proved a profound disappointment for many within the movement. As one participant has recalled, 'mixed up here were political disappointments and organisational disappointment, and physical disappointments, like the fact that it was on glossy paper — a selling out to the consumer society that we were all against'.[58] This remark demonstrates the difficulties which *New Left Review* was bound to encounter. It was produced against the background of diverse, and often unrealistic, expectations. Moreover, the fundamental tensions which lay at the core of this formation had merely been papered over by the euphoria of merger. Uncertainties about the political direction of *New Left Review*, its potential audience, the role of its talented but internally divided board, the relationship between the movement's largest intellectual presence, Thompson, and the centre, as well as the precise role of the overloaded *New Left Review* office, had not been addressed in the hurry to press on with the merger.

The appearance of *New Left Review*'s early editions forcefully raised these questions. It was not just the style and content of the journal which exacerbated tensions within the movement. The merger itself had, as Thompson suggested, not been well handled.[59] A simultaneous financial appeal was poorly organised. Committees had been set up to take care of this and the myriad of activities boldly announced in the journal's first issues. But most of these existed in name only and were increasingly prone to a debilitating organisational torpor. Meanwhile, board members arrived at *New Left Review*'s offices, hoping to lend a hand or to launch an initiative. Instead, they found Hall and Janet Hase hopelessly busy with paperwork and organisational routine. As Hall now recalls, he and Janet Hase felt burdened with the expectations of the whole movement.[60]

By June 1960, Thompson had withdrawn from the editorial team, Hall had given notice to one or two intimates that he wanted the following year to be his last as editor and Janet Hase was turning her mind to employment elsewhere, finding her efforts in the office derided and misunderstood. On the board, the political divisions which had been submerged during the merger returned as the content of the journal came under discussion. By the end of the year and the early months of 1961, this frustration appeared to have spread to the clubs. Membership and attendance figures were reported to be well below the previous year. The downturn experienced by many club activists outside London came to a head at a joint conference of *New Left Review*'s board, editorial representatives and delegates from the clubs, which met in July 1961 at Lyme Hall near Stockport. Criticism was directed at the journal and its editor. The clubs felt they had been ignored by the centre and demanded a journal to service the movement. From this moment the New Left declined as a political force. During this meeting profoundly differing conceptions of this movement were aired. A tetchy and accusatory discussion ensued, which was far removed from the spirit of creative plurality which the New Left publicly celebrated. For Hall this was the final straw.[61] He attempted to outline many of the problems which had beset *New Left Review*. A confusion, he suggested, lay at the very heart of New Left identity: was this a movement of people or of ideas? This, and other questions about the *Review* remained unresolved because they had never been properly or openly addressed. It was impossible for the journal to cater for all the different organisational models which had been brought into the New Left.

He developed these and other ideas about a new structure for *New Left Review* over the following weeks.[62] For the movement as a whole, these appeared too late. By the end of 1961 several of its commercial projects lay in ruins. The Partisan had been sold to a philanthropic sympathiser, the planned move to make the the journal a monthly had been scrapped, the pamphlets committee (set up the previous year to popularise more detailed New Left research) had released only one pamphlet, whilst the ambitious New Left books project had slowed to a halt due to lack of finance. The clubs' committee had quietly gone into abeyance with the result that individual clubs were left to their own devices.

At the *New Left Review*'s board meeting which took place in August 1961, Saville resigned as chair. He was replaced by Thompson who was to oversee the transition to a new structure for the *Review*. Inexorably, these figures were drawn into a desperate struggle to stave off financial and organisational collapse. The board was recast following a host of resignations. Editorial responsibility was passed to an energetic 'troika', consisting of Dennis Butt, the former communist who had left the party in 1956, Raphael Samuel, former editor of *ULR*, and Perry Anderson, one of the group of younger writers employed by Hall in recent issues of the *Review*. They put together an ambitious proposal to revamp its content.[63] The results of this bid were published as a double issue, *New Left Review* 13-14, a project motivated more by intellectual purism than financial responsibility. The issue ran to over two hundred pages, took five months to prepare and went £1000 over budget. Following the severe criticism they received at the board meeting of March 1962, Denis Butt and Raphael Samuel resigned from the editorial team. The 'troika' had seriously reduced the options open to the board. Control of *New Left Review* passed to the wealthy and talented twenty-two year old Perry Anderson.[64] Some board members, Thompson included, saw him as a youthful guardian of their own ideas. In a letter written in March 1962, Thompson indicated that he was trying to keep Perry Anderson on the editorial team, hoping to make him feel that he enjoyed the board's backing.[65]

These final acts in the drama of the transition from the first to the second New Left are still clouded by the recrimination which they have subsequently generated. The two main proponents – Anderson and Thompson – have each told their side of the story, producing largely incommensurable accounts. As early as 1963 Thompson maintained that Anderson had taken hold of *New Left Review* under false pretenses, providing assurances that it would change in emphasis only, whilst, in fact, altering its content until it bore little resemblance to its forebear. This project was sustained, in Thompson's view, by a crude, simplistic and sectarian representation of the first New Left's political interests and ideas.[66] Anderson, on the other hand, in his lengthy reprise of this period, has suggested that a more complex process occurred. The founders of the journal had not been 'dismissed' as Thompson claimed: 'the notion of an editorial coup is a legend'. On the contrary, he argued that the first New Left 'dissolved itself administratively', leaving a vacuum which it was unable to fill: 'no one stepped forward from it to take up the responsibility of rescuing and reconstructing the journal'.[67] Accepting some blame for the turn of events, he presented the journal's shift in tack after 1962 as the product of political and editorial inexperience and an exaggerated sense of 'generational distance' from the 'Old Guard'.[68] As his critique of Thompson's work in the same text made apparent, however, Anderson was unrepentant about the importance of this shift, seeing little of value in the populism and lack of rigour at the heart of the first New Left's politics.

Adjudicating between these different accounts is an almost impossible exercise, though some critics has seen fit to lend weight to the claims of each camp.[69] More realistically, it seems that both were right in some respects and wrong in others. Even this judgement is difficult: disentangling events from surrounding interpretations is always difficult, but in this case the absence of written records, the small number of those involved, as well as the sharp polarisation characterising subsequent recollections, renders an 'objective' account impossible. Yet several questions arise from these competing accounts and are pertinent for analysis of the first New Left. Was this movement's dissolution and displacement inevitable (as Anderson suggests)? To what extent has the polarisation around Thompson and Anderson led commentators and participants to overstate the difference between these projects? (Anderson himself calls for a reconciliation of the two generations in *Arguments Within English Marxism*.) And to what degree has the *animus* of these events distracted from important, earlier moments in the rise and fall of the first New Left? These questions provide the backdrop to the analysis of key aspects of this movement's organisational practice which follows.

Anderson's editorship undoubtedly marked a watershed in *New Left Review*'s history. He began to bring on to the board more theoretically informed contributors and laid out a bold intellectual programme, incorporating a more explicitly internationalist perspective.[70] Having protested in vain, the old board members left, one by one. Thompson was rapidly disillusioned by this mutation from the politics of the old New Left, outlining his objections in a sharp internal memorandum which he circulated among the board in 1963.[71] In this rarely cited document, he criticised the theoretical direction pursued by the journal and attacked the premises of its approach several years before his public critique of *New Left Review*.[72] Above all, he rejected the caricature of the first New Left's ideas and beliefs which had become prevalent within the journal since Anderson's accession: 'it is my impression that Team members are often ignorant of the problems and context of our past work; that they exaggerate our errors, on a most cursory view of the evidence; and tend too often to retreat into certain attitudes, sanctified by ritual phrases, in which our positions are caricatured'.[73] He concluded by attacking the internationalism espoused by this grouping, which resulted in the wholesale importation of continental Marxism and a fetishistic attitude to 'third world' politics. The denial of indigenous terrain as the ground on which the British contribution to a radical, internationalist politics had to be won, was inexcusable: 'While we strain to catch the idioms of the Third World, of Paris, of Poland, of Milan, might there not be a growing discourse around us pregnant with possibilities, not only for us but for other peoples?'.[74]

Thompson therefore anticipated the intellectual argument which was to erupt between himself and Anderson two years later. Already, Anderson envisaged an entirely different direction for the *Review*: the notion of strategic intervention within contemporary politics was displaced by the belief that theoretical work was now the main task for the New Left. Even Hall's 'unsystematic'[75] *Review* was fondly recalled by Thompson as an exemplar of the early New Left's praxis. By the end of 1963, however, the first New Left had been supplanted by its offspring. Yet, as we shall see, its organisational dissolution did not prevent the production of intellectual work broadly in line with the political perspective of this earlier current. Whilst the first New Left ceased as a meaningful political movement after 1962, its intellectual project continued in the work of individuals such as John Hughes until

1964, inspiring a distinctive critique of the politics of Harold Wilson (see chapter five).

## THE NEW LEFT AS A POLITICAL ORGANISATION

The fortunes of the first New Left were determined by a complex of events, ideas and personalities. Most importantly, it was beset by a number of tensions which induced a recurrent crisis of identity. At key moments it exhibited an alarming degree of vacillation and uncertainty over its political direction. Was this, at root, an intellectual milieu, an independent political movement or a lobbying group of the Labour Party? Alternatively, as Hall asked in 1961, was this a movement of people or of ideas? No answer to these questions ever achieved a consensus within the movement.

This confusion was caused primarily by the unfamiliar terrain which the movement occupied. Whilst it was not the first grouping on the left to stand outside the Labour and Communist Parties, its attempt to found a new kind of political organisation which hoped, simultaneously, to challenge the existing political system, was distinctive. The strain imposed by this dual role was ever present. The variety of organisational traditions and expectations within the movement merely accentuated this uncertainty. The success of both the *New Reasoner* and *ULR* brought into existence two poles of attraction from which developed a number of offshoots. Whilst some involved with the *New Reasoner* looked to the radical traditions of the labour movement for inspiration and floated the idea of co-operation with the Labour left (see chapter five), others, including Thompson, looked forward to the flowering of an independent New Left movement. Similarly, some *ULR* activists became more involved within national Labour politics, whilst others manifested a strong empathy for the politics of direct action which were influential within the peace movement. In London, these tendencies were held together, until 1960, by the counterculture which surrounded the New Left Club. Participants recall the unusual atmosphere which characterised this scene. Its cosmopolitan feel was underscored by the international backgrounds of many devotees. The Club also provided a space for social events, particularly musical performances. New Left culture was crafted from a hybrid set of origins, including beatnik ideas, aspects of contemporary youth culture, such as jazz and skiffle, peace movement values and the aspirations of an older generation who harked back to the Left Book Club. In London and Manchester the movement gathered energy and identity from its metropolitan surroundings: in Manchester the New Left reproduced the mix of culture and politics developed in London, influencing, among others, the young Paul Rose and Trevor Griffiths.[76]

Yet it was the gap between the centre in London and the rest of the country which played a central role in the demise of this movement, generating a series of mutual misconceptions. The concerns of New Left groupings in places such as Yorkshire and Scotland differed markedly from those in London. A similar process had been documented by Thompson among radical movements in Britain in the eighteenth and early nineteenth centuries, and characterised as a dialectic of 'intellect and enthusiasm' in which each tradition was enfeebled without the other.[77] This division rarely operated as a creative tension within the New Left, however: the perceived self-indulgence and preciousness of the cosmopolitan milieu in London, as well as the political pluralism celebrated by those around *ULR*, generated a mixture of suspicion and disdain in these locales. Indeed, contradictions around nationhood, class and political tradition were constantly invoked in the day-to-day efforts of co-ordinating the New Left. This geographical tension – almost endemic to radical movements within the British context – was further exacerbated by the balance of forces within the New Left. The informal seniority accorded to the Yorkshire group, based around Thompson and Saville, redoubled the force of their criticisms of the centre. The correspondence between the two was dominated by a suspicion of the motives of those in London.[78] Meanwhile, leading figures in *ULR* found the experience of speaking at meetings in other locations increasingly taxing. The language and assumptions which they took with them were often discordant within these contexts.

These differences would not have proved so insuperable had a viable political organisation emerged from the New Left's attempts to institutionalise its efforts on a national basis between 1959 and 1961. By then, the tendency within this formation to pluralise and diversify, both in its intellectual and practical activity, had become a destructive rather than creative impulse. The movement's strengths – its energy, spontaneity and participatory culture – had become weaknesses, pulling it apart. To understand why a viable organisation did not emerge from these different emphases and to outline provisional answers to the questions posed above about the dissolution of the New Left, it is important to consider how its internal tensions undermined its political goals. To this end, four key aspects of New Left practice are considered here: the break-up of the original *New*

*Left Review* editorial team; the rapid disintegration of the clubs; the problem of New Left relations with other political groupings; and this movement's fleeting attempt to develop an industrially-based politics. These touch on fundamental weaknesses in the movement's political practice but also highlight the prescience of its ideological agenda. This last aspect of the New Left's politics has become more controversial of late, as the experience of women in the movement has been critically reassessed. In fact, as we shall see, the New Left's relationship with feminism was more ambivalent than its critics have suggested.

## The Break-up of the NLR Editorial Team, 1959-60

The central dynamic within the break-up of the team which was to oversee the production of the *Review* was the difficult relationship between Hall, as editor, and Thompson, chair of the board and leading team member. Whilst the key date in the history of the journal is conventionally understood to be 1962 when Anderson gained editorial control of *New Left Review*, the significance of this earlier period has been neglected by those assessing the record of the New Left. In this period a real opportunity existed for a lasting impact on British politics to be made by a bright new journal, articulating the vision of a burgeoning political movement. Instead, the team which was assembled for this important task fell apart with a rapidity which has not been convincingly analysed by later commentators.

The charismatic and influential figure of Thompson lies at the heart of this story.[79] He brought with him a history of difficult working relationships with close political associates. Most significantly, his relationship with Saville, his closest political ally, was at times strained, as is clear from their contemporary correspondence. As early as November 1956, Thompson threatened to end their collaboration.[80] This threat was repeated on several occasions throughout these years. To a large extent, this was illustrative of the rhetorical hyperbole which Thompson used so expressively in his historical writing and later polemical engagements. Many of his letters reveal his moods to be extreme, while his assessment of those around him tended to be either more eulogistic or more critical than Saville's judgements. In this sense, the relationship between the two men was an extremely open and creative one. Ideas were aired and ruthlessly criticised. Their own behaviour, and that of intimates, was rigorously analysed and often condemned. This mode of working was fruitful – the high editorial standards set in both *The Reasoner* and the *New Reasoner* were the outcome of this partnership – yet stressful, as Thompson tended to vent his spleen on the broad-shouldered Saville as a way of clarifying his own ideas. In a letter he wrote at the end of 1956, Thompson delivered a stinging attack upon the weaknesses of the grouping around *The Reasoner*.[81] Saville, along with several other participants, was criticised harshly. The personal costs of this working relationship were occasionally high. Saville not only bore the brunt of Thompson's polemic but acted as a constant brake upon the latter's tendency to imagine slights and declare his frustrations with those around him.[82] With the onset of the merger negotiations, Thompson's sensitivities were acute. On this occasion, his anger was vented not only upon his collaborator but against those at the centre, especially Hall.

Two factors particularly influenced Thompson's political conduct in this period. First, he had developed a working method with Saville which allowed full rein for his more extravagant moods and opinions. He saw no need to behave differently when problems emerged within *New Left Review*. Second, he tended to condense within his powerful personality many of the tensions and anxieties at the heart of the New Left. Unfortunately, this could spill over into self-righteous and petulant behaviour, likely to worsen rather than ameliorate fraught situations. Thompson was an especially potent force when he presented himself as the voice of disillusioned sections of New Left opinion. Both of these factors informed his behaviour throughout these months. He began to correspond with Hall from an early stage in 1959, attempting to make the *Review*'s editor an intimate. For a short period he appears to have succeeded.[83] The slightly strained intimacy is captured in Hall's lighthearted reply to Thompson's concern about the former's mood in a previous meeting: 'I am usually quiet, not for any other reason than that I am usually quiet. Don't for goodness sake think it's because I'm disagreeing or bothered or depressed. The "happy West Indian" is a myth created by bourgeois imperialist writers to confuse socialists and the more advanced sections'.[84] When it became clear that Hall had diverged from Thompson's wishes over the *Review*, the latter's tone quickly shifted to irritation and open opposition. Throughout this period, Hall set out to appease Thompson's wrath, paying several visits to the North and corresponding with him on a frequent basis.

By the middle of 1960 Thompson was thoroughly disillusioned, not only with Hall, but with the haphazard and disorganised way in which *New Left Review* and the office were run. In a revealing letter to Saville, he conflated a personal critique of Hall and Janet Hase with the political direction taken within the *Review* as a whole.[85] Trawling through his history of bad relations with the office, he dismissed Hall's attempts to appease him as the product of the latter's evasive nature (a criticism which, to my knowledge, was made by no other participant then or since). The journal, according to Thompson, had been poorly edited and allowed to drift. The complaints of Hall and Hase were indicative of their oversensitivity to criticism and inability to organise the office. The New Left was too anarchistic: many in London made a virtue out of disagreement. The journal was too eclectic and dominated by cultural and sociological fashions. These tendencies were, he argued, responsible for the appalling mistake involved in the submission to the Pilkington Committee on Television (outlined in chapter three). Many of these criticisms were typically hyperbolic. But his increasingly oppositional behaviour had damaging consequences: he exacerbated tensions lurking under the movement's surface and undermined the *Review* as it became clear that it had lost the confidence of the New Left's leading intellectual.

That Thompson's behaviour was disruptive in this period is evidenced by Saville's relationship with him. For the latter, Thompson's behaviour finally proved too much for a brief period. Thompson declared that Saville had discriminated against him during a meeting of the board and that his perverse machinations were marginalising the *New Reasoner* group during the merger with *ULR*.[86] Saville, meanwhile, buckled under the frustrations of their intellectual partnership of the last few years: 'I myself took a good deal of hammering during the three years of our collaboration ... sometimes I answered back but mostly I didn't ... I don't put you quite on the pinnacle that some do, but my respect for your intellectual ability is enormous and my affection for you is considerable'.[87]

For Hall, Thompson's behaviour was merely one of many problems he was encountering as editor. Feeling his position to be increasingly untenable, he wrote a lengthy letter to Thompson in June 1960, arguing that 'NLR is a journal without a *brief* – and therefore impossible to edit and impossible to defend'.[88] His working methods were hastily improvised, whilst he was left to appease the different sources of opinion and influence within the New Left. The movement, he recalls, was 'full of big, senior figures all of whom were much older and more experienced than me, who had something to say; that's all very well but the deadlines come, you've just put one issue to bed and you've got to produce another'.[89] This sense of being overawed by the towering presence of Thompson, as well as by the task of servicing the New Left as a whole, reinforced the tendency of the journal's early issues to appeal to a broad range of New Left opinion. By the time Hall began to assert a more cohesive editorial style, working conditions within the journal had become almost impossible. Significantly, he relied increasingly, and to the annoyance of some members of the board, on a:

> small editorial group that began to assemble around Carlisle Street. The latter included people like Norm Fruchter, later a founding figure in the American 'New Left', and some of the younger 'New Left' group in Oxford. The latter had followed the original *ULR* generation and produced their own journal, *New University* – the route by which Perry Anderson, Robin Blackburn, Mike Rustin, Gareth Stedman Jones, Alan Shuttleworth and many others first became latched into the New Left.[90]

In his letter to Thompson in June 1960, Hall reflected upon the difficulties which *New Left Review* had experienced throughout the previous year. For these he blamed himself, the hidden agendas lurking beneath the movement and, in limited (and diplomatically stated) ways, Thompson: 'I don't think that you ever quite saw, or yet see, how much I shuttled between trying (against your overpowering image) to create an area of my own ideas which were viable, and yet could never quite pass from the shadow into an equitable arrangement'.[91] Hall's account provides a snapshot of the background against which much New Left work was being conducted after 1960. Personal squabbles were frequent, the board had degenerated into competing factions, and the clubs were crying out for a national organiser and a responsive journal.

The collapse of the working relationship between Hall and Thompson is central to the difficulties which *New Left Review* experienced, though should not be interpreted as their sole cause. Clearly, both made mistakes and were allotted roles for which they were probably unsuitable (the positions of Hall and Thompson might, as the former suggested at the time, have been more successfully carried out if they were reversed). Yet, the conspiratorial and fractious discourse into which Thompson collapsed during this period combined disastrously with the wider frustrations and problems which emerged within this milieu. Simultaneously, the absence of clear direction from the centre, symbolised by the eclecticism of *New Left Review*, allowed full rein to these divisions. With the demise of the original editorial team, the New Left was considerably weakened. An important moment in the history of the British left had passed: some of the nation's most gifted critics had come together outside the auspices of the Labour and communist traditions, yet failed to develop a cohesive and viable intellectual project.

## The Demise of the Clubs

Explanation of the rapid disintegration of this movement must also be sought in the weakness of the clubs. The notion of a movement based upon them was always problematic, despite the rhetorical hopes of writers such as Thompson:

> The merging of ULR and this journal, and the foundation of 'New Left Review', should provide a stimulus and a sense of direction to the movement. But the crucial development must take place in your town and locality; you must decide what form of organisation is most appropriate – reader's discussion or study group, left Club, or regional industrial conference – to bring socialists into association, and from association into confident activity ...[92]

In fact, the clubs were hampered by two powerful constraints. First, they were most successful where they had arisen out of distinctively local roots, for instance the Fife Socialist League (discussed below). Second, they depended for their survival on New Left advance at a national level. These contradictory conditions of existence were the product of a dialectic which operated throughout the New Left, between diversity at the base of the movement and the desire for national success and programmatic consensus at the top. In some ways, this combination was particular, though by no means unique, to the New Left. It encouraged the belief that whilst the movement celebrated diversity, plurality and grassroots mobilisation, success was ultimately defined through advance at the centre, on the national stage. In this sense, its fortunes were deeply affected by the imperatives of British political life – what Raymond Williams termed the 'centralizing pattern of British politics'.[93] The New Left was caught between countervailing impulses: radical decentralisation made political marginalisation all the more likely, yet many activists remained suspicious of the machinations of parties and politics in London. Mirroring this uncertainty, the representatives of the clubs did not call for the restructuring of the movement so that it would draw all its energies from the localities, but demanded to be serviced by the New Left's central institution, *New Left Review*. The experiences of many clubs were, thus, shaped by a matrix of local and national pressures.

Locally, the clubs found that immediate practicalities drained their energy. Paul Rose recalls how a lively socialist club emerged in Manchester following the events of 1956, involving, among others the future Labour

MPs and government members Joel Barnett and Edmund Dell.[94] Shortly afterwards, a coffee bar was opened which became the focus for a variety of political meetings and social activities. Having served on its committee, he recalls the enormity of effort required to run this body. For many of the clubs, organisation was hard to sustain given the financial restrictions they faced as well as the inevitable competition for activists' time and the haphazard nature of New Left commitment.

A further complication emerged from the movement's relationship with the labour movement. Some activists did not wish to operate solely within New Left organisations, so that in some clubs, for instance Cardiff, participants remained closely involved with the Labour Party. In others, such as Croydon, independent New Left initiatives took hold, including studies of local youth culture. In 1960 the Review highlighted the following activities:

> Several of the Left Clubs have been doing detailed work in Study Groups — Nottingham has framed an exciting and challenging scheme for comprehensive education in Nottingham, Edinburgh has made a detailed study of the Central African Federation, the London Club has done important work in Notting Hill and on Education ... There is talk of a pamphlet on the New Towns by the New Left Club in Stevenage and the VFS [Victory For Socialism] group in Harlow.[95]

These interventions were often significant in local terms. In Notting Hill the New Left was involved in the development of projects designed to promote local community organisation. In other locales (Manchester, Sheffield and Edinburgh for example), the breadth of concern articulated by the New Left subsequently influenced radical sections of the labour movement and later Labour administrations.[96]

Yet, all of the clubs were affected to a remarkable extent by the unfolding crisis at the centre of the movement. Whilst *New Left Review* continued to print an impressive list of clubs until 1963, many of these were defunct in all but name. By late 1960 and early 1961, many had experienced a decline in membership and activism. The changing political situation within the Labour Party and the success of direct action tactics in the peace movement pulled activists away from more cerebral New Left activities. Significantly, the clubs failed to transcend the essentially local and particularist dynamics which had brought them into life in the first place. Nowhere was this better demonstrated than in the case of the Fife Socialist League, the most impressive and best known local New Left organisation in these years.

## The Fife Socialist League

The League was founded in February 1957,[97] growing up around Lawrence Daly who had left the Communist Party in 1956, after a lengthy period of local activism.[98] Whilst it maintained close links with the left of the local Labour Party, it revealed its political independence in two ways. First, through the tireless efforts of Lawrence Daly himself, both he and the League came to be known as inveterate opponents of the bureaucratic injustices perpetuated by the Labour council. He led a number of campaigns against Labour and its administrative machinery in this period.[99] He also maintained a vigorous correspondence with the local press on questions of national and international significance.[100] These efforts were rewarded in 1958 when he won the County Council seat of Ballingry, comfortably defeating the Labour and Communist candidates. Equally significantly, given the industrial and political history of this region, he had become a delegate to the area level of the National Union of Mineworkers, the start of a lengthy involvement and career within the union. The second feature of the League which proclaimed its independence was its programme, particularly its support for nuclear disarmament, the nationalisation of key industries and self-government for Scotland.[101] These commitments were blended with an active involvement in the politics of the National Union of Mineworkers (NUM) in Scotland and an inveterate internationalism. All of these themes were boldly juxtaposed in the duplicated monthly it set up in 1960, *The Socialist*.

The League resembled New Left clubs elsewhere only in its general statements of policy (though its argument for Scottish self-government was unique): its history was the product of distinctive local conditions. It caught the attention of the New Left nationally through its decision to stand Lawrence Daly in the general election of 1959. This was the only occasion on which a New Left candidate stood against the Labour Party in a national election in this period. Daly's candidacy prompted a debate within the New Left which is instructive. The case for supporting him was taken up most vigorously by Thompson and Saville, who were in close contact with him before 1959. They took it upon themselves to persuade others of his worth, organising practical support for his election campaign. The terms in which this appeal was made were significant. West Fife, they suggested, was singular: supporting Daly did not involve a declaration of principle that the New Left should fight Labour candidates. On the contrary, the fate of the New Left could only be determined in each locality:

In some places, because of the way the local Labour Party has evolved, the New Left can only grow outside the traditional organisations; in most areas, it is safe to predict, the New Left will be partly within, partly outside the Labour Party; in others again, wholly within the existing Party. We have to recognise that the rebuilding of a socialist movement will be an uneven and bitty historical process; and there are no Sacred Cows which have first to be bowed to.[102]

Yet, some New Left devotees remained unconvinced about supporting Daly in particular and the idea of standing candidates against the Labour Party more generally. Whilst this did not prevent Thompson, his wife Dorothy and Saville lending support during the campaign, it is clear that the implications of their support for Daly went beyond his electoral performance. The Fife campaign raised the question of the desirability and potential of an independent New Left organisation, though Saville remained sceptical about this project.[103] It therefore caused some of the divisions within the movement to surface in a prescient fashion. Thompson went to great lengths to ensure that those who helped in Fife should be politically suitable. He made clear that he did not want the electoral campaign to be disrupted by younger, inexperienced activists who might alienate the local community.[104] Despite his public utterances about the need for a national New Left movement, the discourse of particularism still dominated the politics of Thompson and the New Left as a whole. The ideas and attitudes of the metropolis were, he felt, inappropriate in other contexts.

Whilst Daly's strong performance in the election (he won nearly five thousand votes and defeated the local Communist candidate) boded well for his brand of politics in the locality, and, more importantly, for his future in the NUM, the result did little for the New Left as a whole and for the League in particular. Despite the appearance, in late 1959 and early 1960, of several vibrant Scottish clubs, by October 1961 the Scottish Regional Clubs Committee was complaining about the lack of progress made by the New Left in Scotland.[105] As for the League, the final issue of its journal had appeared in May. Shortly afterwards, it gave up the struggle to survive in distinctive local conditions. Its most important asset, Daly himself, became its principal legacy as he decided to carry his ideas forward within the NUM. With the League's demise, one of the most distinctive and utopian elements of the New Left's organisational strategy ended: the sponsoring of local initiatives against the bureaucratic machine of the centralised party.

## The New Left and its Political Rivals

The League's decisions to stand a candidate in a general election and adopt a clear organisational structure (including educational provision) struck a chord with some parts of the New Left, though not others. This reflected the lack of agreement within the movement about relations with other left organisations. Throughout its life, the first New Left failed to develop a coherent response to the problem of its relationship with other groupings, especially the Labour Party. In one sense this was an unproblematic agenda: activists were happy to retain dual political affiliations, often to local Labour Parties as well as New Left clubs. Indeed, this was the norm in many areas. Yet, such a response begged the larger question of the identity and autonomy of the New Left in British politics. Clearly, by 1959 a current of disparate elements had carved out a separate space from any other political organisation. Thus, the merger of the two original journals raised the expectation that the New Left would begin to cohere as a political movement. Some hoped that a programme would emerge from this process: in late 1961 Thompson floated the idea of a common platform which might be proposed by the New Left in a future election.[106] By 1962 this idea was impossible.

Hopes for a more cohesive organisational structure were raised in many quarters throughout the brief period of the New Left's success. These ideas, however, obscured the sense in which New Left identity depended upon close engagement with the political forces of the left, above all the Labour Party. It was this proximity that inspired some of the New Left's most original and influential work. The movement's intellectuals found themselves free to provide theoretically informed criticism on key political issues, especially when the Labour left had lapsed into doctrinal sterility (see chapter five). This was exemplified in the attempts by a section of the New Left to influence the key debates which took place at the Labour Conferences of 1959 and 1960, through a daily lobby, a photocopied bulletin for delegates and imaginative visual displays. These interventions constituted some of the New Left's most public contributions to political debate. According to John Rex and John Thirlwell in 1960, 'owing to the excellent impressions made by the *NLR* daily 'This Week', the New Left made a considerable impact on the conference and is exceptionally well placed to lead in a counter attack on the anti-unilateralists'.[107]

This engagement differentiated this milieu from its political rivals outside the Labour and Communist Parties. Its maintenance of a political position which was 'one foot in and one foot out' the Labour Party infuriated its critics, then and since, incurring the 'scathing irony ... of some *enragés* of the New Left Mark 2 during the High Noon of 1968'.[108] But this ambivalent political trajectory accurately reflected the New Left's instinctive dissatisfaction with the political categories it inherited: neither reform nor revolution adequately characterised the politics its constituencies wished to pursue. This was not an inward looking sect reliant upon dogmatic purity. In fact, its loose structure and instinctive plurality ensured that Trotskyite groups, especially International Socialism (the forerunner of the contemporary Socialist Workers' Party) and the Socialist Labour League, were frequent participants at New Left meetings, perceiving a 'soft target' for infiltration and influence. In fact, whilst more experienced political campaigners disliked this presence, such groups found the New Left too diffuse and disorganised to take over. The absence of an obvious centre and hierarchical structures within the movement ensured that ultra-left politics remained merely one marginal voice among many others.

The labour movement was a far more important point of reference for many who had come into the New Left: according to Thompson, 'the New Left must not stand aside from the Labour Movement, and from its immediate pre-occupations and struggles, in righteous anti-political purism. The majority of those actively associated with the New Left will, as a matter of course, be active members of the Labour Party and trade union movement.'[109] In addition, the increasing interest aroused within the movement by the parallel growth of the peace movement and the importance of the unilateralist issue reinforced a proximity to Labour politics. Many who had previously been sceptical of Labour became involved in the struggle to convert the party to unilateralism after 1959. This trend was reinforced by the appearance of a new, radical edge to Labour's rhetoric after 1960 (see chapter five).

Notions of the New Left as a strictly independent organisation also contradicted the essential diversity of thought and activity which made up this formation. It was common for activists to shift their attitudes to the Labour Party during this period. A complex series of factors affected the relationship between the two groups (the ideological implications of this are discussed in chapter five). It was rare for any New Left participant to develop a 'finished' position on this question and maintain it in these years. Likewise, the few attempts to agree a programme within the movement foundered upon internal differences. New Left supporters remained highly suspicious of the very notion of an agreed programme. The movement would have had to cohere institutionally and ideologically to a far greater degree for such a process to have gained momentum. The problem here was not just that the New Left unravelled before this process could take place, but also that it arose on the basis of fundamental differences of perspective. Neither the political will nor confidence lay within its ranks for the distillation of common principles. Many found the process of posing questions and constituting new agendas in their political thought or activities exciting. The desire to provide concrete answers within an organisational context was rarely present, especially because the New Left was characterised by competing models of organisation (for instance the expectations of ex-communists in contrast to the quasi-anarchist preferences of peace activists) rather than their complete absence, as some commentators have suggested.

By definition, this movement included a range of opinion and experience. Whether a loose organisational structure could have been developed to help it survive its lean period after 1961 is a moot point for later commentators. This is a misleading way, however, of judging its achievements. The New Left had not surmounted a basic ideological tension between the celebration of localism and specificity, on the one hand, and its desire to engage with mainstream, national politics, on the other.

## An Industrial Wing of the New Left?

The fourth example of New Left practice which illuminates its life and demise was the attempt made after 1959 to establish a foothold in the trade union movement. This is significant, first, because it has become commonplace among later critics of this formation to comment upon its lack of connections with the industrial working class and, second, because its attempt to found a journal in this field involved a shift towards a distinctively New Left strategy in industrial matters.

The movement's social base undoubtedly shaped its political outlook here. Drawing upon a range of occupational backgrounds, its composition was tilted towards professions where a university education was a prerequisite: the New Left appealed particularly to teachers, lecturers and journalists. According to some commentators this characteristic is central to understanding the project which this and subsequent New Left currents have pursued. In this scenario, the New Left represents a variation of the tradition of 'middle class radicalism' analysed by Frank Parkin in his influential study of the peace movement.[110] In addition, the central role played by 'scholarship boys' – the beneficiaries of the 1944 Education Act who attended grammar schools on scholarships – infused this milieu with a sense of social mobility and unease with older patterns of class alignment. Importantly, the New Left put down roots in a number of locations where older traditions, founded on more homogeneous working-class communities, were being rapidly displaced. Clearly, sections of the New Left perceived the importance of understanding the new forms of alienation which thrived in the interstices of the cultures of affluence and classlessness (see chapter two). But simultaneously, the notion of addressing and mobilising the traditional constituencies of the labour movement recurred in this movement's imagination. The experience of adult education tutoring, common to a number of the New Left's leading figures (Raymond Williams, Thompson, Michael Barratt Brown, John Hughes and Kenneth Alexander), shaped this commitment.[111] At times, these different emphases constituted a creative tension which anticipated the concerns of later ideologues to forge links between the labour movement and the new social movements; on occasion, they produced a debilitating contradiction, hampering the articulation of a clear and confident political appeal. The New Left remained fundamentally ambivalent about the relationship between its various constituencies.

For many activists, it was important to 'establish far more contact between the New Left and the industrial working class'.[112] Indeed, the attempt to build an industrial wing of the movement served for some as a bulwark against the currents of rethinking which were present elsewhere in the movement. For others, however, it was important to advance the struggle for New Left ideas on as many fronts as possible and to link older constituencies with newer forces. Intervention within trade union politics was a key part of this strategy. This project made headway in certain areas of the North of England where the New Left was closely allied with radical sections of the labour and trade union movements.[113] In April 1959 an industrial conference, sponsored by the *New Reasoner*, took place. This was attended by thirty trade union officials. Following this early contact, efforts were made to set up a New Left industrial bulletin. This was intended to promote the discussion of key issues in this field and to make the connection between the industrial and the political worlds a central area of New Left commitment. The resulting bulletin, *Searchlight*, ran for only four issues, from January to April 1960. It was published as a monthly newsletter, principally through the efforts of Saville and Jim Roche in Yorkshire.[114]

Following its demise, strenuous efforts were made throughout the summer of 1960 to set up a Northern industrial committee. Jim Roche, in particular, attempted to generate support for a larger industrial bulletin.[115] His proposal, as well as Thompson's suggestion that efforts be channelled into the formation of this committee, were discussed at a meeting attended by, among others, Stan Orme, Eric Heffer and Lawrence Daly, and appeared to hold out the hope of sustained and co-ordinated work in this sphere.[116] In fact, the committee's work folded with remarkable rapidity because the New Left found this agenda particularly difficult. It proved hard to shift the political allegiances of trade unionists and Labour Party members or even to suggest that these might be sustained alongside concern for New Left issues. Undoubtedly, the New Left's praxis was sharpest in some of the newer areas of concern and analysis which it approached. Articulating these emphases alongside more traditional questions within the socialist agenda proved a difficult task.

The New Left achieved more in this area through its sensitivity to the importance of workers' control as part of an expanding democratic agenda in the early 1960s (these ideas are outlined in chapter five). Rustin points to a particularly strong legacy through 'the channel of workers' education — through trade union colleges, research departments, and links with a few significant trade-union leaders, such as Lawrence Daly...'.[117] The influential work of the Institute for Workers' Control over the next decade flowed directly out of the interest taken in this issue by *New Left Review* under Hall's editorship. New Left writers examined the possibilities for an alternative to the dominant traditions within British trade unionism. They were sceptical of the gradualism of the leaderships of many unions and of the economistic militancy of sections of the left. Importantly, the first New Left set out to challenge the undemocratic culture in which such values flourished, opposing the bloc voting system in the Labour Party. Its influence on these questions was, however, small. This strand of criticism proved marginal in the wider labour movement, leaving the dominant traditions of British labourism unscathed.

## Gender in the New Left

Controversy has arisen in the last few years over the experiences of women within the New Left. Critics have suggested that the first New Left's record in relationship to feminism was hardly praiseworthy, an argument that undercuts the claim that the politics of this formation provided one point of origin for the later women's movement. Whilst it is clear that the New Left encouraged the expansion of the social and cultural frame of reference of the left, it did so by generating a new set of images which reproduced the sexism of its political rivals. In particular, the 'angry young men' celebrated in John Osborne's contemporary play frequently represented its imaginary audience. As Lynne Segal has suggested, in the work of 'angry' writers such as Osborne and Sillitoe:

> Women were never to be trusted but treated as part of the system trying to trap, tame and emasculate men. A stifling domesticity had killed the spirit and guts of men, these 'rebels' declared, and women were to blame. What was really happening in most of the Angry literature was that class hostility was suppressed and twisted into new forms of sexual hostility.[118]

In New Left circles these questions were sidestepped by the adoption of a gender-blind approach to male/female relations. Sheila Benson recalls that in the London Club 'secretarial tasks were often shared out within a general atmosphere of spontaneity and co-operation rather than any rigid division of labour'.[119] As several women involved in this grouping have recalled, there were limits to the success of this approach. Women in the New Left often got a poor deal as public speaking, editorial work and political decisions remained the preserves of men.[120] In theoretical terms, Lisa Jardine and Julia Swindells have highlighted the deeply gendered concepts at the heart of much New Left analysis.[121]

Yet, a more contextual reading of this period suggests that this judgement is not wholly appropriate. According to Lynne Segal, 'the left in the fifties was as silent as everyone else on relations between the sexes because it accepted unquestioningly a belief central to the fifties consensus: women's problems had been solved'. The silencing of women in this movement was a small part of a larger process whereby post-war anxieties about the 'domestification' of men combined with highly conservative notions of the 'assumed biological imperative of motherhood and childcare which emerged more strongly in the fifties than it ever had before'.[122] As a result, the public sphere was forcefully 'reclaimed' as a male preserve during the 1950s. Moreover, feminist discourse was almost wholly absent from the left's political culture in this period, despite the appearance of de Beauvoir's *Second Sex*. Jean McCrindle, for example, wrote an article in this period for *The Socialist* (the Fife Socialist League's magazine) in which she argued the case for increasing women's participation in politics, but in terms which indicate the absence of feminist ideas within the movement.[123] This movement undoubtedly reproduced the sexism, and, on occasions, misogyny of the wider political culture. But a simple condemnation of its sexual politics obscures the involvement in this movement of a number of women who came to the fore in the women's movement of the 1970s,[124] as well as the political and conceptual resources it bequeathed for these radicals. These women provide an important indirect connection between the New Left's commitment to a broader conception of the political and later feminist politics.

## CONCLUSIONS

The New Left was hamstrung as well as dynamised by its organisational and ideological diversity. The ideas developed in *New Left Review* after 1960 proved difficult to translate in places such as Manchester or Fife. Here, the frailty of the New Left as a movement was laid bare. A boldly orchestrated decentralisation had not taken place (this might have involved local journals and centres), yet the language of localism and particularism remained the dominant framework for approaching organisational problems. This contradiction was, as we have seen, powerfully intermeshed with others concerning the direction and nature of the movement. The first New Left was prevented from escaping these binds by its inability to constitute a cogent organisational discourse. As a result, its legacy consists more of directions in which its work pointed than concrete political achievements.

More positively, part of the legacy of the New Left lay in the torrent of ideas it unleashed about the very nature of political organisations. The proximity it encouraged between its 'leaders' and activists ensured that the movement was distinctive because its often complex and heavyweight ideas were developed in close relation to its base. A generation of activists was involved in hammering out new ideas concerning class, socialism and culture. In this sense, the tensions negotiated in its journals were similar to those which beset its organisational practice.

The mode of organisation adopted by the New Left, therefore, had some lasting effects. Whilst later historians have complained about the preponderance of intellectuals in its ranks, this movement was striking to contemporaries on two counts: first, because of the narrowness of the gap between its leaders and supporters; and, second, because its intellectuals were constantly struggling to build a bridge between the world of orthodox politics and the realm of ideas. Rejecting the organisational models which surrounded it, the New Left avoided the fetishes of leadership and constitutionalism. In their place a more informal and spontaneous culture was generated. Certainly, the weaknesses of this mode of organisation became readily apparent. In particular, the first New Left found that abolising rules did not mean eliminating hierarchy, a hard lesson that many women were the first to learn. But the range of options available to later radical movements which sought to combine participatory democratic forms with radical political goals were broadened by the efforts of this movement.

NOTES

1   A.J.Davis, *op cit*, pp75-6.
2   C.MacInnes, 'The Anarchists II', *Queen*, 22 May 1962.
3   D. Lessing, *The Golden Notebook*, Grafton Books, London 1972, p437.
4   This criticism has been made most sharply by Raphael Samuel, 'Born-again Socialism', in Archer *et al*, *op cit*, pp39-57.
5   Davies, *op cit*, p198.
6   Barratt-Brown, cited in Davies, *op cit*, p270.
7   D.Stafford, 'Anarchists in Britain Today', *Government and Opposition*, 5, 1970, pp480-500; D.Miller, *Anarchism*, J.M.Dent & Sons Ltd, London, Melbourne 1984, pp141-51; H.Wainwright, *Arguments for a New Left: Answering the Free Market Right*, Blackwell, Oxford 1993, p233; Samuel, *op cit*; Davies, *op cit*.
8   S.MacIntyre, *A Proletarian Science: Marxism in Britain 1917-1933*, Cambridge University Press, Cambridge 1980, p181.
9   *Ibid*, p181.
10  K.Morgan, *Against Fascism and War. Ruptures and continuities in British Communist Politics, 1935-1941*, Manchester University Press, Manchester 1989, p25.
11  J.Lewis, *The Left Book Club: an historical record*, Victor Gollancz, London 1970, p27.
12  R.Samuel, 'Born-again socialism', p54.
13  S.Hall, 'The 'First' New Left: Life and Times', in Archer *et al*, *op cit*, pp13-38, pp14-15.
14  W.Breines, *Community and Organisation in the New Left: 1962-1968*, Praeger, New York 1982.
15  See J.Saville, 'The Twentieth Congress and the British Communist Party', *Socialist Register*, 1976, pp1-23; and 'The Communist Experience: a personal appraisal', *Socialist Register*, 1991, pp1-27; M.MacEwen, 'The Day the Party Had to Stop', *Socialist Register*, 1976, pp24-42; and *The Greening of a Red*, *op cit*; E.Hobsbawm, interviewed by Gareth Stedman Jones, in '1956', *Marxism Today*, November 1986, pp16-23; W.Thompson, *The Good Old Cause: British Communism 1920-1991*, Pluto London, 1992. For a more detailed assessment of the role of ex-communists in the New Left, see M.Kenny, 'Communism and the New Left', in G.Andrews, N.Fishman and K.Morgan (eds), *Opening the Books: Essays in the Culture and Social History of British Communism*, Pluto, London 1995.
16  See E.Hobsbawm, 'The Historians' Group of the Communist Party', in M.Cornforth (ed), *Rebels and their Causes: Essays in Honour of A.L.Morton*, Lawrence and Wishart, London 1978, pp21-47; Saville, 'The Twentieth Congress and the

British Communist Party', *op cit*, p7.

17　This is evident from Thompson's and Saville's contemporary correspondence; Howard Hill file, Saville papers.

18　This problem is discussed in a letter from Rodney Hilton and Christopher Hill to Victor Kiernan, n.d. (1956), which enclosed a copy of a letter of protest signed by, among others, John Berger, Henry Collins, Edward Thompson and Doris Lessing; 'Victor Kiernan' file, Saville papers.

19　Saville, 'The Twentieth Congress and the British Communist Party', *op cit*, p7.

20　R.Samuel, 'The Lost World of British Communism', parts 1-3, *New Left Review*, 154, 156 and 165, 1985-7; especially part 2, pp63-113.

21　MacEwen, 'The Day the Party Had to Stop', *op cit*.

22　Thompson was on the Yorkshire District Executive Committee at this time. At a meeting on 18 August 1956, a motion requesting that he and Saville cease publication was passed by 19 votes out of 21.

23　*Report of the Commission on Inner Party Democracy*, Communist Party, London, December 1956.

24　Cited in Saville, 'The Twentieth Congress and the British Communist Party', *op cit*, p5.

25　Reprinted in *Widgery*, *op cit*, pp66-72.

26　Saville, 'The Twentieth Congress and the British Communist Party', *op cit*, p12.

27　See Thompson's, 'Preface', in MacEwen, *The Greening of a Red*, ppix-xii; Saville, 'The Twentieth Congress and the British Communist Party', *op cit*, p21.

28　Hall, 'The "First" New Left', *op cit*,p23.

29　Thompson, *William Morris: Romantic to Revolutionary*, Lawrence and Wishart, London 1955.

30　Hall, 'The "First" New Left', *op cit*, p18.

31　See F.Mulhern, *The Moment of 'Scrutiny'*, New Left Books, London 1979, pp85-6.

32　J.Strachey, 'The German Tragedy', *ULR*, 3, 1958, pp1-12; E.Gellner, 'Logical Positivism and the spurious fox', *ULR*, 3, 1958, pp67-71.

33　Editorial, *ULR*, 1, 1957, pii.

34　Elections were first held for the Club's executive committee during the Spring of 1959.

35　Both Sheila Benson and Stuart Hall recall this being a preoccupation of their circle; interviews with the author.

36　Hall, 'The "First" New Left', *op cit*, p28.

37　*Ibid*, p35.

38　For a more detailed account of the impact of the New Left's activities in Notting Hill, including the exposure of Rachmanite landlordism, see J.O'Malley, *The Politics of Community Action: a decade of struggle in Notting Hill*, Spokesman, Nottingham 1977.

39　Samuel, *op cit*, p79.

40　See their correspondence with each other, editorial board members and contributors in the following files: 'The Reasoner/New Reasoner 1956-7', 'The Reasoner 1956-7', and 'The New Reasoner 1958', Saville papers.

41　The Partisan was also booming towards the end of 1958.

42　Bamford discusses the problems which arose in greater detail, *op cit*, pp295-302; Nicholas Faith was the benefactor.

43　Benson recalls the BBC's *Panorama* programme featuring the club; interview with the author.

44　Bamford, *op cit*, overemphasises the personal dimension of this dispute.

45　Sedgwick, *op cit*, pp131-55.

46 Several issues of *Forum* were printed in Sheffield from 1957-8, and were edited by Royden Harrison and Michael Segal.

47 See P.Fryer, 'The Wortley Hall Conference', in Widgery, *op cit*, pp78-85.

48 M. Barratt Brown, 'Positive Neutralism: Then and Now', in Archer *et al*, *op cit*, pp81-7, p84.

49 The following letters from their contemporary correspondence provide extensive comment on individuals involved in *ULR*, especially Hall and Samuel: Thompson, letter to Saville and Kenneth Alexander, 15 November 1957; Saville to Thompson, 18 November 1957; Saville to Thompson, 20 March 1958; Thompson's reply to Saville, n.d., (March?) 1958, '*New Reasoner* 1958' file, Saville papers.

50 *Background to the Merger Question* (internal *New Reasoner* memorandum), n.d. (end of 1958?), p2; '*New Left Review* 1959-63 file', Saville papers.

51 Sigal, letter to Saville and Worsley, n.d., (June 1959?), p2, '*New Reasoner* 1958' file, Saville papers.

52 N.Birnbaum, *Toward a Critical Sociology*, Oxford University Press, New York 1971, p323.

53 Mervyn Jones recalls: 'I regretted the merger, and I saw that Edward and Dorothy did too...', *Chances: An Autobiography*, Verso, London, New York 1987, p165.

54 See note 49.

55 Jones, *op cit*, p323.

56 See Thompson's contemporary correspondence with Saville, '*New Left Review* 1959-63' file, Saville papers.

57 Thompson, letter to Saville, 30 November 1959, '*New Left Review* 1959-63' file, Saville papers.

58 Sandy Hobbs, cited in Bamford, *op cit*, p333.

59 *New Left Review*'s 'Ways and Means' committee was a particular target of Thompson's wrath: letter to Saville, 30 June 1959, '*New Left Review* 1959-63' file, Saville papers.

60 Hall, interview with the author.

61 Interestingly, not all representatives from the clubs were hostile to the *Review*'s editor: according to the records of the Fife Socialist League, their delegate (J.Keenan) 'reported on the Stockport Left Clubs Conference. 40 delegates present. He felt the discussion was not practical enough but was impressed by the contributions of Stuart Hall', FSL (rule book), minutes of AGM, 18 December 1960, Daly papers, MSS.302/3/11.

62 Hall, 'Memorandum to the Editorial Board and the Left Clubs Committee', 7 July 1961, '*New Left Review* 1959-63' file, Saville papers.

63 They presented their case at the editorial board meeting of 21/22 October 1961; Bamford, *op cit*, pp381-2.

64 'Minutes of NLR Board Meeting', Keele University, 7/8 July 1962, Daly papers, MSS.302/3/19. At the meeting Alan Hall reported that the £1300 loss incurred over the previous financial year would be made up by £800 from Anderson and a £500 donation from shareholders which Faith would organise.

65 Thompson, letter to Rex, 16 March 1962, Daly papers, MSS.302/3/4.

66 Thompson, 'Open Letter to Kolakowski', *op cit*, pp314-5.

67 Anderson, *Arguments within English Marxism*, *op cit*, pp135-6.

68 *Ibid*, p137.

69 For an account of these events which reproduces Thompson's own views, see B.Palmer, *The Making of E.P.Thompson*, New Hogtown Press, Toronto 1981, pp55-64.

70 Editorial, 'On Internationalism', *New Left Review*, 18, 1962, pp3-4.

71 Thompson, 'Where are we now?' (internal memorandum to the *New Left Review* board), April 1963, Daly papers, MSS.302/3/19.

72 Thompson, 'Open Letter to Kolakowski', *op cit*.

73 Thompson, 'Where are we now?', *op cit*, p1.

74 *Ibid*, p15.

75 *Ibid*, p20.

76 Paul Rose was elected to Parliament, as a Labour MP, in 1964, becoming Private Secretary to Barbara Castle, Minister of Transport from 1966-8. A leading campaigner on numerous issues, not least Northern Ireland, he joined the fledgling Social Democratic Party in the mid-1980s. Trevor Griffith has been one of the most influential and successful television dramatists working in Britain since the 1960s; for an account of his intellectual and political career, see M.Poole and J.Wyver, *Powerplays: Trevor Griffiths in Television*, BFI Publishing, London 1984.

77 Cited in Anderson, *Arguments within English Marxism, op cit*, p35.

78 Thompson celebrated provincial socialists against the machinations of London-based political leaders in 'Homage to Tom Maguire', in A.Briggs and J.Saville, (eds), *Essays in Labour History*, Macmillan, London 1960, pp276-316.

79 For a complete account of Thompson's political activism, see M.Bess, 'E.P.Thompson: the Historian as Activist', *American Historical Review*, 98, 1, 1993, pp18-38.

80 Thompson, letter to Saville, 17 November 1956, '*New Reasoner* 1958' file, Saville papers.

81 Thompson, letter to Saville, n.d. (early 1957?), '*New Reasoner* 1958' file, Saville papers.

82 See, for instance, Thompson's letter of 16 March 1961 to Daly, Daly papers, MSS.302/3/4.

83 Hall, letter to Thompson, 2 June 1959, '*New Left Review* 1959-63' file, Saville papers.

84 *Ibid*, p4.

85 Thompson, letter to Saville, n.d. (1960?), '*New Left Review* 1959-63' file, Saville papers.

86 Thompson, letter to Saville, 17 November 1959, '*New Left Review* 1959-63' file, Saville papers.

87 Saville, letter to Thompson, 16 November 1959, '*New Left Review* 1959-63' file, Saville papers.

88 Hall, letter to Thompson, 20 June 1960, '*New Left Review* 1959-63' file, Saville papers, p2.

89 Hall, interview with the author.

90 Hall, 'The "First" New Left', *op cit*, p22.

91 Hall, letter to Thompson, 20 June 1960, *op cit*, p4.

92 Thompson, 'A Psessay in Ephology', *New Reasoner*, 10, 1959, pp1-8, pp6-7.

93 Williams, *op cit*, p26.

94 Paul Rose, interview with the author. Joel Barnett became Chief Secretary to the Treasury from 1974-9 and Chair of the Public Accounts Committee after 1979. Edmund Dell held a number of posts during the Wilson and Callaghan administrations, serving as Paymaster General from 1972-6 and Secretary of State for Trade from 1976-8; he joined the Social Democratic Party in the early 1980s.

95 'Letter to Readers', *New Left Review*, 5, 1960, p72. For a discussion of the 'Victory for Socialism' grouping in the Labour Party, see Howell, *op cit*, p215.

96 M.Boddy and C.Fudge, 'Labour Councils and New Left Alternatives', in M.Boddy and C.Fudge, (eds), *Local Socialism? Labour Councils and New Left Alternatives*,

Macmillan, London 1984, pp1-21.

97 The League's inaugural meeting took place on 24 February 1957 at the Lochgally Miners Institute. For a full account of the League, see W.Thompson, 'The New Left in Scotland', in I.MacDougall, (ed), *Essays in Scottish Labour History: A Tribute to W.H.Merrick*, Donald, Edinburgh 1978, pp207-25.

98 For a brief account of Daly's career until 1950, see Thompson, *West Fife: Election* (a confidential memorandum to Saville and Hall), n.d. (mid-late 1959), '*New Left Review* 1959-63' file, Saville papers.

99 See *The Dunfermline Press*, 15 June 1960, Daly papers, MSS.302/8/16.

100 For example, Daly had letters published in *The Dunfermline Press* on 3 and 17 July 1958, Daly papers, MSS.302/8/6.

101 J.McCrindle, 'Declaration of Policy', *The Socialist*, 2, 1960, p6.

102 Saville and Thompson, 'A Note on West Fife', *New Reasoner*, 10, 1959, pp9-12, p12.

103 This view recurs throughout his contemporary correspondence; Saville papers.

104 Thompson, *West Fife: Election*, *op cit*, p4.

105 New Left clubs were set up in Aberdeen, Edinburgh and Glasgow.

106 Thompson, letter to Daly, 29 September 1961, Daly papers, MSS.302/3/18.

107 J.Rex and J.Thirwell, circular letter to New Left Clubs' Committee, 19 October 1960, Daly papers, MSS.302/3/3.

108 Hall, 'The "First" New Left', *op cit*, p35.

109 Thompson, 'The New Left', *Peace News*, 18 September 1959, p16.

110 F.Parkin, *Middle Class Radicals*, Manchester University Press, Manchester 1965.

111 J.McIlroy, 'Border Country: Raymond Williams in Adult Education', *Studies in Adult Education*, 23, 1, 1991, pp1-23, p13.

112 Thompson, 'A Psessay in Ephology', *op cit*, p5.

113 Holden, *op cit*, pp263-7.

114 For further details, see Saville, letter to Samuel, 21 November 1959, '*New Left Review* 1959-63' file, Saville papers.

115 J.Roche, circular letter, 15 September 1960, '*New Reasoner* 1958' file, Saville papers.

116 Minutes, Manchester, 22 October 1960, Daly papers, MSS.302/3/2.

117 M.Rustin, 'The New Left as a Social Movement', in Archer *et al*, *op cit*, pp117-28, p126.

118 L.Segal, 'The Silence of Women in the New Left', in Archer *et al*, *op cit*, pp114-6, p115.

119 Benson, 'Women in the New Left', in Archer *et al*, *op cit*, pp105-10, p108.

120 At the 'Out of Apathy' conference, Jean McCrindle described the silence and the 'almost pathological absence of women both in the content of the journals and of women who were writing'; in Archer *et al*, *op cit*, p108.

121 Jardine and Swindells, *op cit*.

122 Segal, *op cit*, p114; see also, the Birmingham Feminist History Group, 'Feminism as femininity in the nineteen fifties?', *Feminist Review*, 3, 1979, pp48-64; J.Lewis, 'Myrdal, Klein, Women's Two Roles and Postwar Feminism 1945-1960', in H.L.Smith (ed), *British Feminism in the Twentieth Century*, Edward Elgar, Aldershot 1990, pp167-88.

123 J.McCrindle, 'Women in Politics', *The Socialist*, 2, 1960, p3.

124 H.Wainwright, 'Moving beyond the Fragments', in Rowbotham *et al*, *op cit*, pp211-53; M.Rustin, 'The New Left and the Present Crisis', *New Left Review*, 21, 1980, pp63-89, p66.

# CHAPTER TWO

# The Politics of Classlessness: Stuart Hall and the *Universities and Left Review*

> The concentration on problems of mass and high culture, of the quality of daily life, and the search for a new socialist ethic seemed both new and relevant. What was remarkable about much of this was that it represented an effort, mainly unintended, to admix British socialist thought with American and Continental elements. The emphasis on mass culture owed much to Dissent, even if the British problem was set in the context of the new prosperity of the British working class... The image of British society developed in ULR bore a striking resemblance to Wright Mills' portrait of America.[1]                Norman Birnbaum, 1971

Norman Birnbaum's description of *ULR*'s project highlights its distinctive combination of indigenous traditions and continental ideas. Working within this broad framework, its writers began to reappraise socialist thinking in a number of areas. One of the most important examples of this process was provided by Hall in an article which appeared in 1958, 'A Sense of Classlessness'.[2] This instigated a brief, yet sharp, debate within the pages of *ULR* between himself, Samuel and Thompson, which reveals much about the New Left's attempt to reappraise the left's political agenda and the theoretical heritage of socialism. In particular, some New Left thinkers rejected the narrow manner in which politics was defined in both the Labour and communist traditions. The diverse realms of social and cultural life lay beyond the reach of orthodox socialist definitions of politics. For many in the New Left, these could no longer be regarded as arenas which merely registered conflicts that were occurring elsewhere. This view engendered, for Hall in this instance, a more critical approach to Marxism.

The significance of this debate has been underplayed by historians of the New Left. In the course of this encounter strikingly different approaches to some of the fundamental concerns of socialism, including class, consciousness and politics itself, were aired. These divisions anticipated some of the intellectual and political differences which have emerged on the left in a later period, especially in the wake of Thatcherism in the 1980s.[3] The debate is instructive because of the important political themes it raised; it also highlighted the internal theoretical divisions within the New Left. It illuminates the range of perspectives brought into the movement as well as the importance placed by participants on the need to 'defend, re-examine and extend the Marxist tradition at a time of political and theoretical disaster'.[4] Whilst some of its activists paid more attention to defending and extending this heritage, others moved explicitly towards re-examination.

Within the *New Reasoner* after 1957, emphasis was placed upon the development of a humanistic politics which might replace the tarnished values of Stalinist orthodoxy. Socialism could no longer be reduced to the crude and formulaic calculations of the CPGB's leadership but was redefined as the expansion of demands for liberty and co-operative existence, inspired by the ethics of socialist humanism. (The implications of this position are outlined in chapter three). Whilst *ULR* was in broad agreement with this approach, its writers shifted to a different set of problematics in response to the political crisis of the 1950s. They grounded their perspective in the 'facts' of contemporary life, especially the changing patterns of working-class consciousness and experience. Their tools of analysis were more eclectic than those of the *New Reasoner*: Marxism was merely one among several competing strands of thought which they deployed. In fact, under the influence of Williams, whose essays '...were amongst those from external contributors which most closely resonated with the *ULR*'s internal project',[5] *ULR* stressed the importance of grasping the whole social process as well as the interaction of different elements within this totality. This project carried a distinctive flavour and was, according to Richard Johnson, part of a larger 'moment of culture' within Western Marxism in this period.[6]

The different directions pursued by the two journals established from the outset a series of antinomies which characterised the first New Left. In some ways, these differences were generated by the conflicting experiences of two separate political generations. As Hall has pointed out, the historical imagination of the *New Reasoner* milieu was shaped by 'the politics of the Popular Front and the anti-Fascist movements of the thirties, the European Resistance movements during the war, and the popular turn to the left reflected in the 1945 Labour victory'.[7] For *ULR*, on the other hand, 'the...centre of gravity was irrevocably 'post-war'.[8] Whilst it is clear that the two journals did not represent fully coherent alternatives, their origins help explain the divergent paths each began to follow. The differences which characterised this movement were increasingly crystallised into divisive antinomies. Divisions between 'culturalists' and humanists, young and old, those who wished to construct a more diverse and cosmopolitan milieu against the labour-movement orientation of others, were associated with the two journals, though they were never, in fact, this clear-cut.

These different emphases were exacerbated when *ULR*'s writers assessed the shifting basis of economic and social life in the 1950s. Many of the changes associated with the decade of affluence seemed intimately connected with the crises experienced by labourism and communism, yet the ideological universe of both remained frozen in the past. In the 1950s, however, change affected the outlook and experience of numerous social groups. The emergence of new towns, the spread of a consumer culture and the transformation of older political loyalties, as Labour's constituency declined, threw into relief the inadequacy of socialist discourse in the contemporary world. Commentators began to wonder whether socialism could survive the transition to the age of mass consumption, increased social mobility and economic boom.[9] Additionally, the shift in social relations occasioned by the impact of the welfare state, as well as the apparent affluence of the 1950s, signalled deep problems for the left. Many of the assumptions embedded in the socialist repertoire looked increasingly questionable. The spectres of capitalist crisis, mass unemployment and severe economic inequality – all central to politics in the 1930s – appeared to have been banished in the age of the motor car and television. Equally, the idea that the solidaristic values of the welfare state would provide a platform for further social advance, as well as the presumption that continued economic redistribution could be overseen from above, once the party had achieved electoral victory, were open to serious doubt by the late 1950s. Significantly, the ideas of Labour's leading revisionist intellectual, Anthony Crosland, stood out as an exceptional attempt to shift the party's thinking in response to these developments.[10]

The Communist Party's political prognoses were equally problematic in the context of the late 1950s. The party had struggled to come to terms with the effects of the Cold War and the virulent ideological campaigns unleashed against it. It had integrated even more closely within the international communist movement and was dominated by the Stalinist outlook which predominated there. Simultaneously, the party had failed to develop a political perspective appropriate for Britain in the 1950s. As conservatism entrenched its political and social dominance in post-war Britain, the CPGB refused to accept that a new strategic direction was entailed, despite its adoption in 1951 of a programme (the *British Road to Socialism*) that recognised the necessity of tailoring socialism to indigenous conditions.[11] The weakness of its political vision accentuated the frustration of much of its membership in 1956. For some who left, the wholesale re-examination of communist ideas was now imperative.

Unlike its counterparts, the New Left therefore stressed the need to rejuvenate the socialist tradition in terms of its ethical commitment and capacity to understand the contemporary world. Outside the orthodoxies of Labour and communist thought, however, this was a perilous enterprise. The extent and nature of this rethinking constituted a source of substantial disagreement within the movement. Whilst some, especially around *ULR*, were ready to move beyond the fringes of socialist orthodoxy in the search for inspiration, for the *New Reasoner*, the project of reconstituting a libertarian communism entailed the rediscovery of older traditions of socialist revolt.

## FROM CLASS TO CLASSLESSNESS: STUART HALL AND THE *ULR*

The debate about classlessness touched many of the points of difference between the two groupings. The exchange comprised four articles within *ULR*. Following Hall's contribution in *ULR* 5, Samuel and Thompson produced replies; then, in *ULR* 7, Hall further elaborated his position.[12] Despite their differences, these antagonists shared many beliefs, for instance the assumption that mass consumption was the creation of post-war capitalism and depended upon the manipulation of falsely created needs.[13] Yet, the unconstrained atmosphere which surrounded the New Left encouraged the expression of important differences on key themes within socialist discourse, in this debate and elsewhere.

Hall set out to challenge the distinction between experience and consciousness central to conventional socialist thought. His analysis began with David Riesman's description of a new phase in the history of the West, consumer capitalism.[14] Alongside the changes which had taken place in the forms and structures of this system, a series of social, industrial and economic shifts had occurred. These were reflected in new social values and popular cultural aspirations. New kinds of exploitation and socialisation within the capitalist nexus had emerged, culminating in the power of a mass media and advertising complex. New values and goals were, Hall argued, propagated through these institutions. These changes had produced a shift in class consciousness and political culture. In his examination of contemporary social relationships, he highlighted the expansion of white-collar employment. Simultaneously, working-class experiences had been massively altered as the shrinking basis of 'core' industrial employment combined with changes to older patterns of community life. These had been transformed by a new matrix of values concerning individual prosperity, status and the culture of consumer acquisition. Hall's thesis depended heavily upon changes in business organisation: the expansion of automation in the workplace and the shift within largescale enterprises towards a more complex culture of 'man management'. More generally, the changing relationship between state and economy, the consumer orientated boom of the decade of affluence and the 'post-Marx recognition on the part of management that if goods are to be sold, effective domestic demand must be kept up, and the domestic market remain buoyant', had all created a culture in which capitalism could (re)present itself as 'People's Capitalism'. Hall also illustrated the impact of developments in spheres other than production. Consumption had become a key mechanism not only for the circulation of commodities but also for the transmission of the value system at the heart of capitalist enterprise. The cultures of status, lifestyle and upward mobility were enshrined within the cycle of consumption and exchange which had become increasingly salient within post-war society. Sensing the reluctance on the part of many socialists to take these developments seriously, he reiterated Marx's theories on the social values accumulated by commodities within capitalist exchange:

> thus in their lives and their work, working class and lower middle class people can *realise* themselves through the possession (on hire purchase perhaps) of 'alien things'. Capitalism as a social system is now based upon consumption.[15]

His argument openly challenged the conventional treatment of the issues subsumed beneath the category of consciousness within Marxist discourse. The breadth of the factors he cited, as well as the more important role he assigned to consciousness, illustrated his rejection of the determinism and reductionism which had characterised much of the social analysis of the Marxist tradition. Criticising the mechanical development of the base and superstructure metaphor, he suggested that a 'freer play' between the two had to be adopted if socialists were to construct their opposition to capitalism on a broad and meaningful basis:

> This is necessary because we are concerned with a changing pattern of life, attitudes and values – particular responses to a particular situation – many of which can best be seen and isolated in what has so far been considered, in vulgar-Marxist interpretations (rather patronisingly), as the 'ideological superstructure'. [16]

This critique of economistic interpretations of historical materialism was standard across the New Left. Yet, Hall's assessment of a range of political, ideological and cultural factors as central in determining historical outcomes, as well as the greater role he assigned to culture and ideology in his account of the constitution of political identity, proved more controversial. The 'break' his article signified was thinly disguised by his frequent reference to Marx's work as sources for his ideas, though these citations prefigure his later excursions into Marx's ambiguous and complex legacy in these areas.[17] Undoubtedly, the rediscovery of the early Marx by writers in this milieu, enabled by Charles Taylor's importation of the *Economic and Philosophical Manuscripts* from Paris in 1958, was influential here.[18] As Charles Taylor demonstrated in the same issue of *ULR*, Marx's development of the concepts of alienation and species being, and belief in the re-creation of the liberated individual, opened a number of avenues for social and cultural critiques of capitalism. Interest in Marx's early work constituted one of the common elements in the political and intellectual outlook of New Left currents across Western Europe at that time. Hall was not alone, therefore, in his theoretical journey. He was also influenced, as was *ULR* more generally, by the writings of Raymond Williams and Richard Hoggart (see chapter four). The journal had become the forum for a body of writing on the arts and popular culture, the educational system, and the shifting patterns of social life which characterised Britain in the 1950s. These emphases reinforced the belief that socialism, both as an analytical tool and political practice, had to be reconstituted. The left should broaden its understanding of political and social developments, atuning itself to the relative autonomy of these spheres.

The left's particular problems at that time also engendered anxiety about some of the core ideas of contemporary socialism, especially the centralist and statist assumptions at the heart of Labour's politics. This lent credence to a populist reading of the left's mission among the New Left:

the task of socialism is to meet people where they are, where they are touched, bitten, met, frustrated, nauseated – to develop discontent and, at the same time, to give the socialist movement some direct sense of the... ways in which we live. [19]

This approach emerged from a profound scepticism about the conventional teleologies of the British left. Socialism had to be constructed in the changing conditions of the contemporary political world: it would not be delivered by an economic crisis, seizure of the state or the slow permeation of national institutions. Between reform and revolution, the New Left conjured up a new strategic metaphor, calling for a 'long revolution',[20] so that alternative values might become dominant throughout civil society:

> We have to get into towns and cities, universities and technical colleges, youth clubs and Trade Union branches and as Morris said – *make socialists* there ... Why should people – naturally – turn to socialism? There is no law which says that the Labour Movement, like a great inhuman engine, is going to throb its way into socialism or that we can, any longer... rely upon poverty and exploitation to drive people, like blind animals, towards socialism. Socialism is, and will remain, an active faith in a new society, to which we turn as conscious, thinking human beings.[21]

With its mixture of older themes (in particular Morris' 'missionary' commitment to 'making socialists') and newer ideas, this perspective proved popular across the New Left, though it was open to differing interpretations. Thompson, for instance, retained the notion of revolution as the political goal of the left, though as Anderson has suggested, he had undoubtedly broken from bolshevik or insurrectionist notions of this process.[22] More generally, the differences which emerged at a later date in the New Left's life were ultimately rooted in the theoretical questions which Hall's article temporarily brought to the fore. Despite his claim to a Marxist mantle, the logic of his argument had taken him to the edges of contemporary socialist orthodoxy. Here, Hall and others in *ULR* turned to Raymond Williams as an intellectual guide. His work offered an alternative conception of the social world, stemming from his rejection of the language and analysis of conventional socialism (see chapter four).

## CLASS AGAINST CLASSLESSNESS

Thompson perceived Hall's article as the culmination of a worrying tendency within the work of *ULR*. This had its origins, he suggested, in a dangerous enthusiasm for the exploration of new agendas. Those attracted to *ULR* were 'more at ease discussing alienation than exploitation'.[23] They were guilty of recklessly abandoning Marxist explanations of contemporary political conditions. In their place, thinkers from this younger generation proffered an eclectic mix of 'educational and cultural therapy'.[24] Whilst Thompson did not directly accuse the *ULR* team on these grounds, his reproduction of comments made about this milieu was a thin disguise for his own views; he concluded, for example, that 'the jibes are not altogether without foundation'.[25] That he sensed the importance of the emerging differences within the New Left milieu was evident both from the sharp nature of his comment and his recognition of the subversive drift of *ULR*'s ideas:

the generalisations – unless they are held in perspective by a sense of history – can lead to attitudes which are both precious and self-isolating;... these attitudes are never dominant in *ULR*; but they are obvious enough elsewhere, and are incipient in certain contributions to *ULR* 5. [26]

He then highlighted Gordon Redfern's discussion of architectural changes in London in the previous issue of *ULR* as indicative of a shift from Marxist methodology.[27] Indeed, he argued that Redfern's (and others') allegiance to the working class movement 'as the ultimate political force which will achieve socialism' was becoming increasingly abstract.[28] The variety of questions which entertained the fascination of *ULR*, as well as its sensitivity to the specificities of political life in Britain, were regarded with great suspicion by Thompson.

This tendency towards expansiveness in analytical terms, at the expense of moral and political clarity and commitment, was, Thompson felt, reinforced by the trend towards cultural analysis and critique in *ULR*. These provided a path away from Marxist language and thought. For Thompson, contemporary popular culture constituted an important matrix, yet was only the latest in a succession of formations which served to hide the real functioning of social relations within capitalist society. Thus, the ultimate explanation of cultural forms was political and historical. Taking a swipe at Richard Hoggart's influential study of working-class culture, he scolded his readers: 'we must discuss the uses of literacy a little less, and the uses of history rather more'.[29] At this early stage within the New Left's life, such emphases were intended as a warning against the dangers of moving too swiftly from conventional socialist analysis. His views anticipated the significant divisions which were to open up across this movement over the themes of culture and history. In particular, the critique of Williams developed by Thompson in the early editions of *New Left Review* were prefigured in this article.[30] Moreover, Thompson's response to the burgeoning tide of cultural analysis and critique provided an early point of origin for many of the disputes which erupted on the left in later years over the significance of culture and ideology within the social process.

Some of Thompson's conclusions were echoed by Samuel in the same issue of *ULR*, an indication of the absence of political unanimity within each journal. Samuel was a joint editor of *ULR* and close associate of Hall. The latter's arguments, Samuel suggested, grated against the work undertaken in the journal to examine the changing nature of post-war capitalism. He felt that Hall's position sat uneasily alongside the tradition of Marxist analysis of the disposition of class power within British society. For Samuel, a practising historian and former member of the Communist Party, the most significant task ahead was to reinvigorate an indigenous radical tradition by emphasising the roots of radical and socialist struggle from the nineteenth century onwards, a project which, in fact, approximated far more closely to the work of the *New Reasoner*.[31] Both Thompson's and Samuel's ideas rested upon a belief in the significance of reconstituting libertarian strands of the socialist tradition, which emphasised the autonomous agency of the working class. They both focused upon the way in which agency had been submerged in the left's political thought. Important historical studies were conducted on similar themes throughout this period. Thompson had already demonstrated the vitality and relevance of the socialist tradition of the late nineteenth century in his study of William Morris.[32] Throughout the late 1950s and early 1960s, he laid the foundations for his pathbreaking text, *The Making of the English Working Class*.[33] Other members of the *New Reasoner* group studied related topics: Saville contributed an important historical overview of the development of the welfare state, arguing that it had functioned strategically to undermine working-class demands within capitalism;[34] and Dorothy Thompson demonstrated the significance of Chartism as an exemplar of radical, popular mobilisation from below.[35]

These ideas were direct continuations of the creative tradition within

British historical writing generated by the Historians' Group in the Communist Party before 1956. Samuel's empathy for this project originated from his own attendance at the meetings of this group. Significantly, in the context of the *New Reasoner*, this tradition sat uneasily alongside the more contemporary focus of writers such as Ralph Miliband. This partly explains Thompson's anxiety to return history to the movement's intellectual agenda. Increasingly though, the analysis by critics such as Miliband of contemporary power relations carried a critical edge which the historicist reading of British social and political development lacked. The New Left's concern to chart the connections between private sector interests, the public sphere of the economy and the state was expressed most cogently by Miliband in this period (these writings are discussed in chapter five).[36] But in the course of his contemporary argument, he moved outside the framework of the *New Reasoner*, questioning the conventional reliance on nationalisation as a core element within a socialist strategy: 'state intervention ... is now the price which capitalism has learnt it must pay as a condition of its survival as a more or less going economic concern'.[37] Miliband's work anticipated the attempts, over a decade later, to construct a theory of the state rooted in the economic conditions of late capitalist societies. More specifically, these ideas substantially shaped the New Left's distinctive contribution to political economy, a project which found its home within *ULR* first of all, and then within the early editions of *New Left Review* after 1960 (see chapter five).

## BEYOND CLASSLESSNESS

In reply to his critics, Hall stressed the complementary features of the agendas of different sections of the New Left, arguing that 'what he [Samuel] dismisses as a contradiction in analysis (power elite analysis on the one hand, classlessness on the other) is a contradiction in the society itself'.[38] He proceeded, however, to repeat the central assertions of his original article. How, he asked, could a society which was dominated by a combination of new and old elites present itself as more open and more 'classless'? The notion of classlessness – the pervading sense of liberation from class barriers, articulated at many points within cultural and political life – was, he suggested, of greater significance than many socialists realised.

Whilst the debate did not result in an explicit rupture at this juncture, it highlighted a number of important political and theoretical differences. The apparent fusion of differing tendencies which occurred following the merger of the two journals in 1959 did not alleviate these underlying tensions. Hall had suggested that the sense of classlessness – the ideological representation of how people lived and worked – might be the primary location of ensuing class conflict and ideological struggle: 'I think that until we admit that this sense of class confusion has become a dominant feature of the Stalemate State... we are likely to take too simple a view of what has happened to the Labour Movement and of how we are to get out of this fix'.[39] He thus called into question the primacy of economic relationships in generating social identity, adding that socialists had to develop ways of intervening strategically within the spheres of cultural and ideological representation:

> the superstructure of ideas... is going to affect directly the course of events. And if the admission of this fact makes us reconsider some of the more primitive notions – still current – of how to interpret Marx's dictum that 'it is not consciousness of men that determines their being, but on the contrary, their social being that determines their consciousness', I for one, can only say, 'Long live the Revisionists'.[40]

For Hall and others, therefore, the critique of socialist dogma led in heterodox directions. But, whilst the formal ties of party orthodoxy might have evaporated within this milieu, it became evident that more informal, hidden constraints had survived the break symbolised by 1956. For Thompson and those who sympathised with the *New Reasoner*, rethinking involved the reconstitution of a libertarian and popular tradition. For Hall, and those whose political imaginations had been formed in the contemporary world, there were fewer binding ties to the orthodoxies and traditions of earlier generations. Their rethinking consequently took on a far more wholehearted character.

The spheres of culture, consciousness and representation constituted largely uncharted areas of analysis, though important exceptions, such as the work of Christopher Caudwell, were available within the Marxist tradition.[41] Raymond Williams' contemporary work became singularly important in mapping and defining this terrain. Exploration of the workings and significance of these spheres offered two particular attractions. It correlated closely with the New Left's belief that socialism had to be reconstituted on a broader basis as a political philosophy. It also opened up areas for analysis which were relatively unencumbered by the analytical traditions associated with the Labour and Communist Parties. At this juncture, in 1958, the perception could be sustained that these differing emphases within the New Left were complementary, not antagonistic. But within a short period of time, the subversive nature of these ideas became far more problematic for the New Left as a whole. Whilst this particular debate did not cause the tensions which beset the movement, it provided a glimpse of the potent divisions which underscored New Left thought.

## CONCLUSIONS

Hall's challenge to the New Left did not lie solely in his theoretical maneouvres. His conclusions carried strategic implications too. Much of 'A Sense of Classlessness' was taken up by his discussion of domination and subordination within contemporary capitalism. Whilst these processes were described in largely economic terms, he also outlined the implications of changes in other areas. These, he suggested, constituted the terrain on which the New Left ought to develop its politics, refusing to restrict itself to orthodox assumptions and conventional economic programmes. Hall's attempt to immerse the left's political imagination within the complex and troubling realities of the contemporary world provided a parallel, of sorts, with Crosland's revisionist reading of the prospects of British socialism. Accordingly, *ULR* retained a keen interest in, and partial affinity for, Croslandite rethinking, though many remained sceptical about revisionism's political trajectory within the Labour Party. Interestingly too, Hall's ideas echoed the insights of a number of continental Marxist theorists – André Gorz, Henri Lefebvre and Herbert Marcuse, among others. In this sense, the theoretical insights of the Frankfurt school and thinkers within the Western Marxist tradition were not wholly absent in Britain, finding a counterpart in Hall's discussion of classlessness, Raymond Williams' writing on totality and the emphasis on the manipulation of false needs which recurred in British New Left writing.

Hall also called attention to the increasing significance of wants manufactured in the sphere of consumption in contemporary society. This provided one source for the pervasive sense of classlessness and underpinned the myth of the 'open society'.[42] This was the terrain on which contemporary society ought to be challenged. Hall's analysis suggested a wide range of sites from which an ethically informed criticism could be launched and alternatives proposed. This view combined with a desire to expand the political horizons of the movement. These ideas underlay the New Left's most aggressive and politically engaged criticism (outlined in chapter five). Whilst the bald facts of class inequality and oppression were subsumed beneath the veneer of affluence and classlessness in contemporary Britain, there was still room, this perspective suggested, for a radical critique of the nature and organisation of the contemporary social system.

Hall's argument was drawn from a variety of sources, yet his synthesis articulated the instinctive drift of many in the *ULR* grouping. Whilst he was reluctant to present these ideas as a rejection of the work produced by other sections of the New Left, it is clear that this debate contained the seeds of more fundamental theoretical rupture. The rapid disintegration of the movement, as well as the conflicts which divided New Left figures after 1960 (between Hall and Thompson in the 1970s, for example), were prefigured in this early and tentative articulation of these themes. Hall's work was distinguished, above all, by his readiness to carry the re-examination of socialist beliefs into the sensitive areas of class and consciousness. The suspicion with which his ideas were received suggests that despite its apparent novelty and rejection of orthodoxy, the New Left was never wholly open as an ideological formation. Many within it remained sceptical about the desirabilty of wholesale revisionism, remaining confident that a coherent indigenous socialism could be reconstructed.

More generally, classlessness lay at the heart of the crisis experienced by the left in Britain in the post-war period. The relationship between class and consciousness posited by classical Marxism looked increasingly unrealistic. Hall's exploration of this connection carried a strongly cultural and ideological flavour; the discourse of culture, he felt, was intimately connected to the political weakness of socialism: 'Somehow our cultural life has become itself a major political fact, but we cannot begin to understand what sort of a fact it is within the framework of our debased political language'.[43] The vulnerability of socialism in these areas was exposed by his analysis. The debate on classlessness therefore constitutes an important and neglected moment in the intellectual history of the British left, when the efficacy of Marxist ideas was, for the first time, explicitly questioned from a New Left position.

## NOTES

1   N.Birnbaum, *Towards a Critical Sociology*, *op cit*, p323.
2   Hall, 'A Sense of Classlessness', *ULR*, 5, 1958, pp26-32.
3   See especially, B.Jessop, *et al*, 'Authoritarian Populism: Two Nations and Thatcherism', *New Left Review*, 147, 1984, pp32-60; Hall, 'Authoritarian Populism: A Reply to Jessop *et al*', *New Left Review*, 151, 1985, pp115-24.
4   Thompson, 'The Politics of Theory', in R.Samuel (ed), *People's History and Socialist Theory*, Routledge, London 1981, pp396-408, p397.
5   Hall, 'Politics and Letters', in T.Eagleton (ed), *Raymond Williams: Critical Perspectives*, Polity, Cambridge 1989, pp54-66, p54.
6   R.Johnson, *op cit.*
7   Hall, 'The "First" New Left', *op cit*, p22.
8   *Ibid*, p22.
9   See, for instance, M.Abrams and R.Rose, *Must Labour Lose?*, Penguin, Harmondsworth 1960.
10  A.Crosland, *The Future of Socialism*, Cape, London 1956.
11  Though James Hinton suggests that Communist Party thinking was, in certain respects, evolving in more interesting and original directions in the 1940s, in Andrews, Fishman and Morgan, *op cit.*
12  Thompson, 'Commitment in Politics', *ULR*, 6, 1959, pp50-5; Samuel, 'Class and Classlessness', *ULR*, 6, 1959, pp44-50; Hall, 'The Big Swipe', *ULR*, 7, 1959, pp50-2.
13  See, for instance, Hall, 'The Supply of Demand', in E.P.Thompson (ed), *Out of Apathy*, Stevens, London 1960, pp56-97.
14  For an evaluation of Riesman, see S.M.Lipset and L.Lowenthal (ed), *Culture and Social Character: the work of David Riesman reviewed*, Free Press of Glencoe, New York 1961.
15  Hall, 'A Sense of Classlessness', *op cit*, pp 27-9.
16  *Ibid*, p27.
17  Hall, 'The Problem of Ideology – Marxism Without Guarantees', in B.Matthews (ed), *Marx: A Hundred Years On*, Lawrence and Wishart, London 1983, pp57-85.
18  Hall, 'The "First" New Left', *op cit*, p27.
19  Editorial, *New Left Review*, 1, 1960, p2.
20  *The Long Revolution*, Chatto and Windus, London 1961, was the title of Raymond Williams' influential contemporary text.
21  Editorial, *New Left Review*, 1, p2.
22  Anderson, *Arguments within English Marxism*, *op cit*, pp190-2.
23  Thompson, 'Commitment in Politics', *op cit*, p50.
24  *Ibid*, p51.
25  *Ibid*, p51.
26  *Ibid*, p51.
27  Thompson, 'Commitment in Politics', *op cit*, p51.
28  G.Redfern, 'The Real Outrage', *ULR*, 5, 1958, pp7-10.
29  Thompson, 'Commitment in Politics', *op cit*, p52.
30  Thompson, 'The Long Revolution', parts 1 and 2, *New Left Review*, 9 and 10, 1961, pp24-33 and 34-39.
31  This perspective is discussed in greater detail in chapter three.
32  Thompson, *William Morris: Romantic to Revolutionary*, Lawrence and Wishart, London 1955.
33  Thompson, *The Making of the English Working Class*, Gollancz, London 1963.

34 Saville, 'The Welfare State: An Historical Approach', *New Reasoner*, 3, 1957-8, pp5-25.
35 D. Thompson, *The Early Chartists*, Macmillan, London 1971.
36 R.Miliband, *The State in Capitalist Society*, Quartet, London 1969.
37 Miliband, 'The Transition to the Transition', *New Reasoner*, 6, 1958, pp35-48, p38.
38 Hall, 'The Big Swipe', *op cit*, p50.
39 *Ibid*, pp50-1.
40 *Ibid*, p51.
41 See, for example, Williams on Caudwell, in *Politics and Letters: Interviews with New Left Review*, New Left Books, London 1980, p127.
42 Hall, 'A Sense of Classlessness', *op cit*, p28.
43 *Ibid*, p31.

# CHAPTER THREE

# The Socialist Humanism
# of Edward Thompson

Whilst the themes of class and classlessness tended to generate discord within the New Left, the discourse of humanism appeared far more consensual. Both wings of the movement adopted a humanist rhetoric to articulate their opposition to the dominant brands of socialism. Yet, in the wake of his break from Stalinism, Thompson developed a particularly influential, appealing and cohesive normative framework for the left. This revolved around the concepts of agency, individual moral responsibility and experience. All of these had been marginalised or devalued by the economistic and deterministic traditions of Stalinism and social democracy: 'socialist humanism... exists by virtue of a continuing polemic, on the one hand with Communist orthodoxy, and on the other hand with liberal and social-democratic ideology'.[1] His alternative provided the framework for much of the movement's social critique and the core of his own subsequent political ideas, many of which were elaborated in the course of his historical work. Significantly, he was, in the late 1950s, simultaneously writing *The Making of the English Working Class*, his influential contribution to the study of British social history. Many of the concerns of this text dovetailed with his more theoretical writing on socialist humanism. Yet, the latter remain largely unexplored compared to his monumental study of the formation of the English working class.[2]

## SOCIALIST HUMANISM

Socialist Humanism was largely shaped by the political context in which Thompson developed these ideas. Together with Saville and other ex-communists connected with the *New Reasoner*, he sought to develop socialist principles outside the parties of the left, and beyond the dominant intellectual positions available to socialists in the late 1950s. His courageous stand against contemporary communism involved an ethical critique of the limitations of mainstream socialist discourse, and provided intellectual and moral inspiration for others to follow in his wake. Indeed, Thompson's political and intellectual biography is central to the history of the pursuit of a 'third way' among British socialists in the post-war period. His contemporary thinking connected him to a new political generation and a wider series of political struggles, offering starting points for a whole series of academic and political reflections which have since become highly influential. In this sense, his ideas formed a bridge between older socialist traditions and newer emphases – on the importance of cultural processes and moral argument, for instance. Paradoxically, however, many of the avenues pursued by those who were influenced by his creative intellectual reflections were disapproved of by Thompson; developments in the discipline of cultural studies after the mid-1970s provide a striking example of this.

These tensions were also present in this earlier period. It became evident that his ideas were insufficiently novel for some of his new political compatriots, especially some of the younger writers drawn to the *ULR*. To some extent, this rift opened because Thompson was dealing with different questions from these other thinkers. For the latter, the concerns of socialist humanism were simply irrelevant to the project which they were pursuing – the articulation of a new kind of politics for the left, founded on a different conception of political mobilisation and social constituencies.

In Thompson's mind, socialist humanism involved the reconstitution of the positive and emancipatory aspects of the socialist tradition, but in new moral terms. The first issue of the *New Reasoner* carried a powerful statement of his humanist standpoint. In this article, 'Socialist Humanism: An Epistle to the Philistines', questions about morality, the role of the individual and the relationship between means and ends were posed with an unusual candour.[3] He began with a critique of the falsity of Stalinist conceptions of politics. Their influence represented a phase in British and European history when the lineage of libertarian communism had been defeated. In ideological terms, this had resulted in the displacement of any notion of creative human agency. Stalinism took the 'make-believe model' of a base and superstructure in human relations and endowed economic laws and objects with their own agency. These were presented as the sole determinants of human behaviour, obviating discussion of the moral capacities of individuals.[4]

Against these ideas he reasserted the importance of ethical commitments for socialists, suggesting several areas in which they should be considered. Socialism was to be reconstituted as the creation of individual human subjects. Accordingly, he was determined to locate the source of moral judgements within the parameters of everyday existence. He countered liberalism's formulation of an abstract set of universal moral principles, and the application of scientific interpretations of Marxism which denied the significance of ethical problems. He asserted the importance of developing a sense of morality which was universal in application and not reducible to class interests. Essential to socialism's advance was its recourse to higher moral standards than those celebrated in either capitalist or Stalinist societies. This perspective challenged Leninist notions of proletarian virtue which had become increasingly prominent in the communist movement. Consequently, he argued that socialism had to provide a broader emancipation than merely achieving the socialisation of ownership and productive relations. A humanistic socialism stood at the head of human history, when the emancipated individual would emerge from 'his' present shackles. In this belief he drew heavily upon the romantic anti-capitalist tradition of the nineteenth century, particularly the work of John Ruskin, Thomas Carlyle and William Morris. Most significantly, he argued that contingency was endemic within moral judgements. Examining the attitudes which socialists should adopt towards violence, he concluded that for socialist humanists an arbitrary and binding commitment such as pacifism was untenable. Violence in many contingencies might be inescapable. Partisan sentiment and class conflicts were inevitable in human history. Indeed, the road to socialism was unavoidably strewn with these. The values of socialist humanism would mean, however, that until such time as recourse to alternatives was impossible, coercive methods would be avoided. With these values as a guide, such contingent actions would never be glorified.[5]

This principle was further elaborated by Thompson several years later. In the wake of the popularity which 'third world' liberation movements achieved among the younger sections of the New Left after 1960, he warned against the celebratory attitude towards violence adopted by some of the leading theorists of this period, especially Jean-Paul Sartre and Frantz Fanon.[6] Thompson compared such attitudes unfavourably with those of Marx and Engels:

> In their elevation of the humanist values of revolutionary pride, Marx and

Engels rarely glorify violence as such... They also assumed (though this is implicit rather than explicit in Marx's passionate humanism) that the morality of the oppressed would prove superior to that of the oppressors. At some places they suggest a relativistic morality, at others they suggest ulterior criteria, a 'fully human' morality.[7]

The need to develop a contextually based, yet deeply moral, revolutionary ethic was, in his view, obscured by the panegyrics of Sartre, Fanon and their New Left followers. Within any revolutionary situation, both humanistic and anti-humanistic currents were bound to emerge. The social advance represented by a socialist revolution would be expressed in a more profoundly moral society. Simultaneously, however, revolution would have to transform deeply unpleasant historical realities. It was important for socialists not to confuse these two characteristics by celebrating actions which impaired the realisation of a higher morality. Violent rebellion was unavoidable in certain situations, yet Thompson warned against the dangers of presuming that this was the only way in which socialism was to be pursued. Those who believed this were in danger of making virtues out of particular necessities: 'If we accept (as indeed I do) that for the enslaved the moment of rebellion is also a moment of the attainment of richer human attributes, we are surely not tricked into believing that rebellion, gun in hand, is the *only* measure of the attainment of humanity'.[8]

Socialist humanism posited a dialectic between historical necessity and moral choice. Thompson suggested that ethical choices could not be understood without reference to contingency, yet contingency and necessity were balanced by the autonomy of humanist values. In particular situations he was confident that a socialist movement which provided the opportunity for open and honest debate would produce the best moral decisions. Creative moral agency was dependent upon self-consciousness. Informed by open discussion and the deployment of reason, moral choices would be enabled in most situations. After his experiences within the CPGB, Thompson implicitly relied upon a context of institutional plurality for the development of a political culture which would engender individual responsibility and informed citizenship. Drawing upon the tradition of civic republican thought, he proffered a vision of a reconstituted public realm as the basis for political and moral renewal. These ideas provided the cornerstones for the moral commitments enunciated in his New Left and later work. His arguments, however, generated some critical discussion within the New Left, principally because he failed to carry his analysis beyond the attempted reconstitution of an indigenous, radical tradition. This is especially pertinent given the development of comparable bodies of thought in other West European countries, which overlapped to some degree with Thompson's humanist vision. Kate Soper cites, among others, the existentialism of Merleau-Ponty and Sartre, the early work of the Frankfurt school and the ideas of the Praxis group in Yugoslavia.[9] Like Thompson, these thinkers sought to reintroduce a humanist and moral vision within Marxist thought. Significantly, these strands found the tensions between these agendas increasingly problematic, lacking the confidence of British socialist humanists in the coherence of a reconstructed Marxist orthodoxy. Furthermore, these currents were connected to a wider series of philosophical and ontological debates which were unavailable within the British intellectual canon.

## THOMPSON'S NEW LEFT CRITICS

Within the New Left, Thompson's exploration of socialist humanism provided the dominant interpretation of the ethical dimension of socialism. Yet, despite the ubiquity of humanist language within this movement, his ideas were not universally accepted. Indeed the serious challenges which emerged later to his version of socialist humanism (particularly by Althusserian Marxists) were anticipated by some of the differences which emerged around this theme within the first New Left. The subsequent disappearance of socialist humanism as a political phenomenon is partly explicable in terms of weaknesses which became apparent at this time.

Concerns over several aspects of Thompson's analysis were soon registered. He encountered disapproval from orthodox Marxists for 'flitting on the perimeter of idealism'.[10] Significantly, a similar accusation was made against him by the next generation of the New Left which came into the ascendant after 1962. In their view, socialist humanism constituted the intellectual justification of the populism and moralism at the heart of this formation. Thompson's perspective was also criticised by socialists who had abandoned the attempt to reconstruct a set of moral standards within Marxism. Some, like Harry Hanson, turned instead to liberalism for a more coherent and established set of ethical principles, chiding Thompson for his refusal to set out the universal moral principles at the heart of socialism. According to Hanson, Thompson's attempt, 'to prove that in Marx's and perhaps in Lenin's ethics there is an ends-means interpenetration deriving from nonclass humanist values' failed because he wished to incorporate circumstance and contingency in his thought.[11] Like Stalinism, therefore, socialist humanism suggested that the means deployed in the struggle for socialism could not be prescribed in advance: circumstance was the ultimate determinant. However genuine the ethical motivations of socialist humanists, moral commitment was ultimately spirited into the future when a more convenient confluence of circumstances could be found. Thompson, according to Hanson, idealised both socialism and the road to it. Hanson finished by questioning the assumption that social experience inevitably led workers towards coherent humanist values.

In addition, Thompson's ideas received critical notices from two notable political theorists within the New Left. Alasdair MacIntyre, who had authored a penetrating study of the relationship between Marxism and Christianity,[12] proceeded to spell out, more fully than Thompson, the implications of a humanist teleology. He reflected on the extent to which humanist values were either perennial, and thus non-partisan, or were rooted in class relationships. For MacIntyre, human values and human nature itself were determined by 'the history of the class struggle'.[13] Meanwhile, the young Canadian theorist Charles Taylor suggested that connecting humanism with Marxism was more problematic than Thompson allowed. Marx's humanistic commitments had been systematically distorted and downplayed by later Marxists. The ideal of the 'brotherhood of man' had not been as influential as the more production orientated notion of the 'realisation of alienated human nature'.[14] Thompson's simplistic assertion that the means socialists deployed were as important as their ends failed to register these ambiguities within the classical Marxist tradition.

The claims of socialist humanism were clearly not universally shared within this milieu. Those involved with the *ULR* wing of the New Left proved even more sceptical, moving in analytical directions which implicitly undermined the coherence of Thompson's humanism. In their concern for the restoration of a genuine sense of community within British political life, these thinkers – including Charles Taylor, Stuart Hall, Norman Birnbaum, Raymond Williams and Rod Prince – attempted a more concrete assessment of the ethics necessary for socialist advance. This project moved them even further from orthodox Marxism. Attention was focused on the reproduction of dominant values in society, such as the widespread belief that the political system was immune to change, and how these might be displaced and replaced by a participatory political culture and a new sense of community. *ULR*'s increasing interest in cultural products and criticism encouraged its writers to challenge the separate status accorded to the economic, political and cultural dimensions of social life. Cultural trends and practices were perceived as indicative of deeper political and social problems. Moreover, this wing of the New Left engaged more closely with the new points of antagonism generated by contemporary society, empathising with burgeoning currents of countercultural revolt among the youth of the 1950s (discussed further in chapter four). Domination was understood to be rooted within cultural as well as political practices, whilst sub-cultures of resistance to dominant values were celebrated in the form of adolescent revolt, the ideas of the 'angry' writers and local community solidarity. These writers manifested an ambivalent attitude to the forces of change moving throughout British society – endorsing modernity's revolutionary attitude to the old order, yet remaining sceptical about its morality. This contrasted starkly with the *New Reasoner*'s approach: its humanism looked to the restitution of the values associated with the romantic moral ideal. Modernity was rejected as worthless, superficial and unsatisfying.

From the perspective of the *ULR*, the humanist agenda of Thompson failed to provide sufficient guidance in several important areas. It did not involve a rigorous examination of social change and the shifting context of British politics. In particular, socialist humanism placed insufficient emphasis upon the increasingly diversified social and political identities of subaltern groups in the late 1950s. Class was merely one of many determinants of political identity and behaviour: age, race and geographical locale seemed increasingly salient. More generally, Thompson's humanism reproduced the teleological assumptions of classical Marxism. This characteristic, together with the romantic and holistic concerns of the *New Reasoner*, proved anathema to this younger generation who wished to build socialism in the contradictory realities of the present. The younger generation turned elsewhere for theoretical inspiration, especially to the work of Raymond Williams. Increasingly, for *ULR*, the realm of the social (the complex of individual and collective experiences, practices and consciousness) required examination in its own right, and could no longer be interpreted as the outcome of class battles, unseen economic forces or elite manipulation. This analysis began to move in new and subversive directions. Some of the conceptual assumptions upon which the political life of the 1950s was founded were called into question: the relationships between private and public spheres; between culture and politics; and between society and economy.[15] This side of the New Left's agenda developed tributaries which flowed at different points and in diverse ways into the radical politics of a later generation.

Thompson quickly sensed the different agendas which were emerging within the New Left, as we have seen in his debate with Hall. In an early edition of *New Left Review* he took Williams to task for overemphasising both the cultural sphere and the evolutionary development of democracy and educational provision in Britain, as well as for his tendency to downplay social conflict. Once again, he warned against the popularity of the concept of alienation as opposed to exploitation among the younger sections of the New Left; this engendered, in Thompson's view, a move away from material questions about poverty, economic inequality and social provision towards issues connected with consumption, culture and communications.[16] Increasingly, the younger generation within this movement perceived the latter as central to understanding the nature of contemporary society. Whilst Thompson's humanist philosophy remained largely unchallenged during these years, it is clear that for sections of the first New Left, socialist humanism provided an unsuitable vehicle for the development of alternative lines of thought and analysis which they perceived as vital for the regeneration of socialism in Britain.

## PROBLEMS WITH SOCIALIST HUMANISM

Anderson's critique of Thompson's humanism, which appeared in 1980, is the most celebrated and complete refutation of these ideas to have emerged on the British left.[17] Much of this response stemmed from the later New Left's commitment to importing historical materialism into British political culture, encouraging a blunt rejection of the supposed moralism and populism which predominated among its New Left predecessors. Yet Anderson's position was, to some degree, prepared by the experiences he gained within the *New Left Review* milieu after 1960, among those sections of the New Left who were most uneasy about socialist humanism. As he later suggested, the increasingly assertive tone of Thompson's humanist discourse in the late 1950s was 'a reflection of unnegotiated strains and difficulties in the New Left of the time'.[18]

Both *New Left Review*'s geographical location in Soho and the preferences of its editor, Hall, ensured that it retained many of the political and stylistic features of *ULR*. For those who had been associated with the *New Reasoner*, the new journal was an intense disappointment.[19] They watched perplexed as the young, harassed and relatively inexperienced editor encouraged a home-grown stable of writers whose interests and talents were drawn from milieux alien to their more experienced comrades in the New Left. Several of these writers had recently graduated from student radicalism, in particular Robin Blackburn and Michael Rustin. One talented writer who flourished in this context was the young Anderson, who announced his arrival with an ambitious comparison of social democracy in Sweden and the ideas of Anthony Crosland.[20] This younger generation was initially characterised by its interest in current social problems, enthusiasm for cultural phenomena and openness to a variety of theoretical sources; these features were all manifested in the *New University*, an Oxford University journal in which they were greatly involved.[21] The silence of socialist humanism in these areas did little to enhance its appeal to this new generation.

This context does not provide a sufficient explanation for Anderson's later attack upon Thompson's ideas, yet certain connections can be established between these earlier debates and his later opposition to what he regarded as the confused and misleading notion of experience within Thompson's conception of socialist humanism. The complex and multifaceted nature of the social world negated, in Anderson's view, the possibility of interpreting experience as the springboard for coherent humanist values. The apparently innocent notions of social experience, common sense and human nature, should, he argued, be seen as ideological battlegrounds.[22] This was a similar position to that reached by *ULR*, following its wide range of articles documenting social changes the late 1950s and sensitivity to patterns of cultural and ideological representation. Thompson, on the other hand, believed that coherent moral values were developed in the course of social interchange informed by reason and self-awareness. But Anderson wondered how moral sense could arise spontaneously in the context of a complex and partisan social world? Indeed, Thompson's belief in the moral responsibility of the individual weakened his own position further. In explaining individual behaviour under capitalism, socialist humanists increasingly turned to concepts such as alienation and domination. Yet, such collective processes inevitably undermined the notion of the moral autonomy of individuals. Anderson was equally critical of the Thompsonian definition of historical agents as the 'locus' of values, beliefs and intentions. In fact, as Kate Soper has suggested, Thompson himself appeared to disregard these at various points in his political arguments. When addressing the moral errors of the Stalinists in Eastern Europe, for instance, he mocked their protested innocence: what mattered were the consequences of their actions.[23] If actions were to be judged on the basis of consequences, however, unintended factors might be as important as the beliefs and intentions of individuals and social groups. Circumstance, structure and chance might be of far greater importance in determining outcomes.

These difficulties were not, in fact, unique to Thompson, but reflected an important trend within the politics of this period. Problems of impersonality, bureaucratism and alienation had become increasingly salient following the development of more rational and centralised patterns of state regulation and institutional organisation in the post-war period. Thompson countered these trends, and the theoretical difficulties they posed for socialists, by celebrating the existential rebellion of dissident individuals who strove to forge alternative political traditions and cultures. The re-establishment of a politically literate and discursive civic culture, involving the re-appropriation of levels of decision-making by the popular classes, lay at the heart of Thompson's belief in the creation of a new, morally conscious citizenry (a precursor for the ideas of the Charter '88 group in Britain).[24] The desire to root this vision in the contemporary customs and 'good sense' of the British people led Thompson to blur a number of theoretical problems, not least the complex relationship between social experience, the ideologies through which this experience was evaluated and political change.

Undoubtedly, socialism had come to be associated with a lack of ethical vision and moral scruple. In this sense, the New Left was merely the first wave of a much deeper crisis which has shaken socialism in Britain and elsewhere since the Second World War. Socialists have sometimes appeared uninterested in concrete moral issues, shallow in their ethical concerns and too willing to sacrifice the needs of individuals to the collective good.[25] For the first New Left, ethical questions were central, whilst for Thompson the survival of socialism depended on its reassertion of the centrality of agency and morals in the lives of individuals as well as social groups. Unfortunately, his instinctive reliance on experience as an analytical weapon in his struggle against the totalitarian effects of high-level socialist theory resulted in a belief in the merits of judgements based upon innate and intuitive, social common sense. This remained the case throughout his subsequent intellectual life. Whilst at times this was a source of great analytical strength, as in his polemic against Louis Althusser's theoreticism,[26] this position often amounted to a refusal to recognise the extent to which experience was constructed by complex ideological and social pressures.

Thompson's insistence on the parity of the necessity/choice dialectic within the sphere of ethics was also problematic. Whilst he opposed the celebration of deeds performed in the context of necessity and projected the importance of an ethically inspired socialism, he proved reluctant to develop the categories of agency and choice to encompass the complex relationship between intention and circumstance and the many 'internal' constraints and influences which shaped the individual subject in society. The implications of this divergence between humanist discourse on the one hand (Thompson's position) and sensitivity to the social construction of political identity on the other (the emphasis of many of his critics), have been profound: an increasingly rigid dichotomy has divided those concerned with the rehabilitation of moral language on the left from those more sensitive to the overdetermined nature of social life. In other words, a stark analytical choice was posed for left intellectuals after this date: either they could believe in and defend the moral sovereignty of rationally self-governing individuals or they could deconstruct the notion of this harmonious individual, using bodies of theory which prioritised the operations of ideological and cultural processes.[27]

To some degree, Thompson's theoretical agenda should be understood as the product of the outlook and experiences of the *New Reasoner* group. Socialist humanism was presented as supranational, an inspirational creed for the New Left and its allies in Western Europe as well as the dissident movement within Eastern Europe. This commitment drew upon the memory of the Popular Front of the 1930s, the experiences of partisan resistance movements in the Second World War and the political shift to the left which took place in several West European countries from 1943-5. Thompson later testified to the importance of these events within his own development, evidenced by his jointly edited collection of his brother's letters (Frank Thompson died fighting with the Bulgarian partisans).[28] Socialist humanism was premised on a set of political conditions which had disappeared by the late 1950s. This vision proved increasingly inappropriate within the changing world order engendered by the Cold War of the early 1950s, and following the emergence of new forces for revolution and change in the 'third world'. Once Anderson became the dominant editorial force on *New Left Review* after 1962, the journal was far more interested in revolutionaries in the developing world than dissidents in Eastern Europe.

This preference can be traced back to differences within the first New Left between the socialist humanism of the *New Reasoner* and the sympathy for new liberation struggles which held the attention of sections of the *ULR* milieu, particularly after the Cuban revolution of 1960 (this tension is explored in greater detail in chapter seven).

Furthermore, the *New Reasoner* emphasised the need to reconnect the contemporary concerns of democratic socialism with older lineages. In particular, the romantic tradition of opposition to the effects and ideologies of capitalist development was celebrated within the journal's pages. Socialist humanism was imbued with images from these moments of opposition, such as the Chartists or the romantic poets. Whilst these were represented in an apparently creative and open fashion, this orientation was also generationally based. Many within the New Left were unmoved by this lineage and felt excluded and marginalised by a tradition which failed to address the complexity of the contemporary world.

Thompson's refusal to systematise the body of socialist humanist theory or to develop its categories in a more rigorous fashion was not, therefore, solely the product of his preference for historical rather than theoretical work.[29] Whilst he presented his ideas as the kernel of a tradition which awaited further systematisation, it is clear that significant political obstacles stood in the way of its development. In particular, he neglected to address three questions which were of great interest to the *ULR* wing of the New Left: how to empower social groups and individuals in the modern context; how cultural and ethical domination was actually maintained within different societies; and how the elaboration of the concept of agency could encompass the elements of social identity subordinated by class analysis.

Conventional socialist thought was weak in all these areas. Thompson's work had shifted the terms of socialist discussion to allow for these questions to be posed. Indeed, his bold defence of the moral autonomy of individuals, alongside his commitment to a humanistic discourse, enriched the political ideas of this milieu. But it was left to those associated with *ULR* and the early *New Left Review* to undertake work in these three areas. This difference did not generate overt theoretical opposition to the socialist humanism of Thompson, so that many of his beliefs remained predominant within the movement. Several of the differences which emerged within the movement after 1959, however, were the products of the shift made by the *ULR* wing of the New Left towards a set of questions which tended to undermine the hegemony of socialist humanist discourse. The sharpness of Thompson's comment in contemporary debates, as well as the suspicion he articulated towards *ULR*, emanated from an instinctive grasp of this. He subsequently recalled that:

> when Raymond Williams' *The Long Revolution* came out, Stuart Hall, as editor of *New Left Review*, commissioned me to write a review article upon it. After reading the book I asked to be relieved of the task, since I found my theoretical differences with Williams to be so sharp that, to express them fully, would endanger the political relations of the New Left.[30]

## SOCIALIST HUMANISM TODAY?

Some commentators have recently argued that Thompson's humanist preferences have been misrepresented and that his ideas remain relevant in the current political climate, given the collapse of the communist project in Eastern Europe and the weakness of social democracy in Britain since 1979. Kate Soper, for instance, believes that his normative principles could provide the basis for the reformulation of socialist thought.[31] Like Thompson, she argues that the natural interpretation of socialist principles is strongly humanist and that the hegemony of non or anti-humanist ideas has substantially weakened the left in Britain and elsewhere. The rehabilitation of Thompson's political ideas, in particular his socialist humanism, is therefore important. Ellen Meiksens Wood develops a similar argument.[32] Already established as the scourge of revisionist currents on the left, she stresses the pertinence of the methodology deployed by Thompson throughout his historical work. This is presented as an essential continuation of Marx's own method. According to Meiksens Wood, Thompson, in deploying the Marxist belief that 'there is a unifying logic in the relations of production which imposes itself throughout a society, in the complex variety of its empirical reality', consistently set himself 'to encompass historical specificity, as well as human agency, while recognising within it the logic of modes of production'.[33] He was a creative historical materialist who perceived structural determination as integral to the historical process. Despite the overwhelming praise accorded to Thompson for his interest in the agency of classes and individuals, his ideas have, in her view, been misunderstood. His historical writings were underpinned by the belief that the relations of production were always acting within the cultural and ideological spheres: for Thompson, the economic sphere was always social.[34]

To illustrate her argument, she cites his development of socialist humanism in the late 1950s. In this period, he demonstrated convincingly that morals and values were central to the construction of socialist arguments and were not simply fictions designed to bolster class domination. Accordingly, socialist humanism provided a neglected and significant manifestation of a genuinely Marxist method.

Soper also focuses upon socialist humanism, though she illuminates a number of tensions which beset this project and the evolution of his ideas. Ultimately, however, she suggests that Thompson easily overcame the criticisms of his position made by both liberal and Marxist contemporaries. In conclusion, she celebrates the relevance of the 'spirit' of socialist humanism for contemporary conditions, emphasising the need for universally applicable ethical positions in the context of the environmental crisis.

## CONCLUSIONS

Soper and Meiksens Wood both believe that Thompson's ideas may offer socialists an escape from their contemporary plight. Yet, neither attends systematically to the gaps and silences within socialist humanism. Nor do they examine the tensions which underlay this project at its very moment of inception, in the first New Left. Socialist humanism was not universally adopted within the movement, particularly because *ULR* generated interests which served to undermine the authority of Thompson's formulation. Much of the later criticism aimed at these concepts was anticipated within this movement. Most importantly, Anderson's critique originated, in part, from his experiences in the movement after 1960. Certainly, the ideological significance of socialist humanism should not be underplayed within the development and formation of the New Left. Simultaneously, the context in which this project emerged accounts for many of its features. For Simon Clarke, 'the 'empiricism' of 'socialist humanism' has to be related to the political and intellectual circumstances in which the project developed'.[35] But, it does not necessarily follow, as Meiksens Wood and Soper implicitly suggest, that socialist humanism would have significantly altered the fate of the left in subsequent years, had it become hegemonic. It contained a series of political and theoretical weaknesses from the outset; these were merely exacerbated by hostile currents of thought, such as structuralism and different strands of critical and cultural theory, which have since become influential on the left.

Above all, Thompson's ideas were deeply imbued with a teleological sense of historical progress and the superiority of socialist values. In terms of the construction of a radical and dynamic humanist agenda, these assumptions, which were inherited from classical Marxism, were problematic. They resulted in the failure to approach the difficult strategic task of disseminating these values to particular social groups and agents. In addition, they generated complacency about the ideological positioning of the themes of individual autonomy, opposition to bureaucratism and the state, as well as humanist discourse more generally. Control of these agendas was seized by the radical politics of the right in a later political conjuncture. This did not occur because the left failed to pay sufficient heed to humanistic ideas, as Thompson consistently argued. In fact, at a key moment when humanistic values were influential, many of the difficult questions in this area were not posed. The confidence with which socialist humanists believed that such themes belonged to the left rendered many socialists badly prepared for the onslaught of the New Right in its libertarian and anti-statist guise.[36] Whilst these two ideological projects clearly differed fundamentally, they shared a commitment to a libertarian ethos which combined a concern for individual autonomy with a critique of the increasingly restrictive and regulative role of the state in its various institutional guises. This led both currents towards anti-state and anti-corporatist positions, refusing the logic of centralised provision on behalf of the people. Similarly, both grounded their visions in the increasing sense of discontent and disillusion with state and society in the post-war era. This parallel suggests that socialist humanists' combination of moral discourse and critique of the post-war settlement touched on some of the key tensions within the political consensus of this period; yet, Thompson and other left humanists were unable to translate their vision into a popular and cogent vernacular, unlike their New Right successors.

Whilst it is important to appreciate the role of a fiercely held moral commitment in Thompson's life and thought (particularly his stand against Stalinism), the wholesale rehabilitation of a flawed agenda will not necessarily benefit the left or help us understand the nature of socialist humanism. In fact, the central features of this perspective – its mobilisation of a radical indigenous tradition, its simple emphasis on individual agency and moral autonomy, and its belief in the compatibility of humanist values and historical materialism – are all questionable. Socialist humanism is more accurately understood as a historically specific project which enabled sections of the British intelligentsia to escape the confines of Stalinist Marxism.

NOTES

1 Thompson, *Where are we now?*, *op cit*, p16.

2 Chun, *op cit*, views these writings as some of the weakest parts of his work, p62.

3 Thompson, 'Socialist Humanism: An epistle to the Philistines', *New Reasoner*, 1, 1957, pp105-43. See also 'Agency and Choice – 1', *New Reasoner*, 5, 1958, pp89-106; 'Socialism and the Intellectuals', *ULR*, 1, 1957, pp31-6; 'A Psessay in Ephology', *op cit*.

4 Thompson, 'Socialist Humanism', *op cit*, p113.

5 This theme has been debated more extensively by other Marxist humanists; see, for instance, N.Geras, 'Our Morals: The Ethics of Revolution', *Socialist Register*, 1989, pp185-211.

6 Thompson was especially critical of the anti-European sentiments articulated by Fanon, *The Wretched of the Earth*, MacGibbon and Kee, London 1965.

7 Thompson, *Where are we now?*, *op cit*, p16.

8 *Ibid*, p17.

9 Kate Soper, 'Socialist Humanism', in H.Kaye and K.McClelland (eds), *E.P.Thompson, Critical Perspectives*, Polity, Cambridge 1990, pp204 – 32.

10 T.Enright, 'Materialism or Eclecticism', *New Reasoner*, 3, 1957, pp105-12, p108.

11 Harry Hanson, 'An Open Letter to Edward Thompson', *New Reasoner*, 2, 1957, pp79-91, p80.

12 Alasdair MacIntyre, *Marxism: an interpretation*, SCM Press, London 1953.

13 MacIntyre, 'Notes from the Moral Wilderness – 1', *New Reasoner*, 7, 1958-9, pp90-100, p95; see also 'Notes from the Moral Wilderness – 2', *New Reasoner*, 8, 1959, pp89-98.

14 Taylor, 'Marxism and Humanism', *New Reasoner*, 2, 1957, pp92-8, p97.

15 Critics, such as Wilson, *op cit*, are therefore wrong to overstress the coherence of this milieu's intellectual agenda.

16 Thompson, 'The Long Revolution – 1', *op cit*.

17 Anderson, *Arguments within English Marxism*, *op cit*.

18 *Ibid*, p157.

19 This is evident from Thompson's correspondence with Saville, 'New Left Review 1959-63' file, Saville papers.

20 Anderson, 'Mr Crosland's Dreamland', *New Left Review*, 7 and 9, 1961, pp4-12 and 34-45.

21 This journal was founded in 1960 and gave a strong emphasis to cultural as well as political writing.

22 Anderson, *Arguments within English Marxism*, *op cit*, pp25-31.

23 Soper, *op cit*, pp211-2.

24 The influence of the civic republican tradition in Western political thought upon Thompson's ideas has been underplayed by commentators on his work; see Taylor's discussion of the absence of this lineage in Western Marxism in 'Marxism and Socialist Humanism', in Archer *et al*, *op cit*, pp59-78.

25 For a lucid and influential discussion of these questions, see S.Lukes, *Marxism and Morality*, Oxford University Press, Oxford 1987.

26 Thompson, 'The Poverty of Theory or an Orrery of Errors', in *The Poverty of Theory*, *op cit*, pp1-210.

27 K.Soper, *Humanism and Anti-humanism*, Hutchinson, London 1986.

28 E.P and T.J.Thompson, *There is a Spirit in Europe: A Memoir of Frank Thompson*, Gollancz, London 1947.

29 Thompson deployed this defence on numerous occasions; see, for instance, 'The

Poverty of Theory', *op cit.*

30  Thompson, 'The Politics of Theory', in R.Samuel (ed), *People's History and Socialist Theory*, Routledge, London 1981, pp396-408, pp397-8.

31  Soper, *op cit.*

32  E. Meiksens Wood, 'Falling Through the Cracks: E.P.Thompson and the Debate on Base and Superstructure', in Kaye, *op cit*, pp125-52.

33  *Ibid*, p134.

34  *Ibid*, p136.

35  S. Clarke, 'Towards a Socialist History', *History Workshop*, 8, 1979, pp137-56, p151.

36  For a discussion of the ideological strands of New Right thinking, see R.Levitas (ed), *The Ideology of the New Right*, Polity, Cambridge 1986.

# CHAPTER FOUR

# Politics and Culture: Raymond Williams' 'Long Revolution'

> The new left has still a great deal to do in clarifying and developing its own positions. It has succeeded in defining the cultural crisis which is perhaps the most specific feature of advanced capitalism and thus opening up a new political perspective.[1]    Raymond Williams, 1965

For the younger wing of the New Left, Raymond Williams provided a methodology for social and political analysis. The development of his own ideas throughout this period is, therefore, vital to comprehending New Left politics and ideas. As will become clear, the conceptual shifts registered in his book, *The Long Revolution* (1961), encouraged sections of this movement to move beyond the traditions of economism and voluntarism which dominated the British left's imagination when it approached specifically cultural questions. More generally, Raymond Williams provided the theoretical tools and guidance for some within the New Left to address the pluralisation of social life and to develop a distinctive assessment of the contemporary world. Here, his emphasis upon the interconnections of the different elements within the social process was highly influential. These ideas were also translated into concrete activities which, though rudimentary, amounted to a serious attempt to construct a cultural politics. This project proved exceptionally fragile and contentious within this formation, yet prepared the way for a number of later intellectual and political developments.

As we have already seen, the New Left was characterised by a protean attitude towards established orthodoxy. Exploration of the cultural provided a suitable terrain for the reformulation of socialist values and the pursuit of a more complex and multi-dimensional conception of social life. As Hall has since suggested, 'the discourse of culture seemed to us fundamentally necessary to any language in which socialism could be redescribed. The New Left took the first faltering steps towards putting questions of cultural analysis and cultural politics at the centre of its politics'.[2] In fact, a key element within this project consisted of a fleeting, yet significant, engagement with popular culture. The work of the first New Left encouraged a more systematic account of popular cultural relations and forms, and prepared some of the ground for the more theoretically inclined reflections of Hall in particular and the Birmingham Centre for Contemporary Cultural Studies in the 1970s in general.

## CULTURE AND THE NEW LEFT

Cultural themes were frequently addressed within the New Left's intellectual practice. The profile which culture enjoyed within this milieu was the product of three particular developments. First, much of the force of New Left criticism of the prevailing orthodoxies on the left focused upon their narrowness. Both Stalinism and contemporary labourism were primarily concerned with redistribution in the economic sphere. Culture, in these perspectives, was viewed either as an appendage to more important considerations or as a purely epiphenomenal entity.[3] For the New Left, these assumptions had weakened the ability of socialism to describe and transform social and political life. The complex and diverse layers of contemporary society could not be adequately registered by such ideas. The second impulse behind this movement's interest in the cultural realm emerged from its emphasis upon the novelty and specificity of contemporary conditions. These were frequently described by its writers in cultural terms. The language of cultural criticism, garnered from the discipline of English literature, remained untainted by economism and reductionism, and consequently appealed to these critics.[4] This tradition, and Leavisite ideas especially, furnished the concepts with which the New Left expressed its concern for the totality of the social process. Third, writers in this milieu recognised the social impact of changes within the nation's popular culture. The onset of mass marketing and advertising, and the revolution in habit and lifestyle engendered by more dynamic consumption patterns, were developments of great social and political significance in their own right.[5] Some of these phenomena had first appeared in Britain in the pre-war period,[6] but their impact was more pronounced in the 1950s and appeared to be part of a much larger change in the social and cultural landscape. For some in the New Left, the reconstitution of socialism depended upon its ability to describe and engage with these processes. In addition, the emergence of new cultural habits (package holidays and television for example) revealed and accelerated the diversification of the social sphere. Increasingly, the New Left focused upon a broader set of social groups and identities whose specific concerns had to be addressed by socialist politics, not subsumed beneath a master category, for instance class, or a single strategic appeal. This formation's sensitivity to the demands of an aspiring youth culture, which is described in more detail below, exemplified its pluralistic vision of the social world.

Thus the work of the New Left in the cultural sphere developed a particularly strong profile. This area of its intellectual practice proved contentious, however, especially because it coincided with Crosland's assessment of the significance of social and cultural change and their implications for Labour. Such a parallel with revisionist currents in the Labour Party was both embarrassing and stimulating for these elements of the New Left. Members of the *ULR* circle remained critical of Crosland's project but simultaneously recognised their shared interests, hence the debates with Crosland and other Labour figures at the New Left Club in London. Both projects were moving into the same territory, though from different directions. Differences of approach, as we have seen, emerged within the New Left over the extent and nature of rethinking necessary to reconstitute socialist thought. The theme of culture lay at the centre of the anxieties experienced by many over the future direction of socialism.

## RAYMOND WILLIAMS

Williams came to the New Left after a period of political inactivity, following his brief membership of the Communist Party and involvement in the Second World War. Invited to speak at the ULR Club, he developed a strong empathy for the intellectual project pursued within the journal's pages. His relatively early break from communism put him at a distance from the *New Reasoner*. Throughout these years he was less directly involved in the New Left than either Thompson or Hall, yet he left his intellectual stamp on the movement in numerous ways. His reflections on the relationship between politics and culture broke new ground on the left, providing inspiration for many of the practical and theoretical endeavours of the younger New Left generation – especially Hall.

Williams provided the intellectual framework for much of *ULR*'s project, especially through his discussion of the interaction between cultural practices and other aspects of the social process. Indeed, his intellectual development before this period ensured that his own work was well in advance of the thinking evident in either of the journals on these questions. As John McIlroy suggests:

> Williams... saw in the emergence of the New Left and its new emphasis
> – conditioned by the new prosperity, the abating of overt class struggle,
> the social stability – on *cultural* struggle to transform the values and
> meanings generated by capitalist society, the opportunity to practice on
> the political plane the ideas he had been developing since 1948.[7]

In *Culture and Society* (1957), Williams attempted to deploy the Leavisite notion of practical literary criticism to interpret social processes.[8] For Leavis, the cultural norms and values of a given society could be criticised and understood with relation 'to a fixed set of standards nominated as Culture with a capital C'.[9] Whilst the Leavisite perspective engendered hostility to popular cultural formations and a generally anti-democratic ethos,[10] it provided a method for analysing cultural systems and products, and an emphasis on the importance of social transformation. According to Hall, it also appealed as a tradition which took culture seriously, unlike the modish dilettantism of the Oxbridge literary establishment.[11] In *Culture and Society* the influence of this perspective on Williams' work was apparent as he strove to construct an unsullied tradition of opposition to industrial capitalism. The authors who made up his tradition displayed differing political allegiances (from Burke to Godwin), yet shared in common a rejection of the terms and norms of industrialisation, as well as a sensitivity to the impact of this process upon society and the environment.[12]

Williams' distance from Marxism and the 'committed criticism' of the Communist Party was evident: 'To describe English life, thought and imagination in the last three hundred years simply as 'bourgeois', to describe English culture now as 'dying' is to surrender reality to a formula'.[13] His response to these writers was predicated less upon their class position than their relationship to an immanent tradition whose contemporary completion lay in the advance of democratic socialism. Significantly, he also rejected the 'respectable' mode of cultural criticism embedded in such organs as the *New Statesman*, criticising the tendency to relegate this dimension of life to the margins. Even then, culture was conventionally presumed to be meaningful only if it was 'high' culture. With his emphasis upon the importance of all levels of the social process, Williams regarded such views as antiquated. He therefore challenged conventional wisdom about the 'triviality' of cultural meaning. The pervasiveness of mass culture had, in the eyes of many, blunted social divisions and eroded older ideological commitments. This was, for instance, the presumption of the 'end of ideology' theorists whose ideas were increasingly influential.[14] According to Williams, however, ideological conflict, far from disappearing, was constantly contesting and being contained by a divided and unequal cultural exchange.

Later commentators have not shared the enthusiasm with which the book was contemporaneously received. From the ranks of the later New Left, Terry Eagleton launched an attack upon this 'idealist and academicist project':[15] Williams' tradition was predicated upon a partisan re-reading of these authors. He was guilty of tapping into a highly ambivalent and romantic populism which obscured the contradictory nature of many of the texts under discussion. Following his critical appraisal of the 'one-sidedness' of many of Williams' political judgements, Terry Eagleton interpreted the latter's utopian emphasis on the creation of a common culture as the logical outcome of a romantic teleology. Indeed, Williams' belief in the possibility of a common culture, as well as his confident assertion of the future transformation of the labour movement into the vehicle of social change, revealed the naivety of the politics which underlay this vision. Whilst Eagleton's polemic was overstated in certain respects, as he himself later admitted,[16] his critique highlights two important aspects of Williams' argument in *Culture and Society*. First, his search for coherent humanist values was undermined by his increasing sensitivity to the political and social ambiguity of the cultural process in this period. Second, the teleology at the heart of this text, moving from early nineteenth-century opposition to liberal political economy to the post-war Labour Party, looked increasingly problematic in the political conditions of the late 1950s. In fact, Williams came to reject some of the assumptions behind this text shortly after its appearance. He subsequently provided, in *The Long Revolution* (1961), a distinctive reading of the social process which challenged conventional socialist ideas about the relationship between culture and politics.

The 'long revolution' stood for the culmination of three connected trends in social development: the democratic revolution (involving movements as disparate as the extension of parliamentary suffrage and the liberation movements of colonial peoples), the industrial revolution and the cultural revolution. This three-dimensional change was reverberating at all levels of

British social life though its direction was neither linear nor predetermined: 'This deeper cultural revolution is a large part of our most significant living experience and is being interpreted and indeed fought out, in many complex ways in the world of art and ideas'.[17] Williams offered a more holistic, anthropological understanding of the social world, illuminating connections between different elements which had previously been separated. Emphasis should be shifted to 'the study of relationships between elements in a whole way of life'.[18] Within this framework, areas of culture conventionally accorded 'special' status (fine art and literature, for instance) were viewed as socially privileged means of communication rather than the repositories of ultimate truth. Focus should be shifted to the way in which dominant values were affirmed within the social process: economistic readings of the cultural and social spheres were therefore rejected, as was the idea that consciousness was determined unidirectionally by economic relationships. The cultural world was more autonomous than was often recognised, whilst the various aspects of social existence had to be perceived as interacting within a larger totality, if the key questions of contemporary politics were to be grasped:

> if socialism accepts the distinction of 'work' from 'life', which has then to be written off as 'leisure' and 'personal interests', if it sees politics as 'government', rather than as the process of common decision and administration; if it continues to see education as training for a system and art as grace after meals... if it is limited in these ways, it is simply a late form of capitalist politics ... [19]

Pre-existing patterns of domination and subordination were not fixed immutably in the economic structures of a given society. A constant process of organisation and containment of the different dynamics of social action characterised modern society. Unconventionally, Williams incorporated the private sphere within his analysis, noting its interrelationships with the public world of conventional politics.

Because of the tension generated in the social process, it was impossible for a dominant culture to contain subordinate groups and ideas in a thorough way, resulting in cultural practices generating values which were contradictory and contestable. Any social or cultural formation could be divided on a tripartite basis into emergent, dominant and residual elements. Because of the uneasy co-existence of these parts, a subversive potential characterised the dominant order. As Edward Said has since noted, this perspective bears some resemblance to Gramsci's understanding of the nature of hegemony within modern societies.[20]

Throughout this text, Williams reasserted the value of approaching political issues from the perspective of totality, rather than the restricted categories of economic performance, political behaviour and cultural development. At present, socialists lacked the analytical vision to develop a cogent political strategy:

> In particular fields we have made some progress with these, but in our most general descriptions we are all still visibly fumbling, leaving an uncertainty easily explained by the blandest version of a natural and healthy evolution and certainly not rendered by such general nostrums as the fight for socialism which remains, after all, in terms of this country, almost wholly undefined.[21]

The left's prospects depended on its ability to understand and provide an alternative to the political effects of the cultures associated with marketing, advertising and consumerism. He warned, somewhat presciently, that 'parts of our very idea of society are withered at root' and, therefore, re-emphasised the concept of community as an alternative ethical principle, though one that was, at present, severely eroded and damaged by modern society.[22]

## COMMUNITY[23]

The concept of community played an important role as the vehicle for the transformation of Williams' ideas in this period. His distinctive political and intellectual history is important here.[24] His interest in the boundaries between communities and outsiders was longstanding; he regarded himself as the product of a border community.[25] In this period he returned to and transformed community as a political metaphor, fashioning a distinctive framework for his contemporary ideas, especially the belief that socialists had to broaden the scope of their social analysis and comprehend the interconnections between the lifestyles, consciousness and experience of social actors. Community was also significant because it lay at the heart of older interpretations of socialism which Williams opposed. Community had been understood as a sense of place and lifestyle, particularly that associated with large working-class communities in cities. This emphasis had always been supplemented by a concern for the symbolic and normative dimensions of community. In fact, numerous overlaps and confusions had arisen through the usage of community in the political discourse of the left. Communist interpretations of the term, for example, tended to impose an idealised version of the physical community on to the second dimension.[26] Socialist discourse implicitly sought to graft one, usually romanticised, form of community life on to the national community as a whole. In the 'them' and 'us' scenario of this logic, 'they' would be defeated and replaced by 'us' and 'our' way of life. In its pure (and crude) form such an approach was unworkable. How coherent were working-class communities in reality? How important were divisions within these communities? Were differences of interest and perspective to be marginalised beneath the presumed solidarities of communal life against outside enemies? Was it possible to extend the values of one kind of communal life, or at least the values the left preferred over others (solidarity against greed, sharing against bigotry), on to a larger scale, in a different context, outside the immediate world in which these values were fashioned?

Variations of these ideas abounded in the left's political thought prior to 1956. Romantic critics, communitarian utopians and pragmatic Fabians tended to share certain characteristics in their conceptions of communal liberation. Many of these theories were premised upon the conflation of individual with communal fulfilment. The political problems of such a 'general will' perspective were enormous, as the New Left repeatedly observed. Simultaneously, socialist intellectuals often deployed a notion of the self which was both highly romantic and essentialist. They implicitly related the construction of an ideal community to the possibility of complete human fulfilment, positing the transcendence of all internal contradictions and the emergence of the liberated, Arcadian individual. It was this simplistic and one-dimensional concept of community that Williams challenged. Enveloped by a sense of the 'border' and of the frontiers between old and new communities, he was acutely aware of the physical and social cohesion of many working-class communities. But his personal and political experiences had also given him an early acquaintance with a more cosmopolitan and transcendental political perspective. It was this tension which first attracted him to the concept of community and subsequently allowed him to rework its pre-existent connotations. This led him towards a different understanding of community from its conventional incarnations.

In *Culture and Society* he advanced community as a metaphor for the organic solidarities of life challenged by capitalism. Yet, an important tension characterised this perspective. In conclusion, he argued for a common culture at the heart of a putative, socialist community. His vision depended upon some sense of potential within contemporary working-class culture and its most progressive embodiment – the labour movement. But he remained deeply ambivalent here. Whilst he recognised that the solidaristic habits of working-class culture were not in themselves sufficient for a new political community, they were perceived as the platform from which this community might be built. His hesitation was caused by his claim that positive elements within the labour movement tradition still persisted. Simultaneously, however, his own critique of contemporary socialist politics and sense of the limitations of the labour-movement model for a dynamic, fast-growing and increasingly complex society, made such a suggestion problematic. In particular, the drift away from more settled social identities, which consumer capitalism engendered, required a new model of communitarian liberation.

This tension was resolved differently by another celebrated communitarian thinker whose work was also important within the early New Left. Richard Hoggart, author of the influential *Uses of Literacy* (1957), suggested that community, in both moral and physical terms, was being corrupted by the forces of modernity. A sense of lost innocence pervaded his text. Nor was Hoggart alone in this view. For many on the left, a nostalgia for a more wholesome and organic life was deeply embedded within approaches to the question of community. Yet, the significance of *The Long Revolution* lay in Williams' movement away from such notions. This was evident from a conversation between him and Hoggart published in 1960, in *New Left Review* 1. For Williams, community provided the basis for a more diverse and democratic communicative practice:

> I think it all centres on the nature of community, and when people say you and I are nostalgic or whatever, I want to get this completely clear... we have learned about community in our own ways, but we're not interested in the business of reproduction, it's the principle that's important. The fact is that communication is the basic problem of our society... It depends if it is to be real ... on real community of experience and the channels open so that all are involved.[27]

Despite the suggestion that he and Hoggart concurred about the concept of community, this comment barely conceals the disparity between their ideas. Whereas Hoggart believed in the re-creation of older communal loyalties and values in the face of an alienating and superficial modernity, Williams investigated the impact of modern values and cultures and their complex relationship with older traditions and ways of life. When interpreted simply as the nostalgic call for a lost world, community was an inadequate basis for opposing this new social order. The difference of tone and substance between the two men on this subject is significant because Williams was criticised in this period for replicating the organicism of Hoggart's ideas on community. In 1961 Richard Wollheim authored a Fabian Society pamphlet (*Socialism and Culture*) in which he conflated their ideas on culture and community.[28] In *The Long Revolution* Williams offered a confident reply to these criticisms. Indeed, he adopted a new framework to do so. In addition to his complex intellectual development, he was affected by two attributes of the early New Left here. First, as we have already seen, the *ULR* wing of this movement was fascinated by the question of political identity, challenging socialist axioms about consciousness and the relationship between class and politics. Against the traditions of economism and reductionism, writers in *ULR* analysed the 'subjective' elements of social life and worked from and with these as points of departure for a new and radical politics.[29] They disagreed with orthodox Marxist emphases here: social life was not a surface through which one looked to find the real course of history and politics; it constituted a complex terrain which the left had to comprehend and transform. Second, the New Left placed tremendous emphasis upon democracy, spontaneity and initiative from below. This motivated much of its opposition to communism and social democracy. Fear of the 'machine' lead to a celebration of difference, activity and democracy. Pluralism did not have to be surrendered to liberals. Was it possible, New Left writers implicitly asked, to reorganise society along socialist and pluralist lines? The New Left combined this sensitivity to the density and breadth of civil life with scepticism about statist forms of socialism. Both of these emphases provided Williams with the degree of political vitality required to develop new ways of tackling some longstanding problems for socialists.

In his hands, therefore, community became a metaphor for addressing social subjectivity and pluralism. In *The Long Revolution* he asserted more boldly that any communal extension must involve the provision of resources and abilities for a diversity of cultural and political perspectives. Here, community worked explicitly against the archaic meanings it possessed in Hoggart's work, as well as the socialist tradition more generally – a point supported by Charles Taylor's powerful contemporary critique of the 'jacobinical' assumptions of Marxist communitarianism.[30] The creation of a common culture involved the democratisation of Britain's political institutions so that the benefits of individual and collective participation could be reaped. Significantly, Williams did not pinpoint the contemporary labour movement as the vehicle for this transformation in this text. Instead, he provided criteria by which 'the open society' might be attacked, beyond the conventional grounds of efficiency, competence and material inequality. Through the principle of community he proposed a wider set of social goods and political sites from which contemporary society might be opposed and radical political interventions made. Like Thompson, Williams believed that the renewal of socialism was dependent on a more complex and meaningful discourse of values and needs, yet his political vision involved the transformation, rather than the rejection, of modernity.

Community, for Williams, meant more than the lifestyles and experiences of the working classes. As a political metaphor, it could no longer be anchored in the myth of the undifferentiated experience of ordinary people. Older senses of community were increasingly displaced by new ways of living. Against these trends he called for a new sense of belonging and meaning for both individuals and social groups, expressed through democratic, participatory and egalitarian cultures. Until socialists in general, and the Labour Party in particular, addressed the problems of workplace democracy, the degradation of the social environment, the decline of genuine social communication and the difficulties of social interaction, contemporary social developments would continue to undermine the Labour Party and movement:

> Caught in these many currents, the men and women of the newer communities are living out, explicitly, a pattern of learning and response which is also involving the society as a whole. I am not greatly surprised that contemporary Conservatism, in part directing just this complex, makes sense as an interpretation of it to very many people.[31]

Labour's political frustrations were reinterpreted, therefore, as the product of its failure to challenge the social and cultural myths and images through which conservatism reshaped the popular imagination. The analysis Williams offered was not restricted to cultural matters. It concerned the fortunes of socialist politics in Britain: the sense of apathy permeating British political life and its institutions, the increasing tendency to social fracture around styles of living rather than workplace consciousness, and the prognostications of the 'end of ideology' theorists, would increasingly work to undermine the left unless it broadened its moral and political outlook and organised interventions in all of the spheres of the long revolution. Its democratic task should be the renovation of the pre-modern forms of much of Britain's public life, an interesting precursor of the arguments of Anderson and Tom Nairn in the mid-1960s. Its cultural goal should be the supercesssion of the arcane and immobilising divisions between elite and popular cultures.

The importance of this text lies in the breaks it established with pre-existing modes of thought, though elements of continuity were also evident. Its status as a 'text of the break'[32] is enhanced by consideration of the political background to Williams' work, particularly his New Left involvement, and by the influence he exerted over the cultural politics and analysis pursued within this milieu. His adoption of an unsettled and idiosyncratic vocabulary in this book suggested that the uncertainties of the left in this period had extended into the very language of socialism. In this sense, *The Long Revolution* was a somewhat experimental text. Williams abandoned some of these ideas shortly afterwards and began his theoretical journey towards a more Marxist cultural materialism. Yet, aspects of this project persisted in his later work, not least, as Hall suggests, a commitment to the 'impossibility of separating out the different lived systems and according one any prior determinacy'.[33] For the first New Left, however, this text provided a rough methodology for its cultural practice and analysis. For numerous academics and cultural critics after this date, *The Long Revolution* constituted a landmark in its recognition of the deep interconnections between culture and politics.

## THOMPSON'S RIPOSTE

These ideas encountered a good deal of opposition within sections of the New Left. Thompson, for instance, developed a sustained critique of Williams' position in consecutive issues of *New Left Review*.[34] In both articles he attempted to limit the movement's exploration in these areas and challenged the cultural emphasis of Williams' outlook. As Gregor McLennan has observed, for a number of later commentators Thompson provided the definitive critique of 'the idea that culture (or 'communications') determine social being', arguing that 'to imply as much (as Williams did) is to abandon crucial notions of struggle, of power, of ideology, and of materialism'.[35] In fact, as we have seen, Williams' analysis did not entail a retreat from politics and power, but a different understanding of their operations. Thompson, however, berated the absence 'of a frontal encounter with historical materialism' in Williams' work and the overconfident assertion of the 'whole way of life' as the primary conceptual tool for social as well as cultural analysis. The results of this were, Thompson suggested, particularly disfiguring. It had induced a tendency to rewrite history not as a process of struggle and choices but as the 'record of impersonal forces'.[36] Moreover, the gradualist perspective bound up in the notion of the long revolution coalesced with this tendency so that 'there are no good or bad men in Mr Williams' history, only dominant and subordinate "structures of feeling". As a result we are left with a general euphoria of "progress".'[37] Whilst he shared some of Williams' interests, in particular his renovation of the cultural sphere as a significant arena of political contestation, Thompson suspected that Williams had overplayed the significance of cultural questions, hence his failure to provide a convincing account of social conflict.

It follows from this criticism, which has reappeared in various guises amongst later commentators, that Williams' emphasis on a common culture, as well as his usage of the community metaphor, represented a confused retreat from the harsh realities of institutional and class power. Thompson articulated these sentiments powerfully for many New Left activists. The emphasis upon cultural analysis pioneered by *ULR*, and evident in *New Left Review* after 1960, made some uneasy. For Thompson and the *New Reasoner* group, the commitment to rediscovering indigenous radical traditions and connecting these with present-day struggles was threatened by the shift in analytical and political focus which such ideas engendered. Cultural critique, was, at best, a pleasant diversion from this more serious project. Thompson's ability to articulate these sentiments was significant because it provided a political focus for the airing of differences across the movement. His critique constituted the clearest exposition of the differences that developed around the New Left's cultural praxis. For many involved with *ULR*, political ideas and identity could no longer be deduced from class location: politics was increasingly intertwined with cultural and social developments. Culture, itself, was redefined as a politically contested arena. These commitments opened fissures within the New Left's thought, especially as Williams' work continued to provide an alternative perspective which encouraged the development of novel approaches to politics and culture.

## CONNECTING CULTURE AND POLITICS – COMMITMENT?

One of the most provocative aspects of the younger generation's exploration of the interface between politics and culture arose from its interest in the longstanding and troublesome question of the nature of political commitment for left-wing cultural producers. As both politics and culture were increasingly viewed within this milieu in more complex and theoretical ways, the notion of the radical artist or cultural intellectual either speaking on behalf of the labour movement or aligning their work with its political goals, seemed ever more problematic. Could such individuals be regarded as the point of fusion for the political and cultural? If not, what were the implications for the cultural wing of the contemporary intelligentsia?

The pertinence of this issue was reinforced by a range of artistic and cultural initiatives which were loosely allied to the New Left. The New Left provided a home for some of the leading intellectual and cultural dissidents of this generation because of the revolt against orthodoxy which it championed and its willingess to explore the connections between culture and politics. The implications of this relationship have been largely ignored by later commentators, even though it provides one of the defining characteristics of the milieu. The New Left empathised with the social critique which emerged from the work of a number of contemporary writers, dramatists and film-makers, including Lindsay Anderson, John Osborne, Dennis Potter, Shelagh Delaney, Doris Lessing, John Braine, Kenneth Tynan and Alan Sillitoe. In some cases, for instance Lindsay Anderson and Doris Lessing, this relationship extended to active participation in the New Left. Not all of these critics were committed socialists, yet the New Left was sufficiently eclectic and devoid of conventional, bureaucratic political pressures to prove amenable to a range of radical cultural practices. Moreover, the anger, frustration and passion of writers such as John Braine and John Osborne appealed strongly to New Left sensibilities. David Marquand recorded an occasion at Oxford which illustrates this appeal: "'Look Back in Anger", one prominent University left-winger shouted at me recently, his voice almost shaking with passion, "is a more important political document than anything the Labour Party has said since 1951".'[38] This empathy may also have involved a shared sense of 'masculine rage' which often reinforced male dominance within the New Left's politics.

This temporary period of co-operation between disaffected sections of the intelligentsia committed to exploring the contradictions and anxieties embedded within welfare capitalism more deeply than conventional politics allowed, generated a brief yet significant dialogue with the New Left. Sensing the important and unresolved questions about the relationship between culture and politics which the left had failed to address since the 1930s, *ULR* sponsored a series of discussions about the nature and terms of political commitment for artists.[39] Beneath this theme lay the increasing sensitivity of this milieu to the meaning and significance of movements within the cultural sphere. In the course of this exchange, it became clear that older traditions of relating cultural practices to political causes were inadequate in the contemporary world. The suffocating constraints imposed upon artistic initiative by the tenets of socialist realism in the communist bloc had proved unbearable.[40] Simultaneously, the betrayal and disappointment felt by radicals over the Labour Party's performance in office, and then in opposition, resulted in the severance of its connections with many radical artists and intellectuals. Even the Popular Front 'model' of a progressive alliance embracing cultural and literary revolt against the orthodoxies of the day was now problematic.[41] As contributors to the *ULR's* debate and to an important collection of essays by contemporary artists, *Declaration*, made clear, artistic enterprise could not be marshalled behind a political struggle whose goals and alliances had been set in advance.[42] Yet, despite the gulf between artists and orthodox politics, many cultural practitioners increasingly viewed themselves as the voices of the incohate anger and frustration of the disempowered and alienated. As John Osborne rhetorically demanded: 'What is the meaning of the work they do? Where does the pain lie? What are their expectations? What moves them, brings them together? makes them speak out? Where is the weakness, the loneliness? ... Experiment means asking questions, and these are all the questions of socialism'.[43] For David Marquand, writing in the first issue of *ULR*, the sentiments of the 'Angry' generation 'were certainly more widely shared than either the ponderous philanthropy of the traditional left or the conventional smugness of the traditional right'.[44]

Undoubtedly, as the various contributors to *Declaration* indicated, the New Left's brand of socialism did not necessarily appeal either: some articulated spiritual concerns, while others stressed the non-political implications of humanist values.[45] These explorations were open-ended and did not respect orthodox political allegiances: John Osborne's work, in particular, contained traces of nihilism, misogyny and misanthropy, despite his ostensibly socialist commitments. These contradictions illuminated the dilemma facing contemporary, left-leaning artists. Their 'commitment' consisted of a deeply felt critique of the society and culture in which they lived, yet the orthodox political world looked dull and remote from these problems, even though it constituted the only meaningful realm for the construction of any social and cultural alternative. Socialism increasingly lacked appeal for those facing these pressures. The contributors to *Declaration*, likewise, highlighted the role of pleasure within popular cultural practices and the left's silence on this score. Kenneth Tynan and Lindsay Anderson pointed out the associations made by many ordinary people between socialism and puritanism.[46] The connections they charted between culture and entertainment drew attention to the pleasures involved in cultural consumption. This was an especially difficult area for socialists. For Tynan, socialism had been divested of its emphasis on the expansion of individual enjoyment and energies in the dreary halls of Westminster and the puritanical impulses of many activists.[47] Examination of the pleasure embedded in cultural practices challenged the passive associations of consumption (of capitalist commodities) which recurred in socialist analysis.

This dialogue with artists and writers also led the New Left to reflect upon the nature of cultural production. Critics and practitioners questioned the degree to which artists were engaged in communicating a reality which lay outside their own work. This had been the view which underlay the growth of the genre of social realism in photography and literature for instance, yet practitioners were increasingly self-conscious about the political and social meanings of their art, the dramatic content of even the most 'realist' work and the principles of selection which informed a particular artistic product. The photographer Roger Mayne, who took the photograph on the cover of this book, reflected that 'a photograph of boys leaping for a football in a street might be suitable for a Labour poster. But the attitude of aspiration might equally well express Conservative ideals'.[48] Following the ideas of Williams, as well as critical work in other fields, for instance John Berger's pioneering reading of fine art (which was keenly discussed in *ULR*),[49] the notion of the social construction of cultural products was far more pervasive. Artists increasingly viewed their work in the context of their social, cultural and aesthetic surroundings.

Once the role of social and political determinants was accepted, however, the confidence of the author of a work in its integrity, coherence and meaning was increasingly called into question. Genres such as social realism seemed anachronistic, a process accelerated by the proliferation of media and improvement in technical quality of broadcasting. Simultaneously, the relationship between form and content in the arts came in for radical re-evaluation. In his contemporary review of John Mander's book on the nature of political commitment for artists, Hall criticised the latter for failing to address this central issue.[50] He spelt out his own view of these difficulties: to consider the novel as an objective reflection of a reality outside it was woefully inadequate. The novel dramatised values and, at the same time, 'makes us know them in ways which it is impossible to know by other means'.[51] Greater emphasis should be placed on experimentation in the forms of artistic practices. Language itself constituted a key medium through which ideas were moulded and values represented. He therefore rejected conventional interpretations of commitment. With their tendency to present texts as coherent expressions of an exterior reality, previous interpretations mediated against attention to forms and language: 'what I am saying is that form and content are indivisible, and that the great danger of the word "commitment" is that it invites us to make a treacherous dichotomy between them'.[52]

This rethinking of orthodox approaches to the cultural was informed by the arrival of 'mass culture' in the post-war period. In fact, changes in the cultural practices and attitudes of the subaltern classes in British society were far more complex and elaborate than the notion of mass culture suggests. The arrival of television and its cross-class audience, the increased spending power of many young people, and a pluralisation of the sources of social identity, along the lines of age, race and access to consumer goods and styles, combined to erode older patterns of behaviour. These changes threatened the more stable cultural boundaries of previous generations. Culture as a class or regional entity was increasingly replaced by culture as access to consumer values and goods. This was particularly perplexing for the left. Older ways of life, for many associated with areas of traditional labour movement strength, were being rapidly transformed by new towns, consumer goods and mass entertainment.[53] Most worrying of all, these changes were apparently welcomed by the working classes. It was this revolution in the popular culture of the nation which inspired the New Left's cultural politics. Popular culture, which for so long had been the butt of liberal and left criticism, no longer stood as an arena in which the logics of domination and alienation held complete sway. Following Williams' analysis in *The Long Revolution*, culture constituted a key site on which social values were both affirmed and contested. From this perspective, changes in the form and content of advertising, television and popular entertainment were significant developments in their own right.

# PILKINGTON

The New Left developed its cultural politics in distinctive ways; its engagement with the changing pattern of contemporary popular culture marked a significant departure from older socialist ideas – a break well illustrated by its submission to the Pilkington Committee on Television and Broadcasting in 1962 (outlined below). The Committee sought to examine the implications of the new medium for British society and culture; its final report set the agenda for broadcasting policy throughout the 1960s, as well as the framework for considering cultural questions among key sections of the intelligentsia. The Committee provided the opportunity, in the minds of some of the New Left's younger 'modernists', for radical voices to be heard by those overseeing the development of British television. In its submission to the Pilkington Committee, the New Left's cultural politics were thrown into relief, both because of the hostility which this document aroused among sections of the movement,[54] and due to the influence which some of the ideas appear to have exercised over members of the Committee.[55]

Throughout its life, the New Left fused culture and politics in more imaginative ways than its contemporary political rivals. *ULR* was distinctive as much for its look as for its content; surrounded by bold, modernist lines and embellished by documentary photography, its design resembled commercial magazines more than its socialist counterparts. In addition, the New Left Clubs in London and Manchester were also places of entertainment, where music and poetry were heard and exhibitions were held on cultural topics. As several participants have since attested, this proximity helped promulgate Williams' notion that culture needed to be understood as an integral feature of social life, experience and identity. Hall's description of the *ULR* Club in London exemplifies this:

> The cultural debates and activities were considered as important as the more 'political' ones. Arnold Wesker and John Arden connected us to the 'new drama' and its home at the Royal Court; Lindsay Anderson, Karel Reisz and Alex Jacobs to Free Cinema, the British Film Institute and the National Film Theatre; Paddy Whannel and others to the London jazz scene; Roger Mayne to new movements in documentary photography; Germano Facetti and Robin Fior to new ideas in design and typography. There were visits to and discussions at new venues like the Whitechapel Gallery.[56]

The movement also sponsored and encouraged a number of cultural initiatives, often of an experimental nature; the Free Cinema movement at the National Film Theatre (launched by Lindsay Anderson) most notably. The London New Left milieu championed cultural genres associated with modernist values and aesthetics, such as jazz. This taste for modernist art and design clashed with the aesthetic interests of the older generation.[57]

These new preferences engendered a strong interest in the new popular cultural practices of the early 1960s. The nature of the New Left's engagement with these is illustrated by its submission to Pilkington and the reaction this document elicited within the movement. Indeed, its appearance arguably presaged the movement's complete breakdown. For some activists, any engagement on the terrain of popular entertainment smacked of triviality, if not capitulation. It is clear from Thompson's contemporary correspondence that he viewed the analysis and reformist recommendations of this submission as the direct product of *ULR*'s 'culturalism'.[58] This criticism has been reproduced by a recent commentator who laments the naive statism evident within this movement's cultural politics:

> The demand was for the state, in response, to become far more a cultural welfare state, regulating the tendencies to commodification, redistributing cultural benefits, building on the basis of the development of existing institutions such as the Arts Council, the BBC, the 1944 Education Act, a new cultural prosperity open to all sections of society. This would require an extension of public ownership and greater regulation of the media and the advertising industry. These ideas gripped a wider constituency than those grouped around the journals and clubs.[59]

A similar criticism has been made of the New Left's reformism and statism in other areas, especially in its economic policy recommendations for Labour (outlined in chapter five). Yet, according to some commentators, 'it is in the field of "culture" as usually understood that the new left achieved more tangible success via its influence on the Pilkington Committee on broadcasting'.[60] Certainly, the final report produced by the Committee revealed the influence of the New Left's critique of television genres, though it showed less evidence of the radical proposals for democratising this medium which the New Left's submission included. More generally, the movement's cultural politics were more complex and ambivalent than the reformist or statist labels suggest.

The submission drew heavily on Williams' thoughts about popular culture, though he was cited merely as an adviser on the final draft. His ideas in this area were thoughtfully laid out in an article he wrote in 1960, 'The Magic System'. In this he developed an anthropological reading of advertising, a key component within popular culture.[61] Rejecting crudely deterministic readings of advertising, he suggested that it constituted an important medium for the reproduction and imaginary resolution of profound social tensions. To comprehend its meaning and significance it had to be juxtaposed with other elements in the social process:

> we shall only understand it with any adequacy if we can develop a kind of total analysis in which the economic, social and cultural forms are visibly related. We may then also find, taking advertising as a major form of modern social communication, that we can understand our society itself in new ways.[62]

Like magic, advertising sought to address people in their various social locations whilst responding to real social needs and interests:

> If we look at the petrol with the huge clenched fist, the cigarette against loneliness in the deserted street, the puppet facing death with a life-insurance policy, we are looking at attempts to express and resolve real human tensions which may be crude but which also involve deep feelings of a personal and social kind.[63]

Advertising worked through the ideological construction of social agents as 'consumers' and of classes as 'masses'.[64] But, in Williams' mind, a deeper, more authentic reality lay behind its glossy surfaces, though this was currently obscured by the distortion of human priorities which advertising legitimised.

Williams' argument greatly influenced the approach to television taken by the submission's authors. Significantly, they reproduced his ambivalence towards the new forms of modernity, regarding television as replete with new opportunities as well as reproducing longstanding dangers. The authors drew heavily on Williams' recognition of the complex relationship between popular cultural practices and ideological effects. The submission to Pilkington consequently stood out from conventional approaches to television. Locating television within the complex currents of popular culture, towards which 'a condescending or contemptuous attitude... is found at many influential points in our society',[65] the submission provided a detailed critique of the most common genres in television, paying particular attention to the value systems through which popular pleasures were transmitted. By drawing attention to the ideologies which underlay television programmes, this document developed points of genuine originality. At the same time, it sought to bypass more traditional approaches which emphasised the role of false consciousness within these areas: 'Such features dispose once and for all of the opinion that this type of programme is simply a diversion, a form of escapism, to which moral or aesthetic criticisms do not apply'.[66]

In a contemporaneous article, 'Television in Britain', Williams pursued this aspect of the submission, presciently citing television as the location for an important ideological battle between 'a traditional pattern of responsible paternalism and a very powerful pattern of market culture'.[67] Engaging with the various genres which dominated television, he applied his analysis of advertising to the small-screen:

> The viewer does not really identify with the criminal, with the detective who behaves like a criminal, or with the Western hero who is character-istically misunderstood and on his own. These figures catch the sense of isolation, tension, and the permanently hostile environment which is society, but instead of exploring these facts of a real society in substantive terms divert the feelings into the safe channels of fantasy.[68]

Television was preoccupied with the imaginary resolution of more fundamental conflicts and anxieties within society, yet was only capable of generating an inadequate and artificial cultural language. It amounted to:

> the restless expression of a society ... deeply afraid even to try to understand itself. ... Both elite and masses – the people of the society in their characteristic relations – are caught up in a deep failure: essentially that nothing that unites them seems real or satisfactory, and then the tension, the fear, the disillusion must be played over again and again ...[69]

Against the fears of those, especially on the left, who regarded television as the agent of the '"massification" of society',[70] creating a malleable and passive populace, he pointed to the tensions which constantly disrupted the medium's attempt to construct and control its audience: 'In all these ways, majority television operates against consciousness, not as a form of thought-control, but as an expression of the basic illusions, the dark areas and the formulas that cover them, of the society itself'.[71] This line of analysis constituted a significant departure from the left's traditional response to popular culture in Britain, shaping the agendas of the subsequent discipline of Cultural Studies and the pedagogic approach to popular cultural texts manifested by the Open University's pioneering courses in this field in later years.[72] In this earlier period, Williams' ideas allowed some within the New Left to present themselves as radical and engaged populists outside the traditions of economism and voluntarism through which the left had traditionally approached popular culture. The submission to Pilkington confidently outlined a more democratic future for television, including proposals concerning community access and input into programme making and scheduling, a project which bolstered arguments for a minority channel on British television: the subsequent establishment of Channel Four represented a long-term realisation of these recommendations.[73]

Simultaneously, however, the authors of this document, like Williams, retained a high cultural critique of television. Deploying the notion of 'quality', they continued to disparage the vast majority of programming on BBC 1 and the newly created commercial channel as the detritus of mass culture. Whilst they were determined to challenge the divide between high and low cultures institutionalised within television, the recourse to 'quality' illustrated the continued significance of the tradition of moral disapproval of 'mindless' popular pastimes.[74] Significantly, this emphasis was reproduced in the Committee's final report which set the tone for BBC policy over the next decade.[75] Joan Seaton and James Curran argue that the Pilkington report depended on 'a crude view of the power of the media to influence individual behaviour'.[76] Programmes were judged by the report's authors according to their educational, informational and social content – their ability to address the 'real' needs of the audience and, thereby, raise its consciousness.[77] Underpinning these beliefs lay a romantic commitment to 'a concept of folk culture', a yearning for a more authentic mode of cultural expression.[78] This 'golden ageism', the conceptual division between real and false needs and the disdain for aspects of popular culture, were reinforced by, and possibly derived from, the New Left's arguments. Its submission to Pilkington tallies most closely with the final report in these areas.

In Williams' later article, this disparagement was taken further, so that:

> the failure of democratic culture in Britain, by the restriction of
> education both absolutely and along class lines, has left a vacuum which
> pseudo-Americanism seems to be rapidly filling. If we add the fact that
> much of the most easily exported and standardized American culture is

itself synthetic ... we are in a position to begin understanding the extremely low cultural level of majority British television.[79]

Hostility to the 'synthetic' aspects of American culture, the resentment of British intellectuals towards perceived American cultural imperialism and anxieties about the worth and meaning of popular culture were neatly combined in this argument. Clearly, the ideas bound up in the New Left's cultural politics were compatible with more hostile attitudes towards popular culture; even so, important breaks had been registered with traditional ideas in the socialist repertoire in this area.

## CULTURE AND MODERNITY

The submission to Pilkington highlights one overriding contradiction which characterised the New Left's cultural politics. On the one hand, the movement's critics continued to draw upon the critique of contemporary culture as mass culture which needed to be replaced by more worthwhile and wholesome pursuits.[80] On the other, some elements within the New Left became fascinated by the emergence of new modernist currents within the social and political world of the late 1950s, moving away from this older emphasis. A similar dichotomy characterised the left's response to popular culture in earlier periods. As Chris Waters demonstrates, a much earlier period, the 1890s, witnessed the emergence of similar responses to popular cultural practices among some British socialists.[81]

According to some critics, in particular Samuel, this empathy with modernity provides the key to understanding much of the New Left's political identity: its modernistic zeal was potentially elitist and Fabian in inspiration, anticipating the culture of expert planning which came to dominate social provision in the 1960s.[82] Undoubtedly, this movement did display a keen interest in modernist aesthetics and, on occasions, called for the construction of new urban landscapes which would abolish the problems of older communities. Samuel highlights an article by the architect Graeme Shankland in the first issue of *ULR*: 'it was the burden of his argument that 'piecemeal' slum clearance was a license to anarchy, and that only large-scale redevelopment – undertaken 'in a great combined operation' and under a single directive intelligence – could prevent what he called the 'monotony of muddle'.[83] Moreover:

In housing and town planning we stood for comprehensive redevelopment, advocating 'islands of compact buildings' or 'towns within cities' as an alternative to 'subtopia' and sprawl. Vallingby, Stockholm, was one of our models, 'the new attractive LCC flats at Roehampton' another – high-rise blocks on a site 'formerly ... wasted by crumbling, decaying and totally uneconomic Victorian mansions'... We also presented ourselves ... as avatars of the motorcar age, praising, in *ULR* 2, the 'great sculptural beauty' of the new Los Angeles flyovers and attacking the British road system as 'archaic'...[84]

Yet such sentiments were counterbalanced by the emphasis upon community control and involvement dear to many in this movement. In a controversial analysis of the relationship between architecture and the urban environment in *ULR* 5, for instance, Redfern highlighted the neglect of London's social and physical environment, the obstacles to planning brought about by market pressures and the reluctance of central government to intervene.[85] Calling for a democratic, community-driven planning strategy, he argued that the needs and wishes of local residents affected by dereliction and reconstruction programmes should be primary. Significantly, he continued to advocate the virtues of community planning and architecture, particularly in debates about 'new towns' of the late 1960s.[86] In Notting Hill, George Clark and a number of other New Left activists were involved in the development of a network of local community institutions. Overall, therefore, a more complex position than Samuel allows persisted within the first New Left concerning cultural practice and social change. The early New Left was torn between its desire to defend the interests of community organisations and perspectives and its attraction to the modernistic edges of contemporary culture.

This tension reappeared throughout the movement's cultural politics. For those drawn to the *New Reasoner*, culture represented the coherent articulation of already known socialist truths through established high art genres, such as poetry and fiction. For the more cosmopolitan milieu around *ULR* in London, jazz, drama and architecture encouraged the development of a European, avant-garde sensibility: as Samuel recalls, 'in art politics, the New Left – or at any rate the *ULR* end of it – was on the side of the avant-garde, one of the invisible differences with our elder brethren on the *New Reasoner*'.[87] But fascination with the modern also led in a different direction altogether. Inspired by Williams' attempt to comprehend the contours and contradictions of contemporary popular culture, some began to engage with popular culture outside the critical framework which their socialist forebears had often deployed. Popular culture was increasingly regarded as a key resource in the construction of political identity and a contradictory and complex formation in its own right. This tension between the avant-garde and the popular within socialist attitudes to culture has been visible throughout the post-war period. Clearly, some participants in this formation were affected in their subsequent careers by the New Left's treatment of these questions. The playwright Trevor Griffiths, for example, who was active in the New Left in this period (he was at one time chairman of the Manchester socialist club), dramatised exactly this tension within socialist approaches to popular culture in his later television play *Comedians* (1976). Within the New Left, this tension was never clearly defined or tangible. It persisted across the movement and within the cultural preferences of many of its activists. Tony Bennett, for instance, has drawn our attention to this antinomy in the very first edition of *New Left Review*, contrasting the editorial's recognition of the importance of new political antagonisms and sites of revolt with Paddy Whannel's hostility to 'rock'n'roll' as a worthless musical genre in his article in the same issue.[88]

## THE YOUTH AGENDA

This fragile and rudimentary cultural politics encouraged some in this milieu to disaggregate the left's constituency. Cultural engagement engendered familiarity with the many particular identities contesting the social world, as well as a recognition of the limitations of appealing to all these groups in a single or universal discourse. Understanding the needs and interests of different social actors produced a more complex and fragmented political response. An important example of this process can be observed in the New Left's attempt to respond to young people as a separate and specific social constituency. The New Left's realisation that youth constituted one of the key constituencies within society and that this group had been poorly represented by the politics of the traditional left was informed by changes which occurred throughout the 1950s. In particular, the arrival in the late 1950s of the 'teenager', the product of the expansion of consumer markets and the economic independence of many young workers, combined with the representation of youth as a metaphor for the country's ills – a process described by Bill Osgerby.[89] For some, concern for young people arose from an empathy with revolt against the worlds of apathy and consensus, as well as the belief that decoding youth culture might provide the key to unlock the creative energies of the contemporary social system. Understanding the 'problem' of youth would generate an important insight into the failings of society, culture and even the Labour Party. As Colin MacInnes, a sympathiser with this wing of the New Left, lamented, 'when I read Labour propaganda addressed to youth and then think of the kind of teenagers I've met in coffee bars, in jazz clubs, at the palais... I have the feeling of a total failure of communication'.[90]

In an article in 1959, 'Absolute Beginnings', Hall ruminated on the interrelations between youth, education and social change.[91] Avoiding conventional representations of young people either as loosely bonded within society, and thus open to the lures of criminality, or as zealous consumers – the 'darlings' of the advertisers – he explored the social, educational and cultural dimensions of the 'problem' of youth. Linking the failure of many Secondary Modern schools to enhance the creative abilities of their students with the development of networks of youth subcultures, he suggested that 'much of the aimless frenzy of their leisure life is a displacement of the energies and aspirations which have been trained or drained out of them by school and work'.[92] The left's starting point should be the cultural deprivation which occurred in the interstices of 'modern education' and 'an old school environment'.[93] Education was perceived as the means of adjusting children to their 'proper social and cultural position'.[94] This was an area of social communication in which roles were fixed and expectations compressed. Simultaneously, mass culture reproduced the dichotomy between alienation at school and fulfilment through leisure. It was in this latter sphere that the emotional vitality and creativity of increasing numbers of young people were channelled. This perspective raised an important paradox in Hall's thought. Whilst feeling for the essential worth of young people, he was less enthusiastic about the forms in which such energies were articulated. In one sense, this was a recurrent part of the left's dilemma about the content of social revolt. Violence, prejudice and a narrowness of vision were all 'unpleasant' distortions of the 'flow between human beings'.[95] More generally, a crisis had emerged in a society committed to the ideals of affluence and classlessness around the passage from youth to adulthood. Only by understanding this crisis in more general social terms, rather than primarily moral or educational ones, could the real needs of different social groups be administered.

In July 1959 the New Left submitted an imaginative assessment of the youth agenda to the Labour Party's Youth Commission, attempting to challenge its ideas on this issue. This document clearly reflected its *ULR* origins, building upon Hall's analysis to present a cogent set of proposals. It explored more fully the nature of the youth revolt: 'Young people ostentatiously set out to create their own youth culture which is in many ways an anti-culture, and this phenonemon is not merely an out-growth of individual problems of individual adolescents... It is the society, not merely one's parents, which is being rejected'.[96] Youth culture constituted a response to the powerlessness experienced by the young and was organised according to its own internal codes and laws, many of which were meaningless to the external observer. The submission described in unusually sympathetic terms the 'dreamworld' inhabited by the average teenager. Traditional political language and modes of address were unable to penetrate the boundaries of these cultural communities, especially from a party which was deeply compromised by its association with the bureaucratic and cumbersome institutions of the welfare state. The role of schools was critical: education had to be broadened to include the development of all aspects of the adolescent's personality. Imaginative suggestions for schools to become social as well as educational centres were juxtaposed with the call for a national apprenticeship scheme.[97] Whilst these ideas fell on deaf ears in the contemporary Labour Party, they clearly enjoyed some impact, in the longer term, in debates about educational provision. Several passed into the repertoires of teachers and educational authorities from the late 1960s onwards.[98]

Yet, older suspicions and traditions persisted too. In the absence of a coherent alternative language to express its social observations, the submission, and the movement more generally, frequently resorted to cliché and weak generalisation: thus, when describing the 'normal' stages of adolescent development, it was unthinkingly argued that 'the next important phase begins with marriage'.[99] Additionally, the authors felt compelled to denounce the teenage dreamworld in strong moral terms: 'if this is all a world encourages you to do seven days a week, what can be the outcome?'.[100] Likewise, the dreamworld stifled revolt and induced passivity in the young, softening them up for the blandishments of the advertisers. The New Left did not, therefore, shift entirely from attitudes of disapproval for the 'empty' and 'inauthentic' aspects of everyday culture. But, it moved considerably from the paternalist assumptions which often characterised the left's attitude towards the young. Hall concluded his article with a lively analysis of the changing nature of youth styles and fashions, from the 'atavistic' Teddy boy of media demonology to the more urbane and sophisticated teenage consumer celebrated in Colin MacInnes' novel, *Absolute Beginners*.[101] These changes represented more than mere variations on the themes of false consciousness and alienation. They were characterised as shifts and responses to a complex set of social and cultural pressures. This approach consequently threw light upon elements in youth culture which had been neglected previously, laying the foundations for later academic reflections on the nature of subcultures, and bequeathing a mixture of sensitivity to their rejection of the dominant culture and a continuing search for an authentic expression of working-class life (an assumption which later critics, such as Angela McRobbie, have criticised).[102] In this period, these ideas challenged assumptions about the coherence of the left's constituency as well as the adequacy of socialist images of contemporary society.

## CONCLUSIONS

The emergence of profound differences between and within communities, as well as the more diverse and densely layered social life which characterised post-war British society, were directly anticipated by Williams' work in this period. *The Long Revolution* located its analysis in the 'grain' of contemporary social developments, yet was deeply critical of the form this modernity was taking. Undoubtedly, he found it difficult to develop an indigenous theoretical language to express his interest in social totality and begin the task of increasing the range and depth of socialist values in a modern context. His ideas encompassed a wide range of social phenomena; power and conflict were at the centre of his analysis, though Thompson was perhaps correct to suggest that they were not immediately visible. According to Williams, the left had to decode the cultural forms of underlying social changes. At the same time, developments in the cultural sphere were relatively autonomous and required analysis in their own right. Reflecting on his work in this period, Williams suggested that:

> in understanding cultural hegemony and in seeing it as the crucial dimension of the kind of society which has been emerging since the war under advanced capitalism, I felt the need to break both from mainline Marxism and even more from the traditions of social democracy, liberalism and Fabianism, which had been my immediate inheritance.[103]

Like Hall, he provided an indigenous version of the work of various continental theorists: his notion of community as the basis of an alternative to instrumentality and alienation, for instance, resembles the more extensively theorised work of Jürgen Habermas on communicative action.[104] According to the critic Fredric Jameson, Williams' ideas from this and later periods surpassed Theodor Adorno's reflections on the culture industry.[105] Significantly, these reflections were developed in empirical terms and in ways which appeared to conflict with the Marxist canon. Crucially, Williams convinced numerous contemporaries that social diversity, political identity and consumerism were central to the concerns of socialists.

Yet, the limitations of the New Left's attempt to engage with popular culture should also be evident. Restrained from the beginning by the weight of argument deployed by Marxists and traditional socialists within the movement, the 'culturalist' parts of the New Left were also hampered by the survival of a tradition of hostility to popular culture. Similarly New Left ideas in this field were sometimes confused and derivative. Williams, for instance, did not break completely from the optimistic, social democratic teleology of *Culture and Society*: in *Communications* (1962), for example, he argued that 'a cultural revolution, proceeding through gradual institutional reforms, would qualitatively deepen democracy and produce a learning society', and produced an optimistic analysis of the 'kind of reforms a Labour Government might introduce'.[106]

Despite the continuing purchase of these older traditions, however, it is clear that pioneering work was undertaken in this period. The first New Left prepared the ground for the later discipline of Cultural Studies with its thoughtful analysis of popular culture, its conception of a plurality of social forces within contemporary politics and its interest in the processes of ideological and cultural representation. The history of the impact of Gramscian theory upon the development of Cultural Studies in the academy, which has been crudely attacked by one recent commentator,[107] is clearly more complex than has been suggested. The younger wing of the New Left developed an indigenous and unsystematic body of ideas which in some ways resembled the work of theorists in the Western Marxist tradition, not least Gramsci. The similarities stemmed from their break with economism and reductionism, and more expansive conception of the importance of culture. As *ULR* declared in 1958: 'We want to break with the view that cultural or family life is an entertaining sideshow, a secondary expression of human creativity or fulfilment'.[108] Indeed, the 'culturalist' wing of the New Left came close to Gramsci's influential notion of hegemony in its emphasis on the constant struggle for command of the moral, political and cultural worlds, though it lacked the theoretical precision and language of continental thinkers. The imaginations of figures like Hall were, therefore, opened to theoretical influences on these questions by experiences in this movement as well as by subsequent influences. In terms of theoretical sophistication, however, the first New Left offered only rudimentary guidance to those pursuing work in this area.

Whilst analysis constituted a central part of the cultural politics developed by the first New Left, its practical interventions also render it relatively singular within the political history of the British left. This period should not be interpreted simply as a time when popular culture was rejected by the radical intelligentsia – the impression bequeathed by Dick Hebdige, for example.[109] On the contrary, it was the desire to engage and interpret, and ultimately to inflect, the cultural practices of the people which allowed this movement's radical wing to recast the socialist imagination in a more pluralistic vein and to present civil society as the natural habitat of left politics. Lacking the political will or the theoretical tools to pursue these instincts, the New Left imploded as a political movement before these interests could be further developed.

NOTES
1   Williams, 'The British Left', op cit, p26.
2   Hall, 'The 'First' New Left', op cit, pp25-6.
3   Hall, 'The Culture Gap', Marxism Today, January 1984, pp18-22.
4   Jardine and Swindells, op cit, p4.
5   B.Waites, T.Bennett and G.Martin (eds), Popular Culture: Past and Present, Croom Helm, Open University Press, London 1982.
6   B.Osgerby, '"Well, it's Saturday Night an' I Just Got Paid': Youth, Consciousness and Hegemony in Post-War Britain', Contemporary Record, 6, 2, 1992, pp287-305, p292.
7   McIlroy, op cit, p6.
8   See Williams' observations on Leavis in Politics and Letters: Interviews with New Left Review, New Left Books, London, 1979, pp44-5, 66-70.
9   Hall, 'Cultural Studies and the Centre', op cit, p19.
10  For an extensive assessment of the Leavisite tradition, see F.Mulhern, The Moment of 'Scrutiny', New Left Books, London 1979.
11  Hall, 'Politics and Letters', op cit, p57.
12  Williams, Culture and Society, op cit, p4.
13  Ibid, p19.
14  See especially D.MacRae, Ideology and Society, Heinemann, London 1961; D.Bell, The End of Ideology, Collier, Macmillan, New York, London 1965.
15  T.Eagleton, 'Criticism and Politics: the work of Raymond Williams', New Left Review, 95, 1974, pp3-23, p10.

16  For a careful reassessment of Williams' political and theoretical ideas, see
    T.Eagleton, 'Base and Superstructure in Raymond Williams', in Eagleton (ed),
    *Raymond Williams, op cit*, pp165-75.

17  Williams, The Long Revolution, *op cit*, pxii.

18  *Ibid*, p69.

19  *Ibid*, pp113-4.

20  E.Said, 'Foucault and the Imagination of Power', in D.Couzens Hoy (ed), *Foucault,
    a Critical Reader*, Blackwell, Oxford 1986, pp149-54, p154.

21  *Ibid*, p294.

22  *Ibid*, p298.

23  For a more extensive assessment of this theme in Williams' work, see M.Kenny,
    'Facing up to the Future: Community in the Work of Raymond Williams in the
    Fifties and Sixties', *Politics*, 11, 2, 1991, pp14-19.

24  See especially S.Hall, 'Only Connect: the life of Raymond Williams', *New
    Statesman*, 5 February 1988; F.Mulhern, 'Living the Work', *The Guardian*, 29
    January 1988; R.Samuel, 'Philosophy Teaching by Example: Past and Present in
    Raymond Williams', *History Workshop*, 27, 1989, pp141-53.

25  Williams, *Politics and Letters, op cit*, pp21-39.

26  *Ibid*, pp91-3.

27  R.Hoggart and R.Williams, 'Working Class Attitudes', *New Left Review*, 1, 1960,
    pp26-30.

28  R.Wollheim, *Socialism and Culture*, Fabian Society Tract, no.331, 1961, p10.

29  This commitment was common across the New Left; see, for instance,
    E.P.Thompson, 'Revolution', *New Left Review*, 3, 1960, pp3-9.

30  Taylor, 'Alienation and Community', *ULR*, 3, 1958, pp11-18, p17.

31  Williams, *The Long Revolution, op cit*, p333.

32  Hall, 'Cultural Studies and the Centre', *op cit*, p36.

33  Hall, 'Politics and Letters', *op cit*, p62.

34  Thompson, 'The Long Revolution – 1 and 2', *op cit*.

35  G.McLennan, 'E.P.Thompson and the Discipline of Historical Context', in
    R.Johnson *et al* (eds), *Making Histories: studies in history writing and politics*,
    Hutchinson, London 1982, pp96-130, p118.

36  Thompson, 'The Long Revolution – 1', *op cit*, p31.

37  *Ibid*, p28.

38  D.Marquand, 'The New Left at Oxford', *The Guardian*, 18 August 1958.

39  C.Logue *et al*, 'A Commitment Dialogue', *ULR*, 4, 1958, pp15-20.

40  See 'Socialist Realism – extracts from a document by a young Soviet writer', *ULR*,
    7, 1959, pp57-67.

41  See A.Croft, *Red Letter Days: British fiction in the 1930s*, Lawrence and Wishart,
    London 1990.

42  T.Maschler (ed), *Declaration*, MacGibbon & Kee, London, 1957, with contributions
    by Colin Wilson, William Hopkins, Stuart Holroyd, Doris Lessing, Kenneth
    Tynan, Lindsay Anderson and John Osborne.

43  Osborne, in Maschler, *op cit*, p54.

44  Marquand, 'Lucky Jim and the Labour Party', *ULR*, 1, 1957, pp57-60, p57.

45  Wilson, Hopkins and Holroyd adopted a more spiritual approach, whilst the
    others addressed political and ethical questions.

46  Tynan, Anderson in Maschler, *op cit*.

47  Tynan, in Maschler, *op cit*, p120.

48  R.Mayne, 'Photography and Realism', *ULR*, 6, 1959, pp42-4, p42.

49  M.Armstrong, 'Review of Permanent Red by John Berger', *New Left Review*, 8,

1961, pp8-15.

50 Hall, 'Commitment Dilemma', *New Left Review*, 10, 1961, pp67-9.

51 *Ibid*, p68.

52 *Ibid*, p69.

53 Hall, 'A Sense of Classlessness', *op cit*.

54 Thompson, letter to Saville, n.d. (1960?), '*New Left Review* 1959-63' file, Saville papers.

55 Though it is hard to find concrete proof of the influence of the New Left's submission on the final report.

56 Hall, 'The "First" New Left', *op cit*, p29.

57 Thompson, letter to Saville, n.d. (1960?), '*New Left Review* 1959-63' file, Saville papers.

58 *Ibid*.

59 McIlroy, *op cit*, p7.

60 G.Hughes, *op.cit*, p132.

61 Williams, 'The Magic System', *New Left Review*, 4, 1960, pp37-42.

62 *Ibid*, p27.

63 *Ibid*, p29.

64 *Ibid*, p28.

65 K.Coppard, 'Which Frame of Mind? TV and Broadcasting: Evidence to the Pilkington Committee', *New Left Review*, 7, 1961, pp30-48, p34.

66 *Ibid*, p40.

67 Williams, 'Television in Britain', *Journal of Social Issues*, 18, 2, 1962, pp6-15, p9.

68 *Ibid*, p12.

69 *Ibid*, p13.

70 *Ibid*, p14.

71 *Ibid*, p13.

72 This connection is assessed in D.Harris, *From Class Struggle to the Politics of Pleasure: The Effects of Gramscianism on Cultural Studies*, Routledge, London 1992.

73 J.Curran and J.Seaton, *Power Without Responsibility: The press and broadcasting in Britain*, Routledge, London, New York 1988, pp195-92.

74 For a discussion of the hostility to popular culture embedded in socialist thinking in Britain, see C.Waters, *British Socialists and the Politics of Popular Culture, 1884-1914*, Manchester University Press, Manchester 1990.

75 Curran and Seaton, *op cit*, p192.

76 *Ibid*, p188.

77 *Ibid*, p190.

78 *Ibid*, p190.

79 Williams, 'Television in Britain', *op cit*, pp10-11.

80 See, for instance, Taylor, 'Alienation and Community', *op cit*.

81 Waters, *op cit*.

82 Samuel, 'Born-again Socialism', *op cit*, p49.

83 *Ibid*, p49.

84 *Ibid*, p42.

85 Redfern, 'The Real Outrage', *op cit*.

86 See, for instance, 'Housing in New Towns', a paper he delivered to the Royal Institute of British Architects' Conference: 'Living in Britain', Brighton, 12-15 July 1967.

87 Samuel, 'Born-again socialism', *op cit*, p42.

88 T.Bennett, 'The politics of 'the popular' and popular culture', in Waites *et al*, *op cit*, pp6-21, pp9-10.

89  Osgerby, *op cit*, p290.

90  MacInnes, 'Labour and Youth', *Socialist Commentary*, December 1959, p20.

91  Hall, 'Absolute Beginnings', *ULR*, 7, 1959, pp16-25.

92  *Ibid*, p18.

93  *Ibid*, p19.

94  *Ibid*, p20.

95  *Ibid*, p21.

96  *Labour Party Youth Commission: Evidence Submitted by ULR*, July 1959, MSS.YC/29 (National Museum of Labour History).

97  *Labour Party Youth Commission: Evidence Submitted by ULR, op cit*, p5.

98  See, for instance, B.Gross and R.Gross (eds), *Radical School Reform*, Penguin, Harmondsworth 1972.

99  *Ibid*, p5.

100 *Ibid*, p16.

101 MacInnes, *Absolute Beginners*, MacGibbon & Kee, London 1959.

102 Osgerby, *op cit*, p72.

103 Williams, 'You're a Marxist Aren't You?', in B.Parekh (ed), *The Concept of Socialism*, Croom Helm, London 1975, pp231-42, p241.

104 T.McCarthy, *The Critical Theory of Jürgen Habermas*, Hutchinson, London 1978.

105 Jameson is cited in Chun, *op cit*, p120.

106 Cited in McIlroy, *op cit*, p10.

107 Harris, *op cit*.

108 Editorial, *ULR*, 4, 1958, p3.

109 Hebdige, 'Towards a Cartography of Taste 1935-1962', in Waites *et al*, *op cit*, pp194-218.

# CHAPTER FIVE

# Political Economy

The early New Left has been repeatedly criticised for the inadequacies of its social and political analysis. It is a commonplace for many commentators that whilst this movement developed interesting and novel ideas about alienation, culture and community, it failed to provide a systematic or convincing account of the political and economic worlds. According to Willie Thompson, for instance, 'the New Left's principal strength lay in the area of cultural critique, particularly in the explorations conducted by writers such as Stuart Hall, Richard Hoggart or Raymond Williams of popular culture... and the life-styles of particular communities or social groupings.'[1] The later New Left's unflattering presentation of this earlier movement's populism and inadequate discussion of power relations has proved extremely influential here.[2] For some critics, these failures can be explained by the hold of older traditions, ranging from anarchism to Fabianism, over the first New Left's political imagination.[3] The reformism of this movement, evident in its frequent policy recommendations for Labour, has, therefore, been criticised by those who argue that the New Left should have mobilised outside the conventional political system. For those who lament the utopianism and libertarianism of this movement, on the other hand, it placed far too much emphasis on the notion of community, ignoring the concentration of power in central institutions, not least the state.[4]

These readings tend to obscure the diversity of New Left work as well as the connections between different parts of this movement's intellectual agenda. Without overstressing the coherence of its ideas, it is important to appreciate the influence of the social, cultural and ethical ideas discussed so far upon the New Left's political and economic thought. Indeed, the insights of Williams' contemporary project (see chapter four) enabled an important methodological shift. Simultaneously, the differences which, as we have seem elsewhere, characterised this formation, were also present here. Despite these, a collective project of sorts did take place in these years, which anticipated some of the key issues in the political history of subsequent decades and left some important intellectual legacies.

The eclectic nature of New Left analysis has been readily cited as a sign of weakness by a number of its later critics. But this diversity was largely the result of the unusual extent of this formation's engagement with the contemporary orthodoxies of the left. A constant dialogue was opened with rival political and intellectual traditions. Inspite of this process, however, writers in the New Left staked out an increasingly coherent series of positions, exploring an intellectual and methodological space between the poles of social democratic and communist thought. The distinctiveness of this thinking emerged from the fusion of different kinds of analysis which were conventionally regarded as separate. Its later critics have, on the whole, been reluctant to adopt a similar approach. Nor have they paid sufficient attention to the complex political context in which New Left praxis developed.[5] In the assessment which follows, contemporary political and economic circumstances provide the background to an analysis of New Left ideas in this area; this approach allows for a more sympathetic appreciation of the methodological and theoretical shifts marked in New Left thought and, finally, a more balanced appraisal of the critical worth of these ideas and their legacy.

Understanding the political context in which the New Left operated is central to assessing the purchase of its ideas, in particular the nature of the 'affluent society' of the 1950s and the response this elicited from the Labour Party. The New Left was closely involved in the party's internal struggles in this period, developing an important critique of the limitations of contemporary Labour politics. Following an assessment of the political context, this chapter then examines the substance of the New Left's contribution to debates about political economy, especially its 'revisionist' description of the elite in contemporary society; its critique of the public sector and the limitations of the welfare state; its reflections upon the nature of planning; and its attempt to shift the left's traditional understanding of how to overthrow the dominant order. Throughout this discussion, the following themes recur: the New Left's move away from both orthodox Marxist and empirical descriptions of power relations, and adoption of a more expansive, quasi-hegemonic conception of the interrelationships between politics, society and the economy; its sensitivity to the multiplicity of points of antagonism between the elite and the popular classes; and its recognition of the importance of the theme of modernisation in contemporary politics. These ideas were characterised by a central tension which provided the creative source for many of its writers' reflections, yet ultimately prevented the formulation of a more coherent project in this area. This tension emerged from the concern of some participants that the New Left should furnish more rational and effective policy ideas for a future Labour government, and among others, the instinctive celebration of community, generating enthusiasm for political and economic decentralisation. These contradictory emphases were, to some degree, associated with particular individuals, yet, more accurately, they were entangled within the politics of nearly all New Left participants.

## THE POLITICAL BACKGROUND

### Tory Affluence

The most important benchmark for the New Left's analysis of contemporary politics was the post-war Labour government. Clement Attlee's administration had profoundly altered the framework of British politics through its enactment of the Beveridge Report and expansion of the public sector of the economy. The Conservatives, by and large, adapted to this new situation, accepting the boundaries between the public and private sectors of the economy and continued expenditure on the welfare state. Yet, important shifts of power and influence within the post-war settlement began to take place after 1951. By the end of the 1950s, the conditions of affluence generated a number of anxieties for the left. Many began to question the assumption that the political world created after 1945 necessarily favoured the Labour Party.[6]

Capitalism had clearly survived the period of Labour rule although it operated on a new basis, both in terms of its unit size and access to a wider range of technological resources. Both of these trends had, in fact, been evident before the Second World War.[7] Yet the post-war world differed markedly from the political and social order of the 1930s. Business now co-existed with the structures and values of the public sector. The political economy of post-war Britain revolved around a new series of issues and conflicts, deeply embedded within the mixed economy. Despite the apparent policy convergence between the two main parties,[8] the institutions of the public sector initially remained the targets of Conservative hostility, especially the 'inefficient' nationalised industries and the 'wasteful' Health Service. The counterpoint between these Labour sectors and the Conservative highlands of initiative, prosperity and affluence, provided the central dynamic to political debate until 1959. Politics in the 1950s, at least until 1958-9, were marked by the general ascendancy of Conservative fortunes and economic buoyancy. Thereafter, a new conjuncture unfolded in which Conservative attempts to manage the political and economic arena were increasingly fraught.

In economic terms, the period after 1958 was increasingly difficult for the government. With hindsight, it is clear that Britain's comparatively weak industrial base hampered the attempt to move to 'the condition of an advanced productive ... economy.'[9] The foundations of the economic boom of the 1950s were relatively brittle though substantial economic growth occurred during this period. The government's attempt to maintain sterling's role as a top international reserve and financial medium and to continue to operate as an economic superpower with worldwide commitments decreased its room for manoeuvre. This problem was exacerbated by a balance of payments deficit as imports poured into the country, prompting the government to deflationary measures.[10] These resulted in minor economic slumps, followed by brief surges in prosperity – the 'stop-go' cycle. The rhythm of industrial peace, easy wage settlements and the rise in living standards, which had characterised the 1950s, gave way to inflation and mini-slumps, though the overall trend towards economic growth continued. By the early 1960s clouds had begun to gather on the horizon for the British economy, in particular a decline in relative international competitiveness.[11] Yet, until 1960 such developments were overshadowed by the pervasiveness of affluence, economic growth and the 'managerial revolution' – the shift in the pattern of ownership and control of many firms, resulting in an enlarged role for managers who did not directly own these companies. Combined with the capacity of the British economy to enhance working-class consumption levels, these developments allowed the Conservative Party to command sufficient political loyalty for the convincing electoral victory of 1959.

Soon after the election, as economic conditions deteriorated, Conservative thinking emphasised two different solutions to the problems which the British economy faced. One resulted in the bid to join the fledgling Common Market in the hope that the business community would cope more successfully in partnership with European capital. The other strategy consisted of the attempt to stabilise the conditions for accumulation, especially for the large units of corporate capital, through a new emphasis on state regulation and intervention. After 1961 the government began to implement programmes to encourage rationalisation and some degree of industrial modernisation. It imposed a pay freeze in the public sector without consulting the unions and instituted an incomes policy to encourage wage restraint. This path was fraught with dangers. The drift towards further state expenditures, when resources were already stretched, proved unpopular in the party. Simultaneously, the administration became vulnerable to working-class wage demands as the cost of living rose and real wages lagged behind. The period from 1962-4 was, therefore, marked by an upsurge of industrial demands and trade union militancy in both the private and public sectors of the economy. Within three months of its installation, the incomes policy collapsed as the government proved unwilling to face the consequences of widespread labour unrest.[12] The consensus which the Conservatives had forged around their ideas in the late 1950s gave way to the unsuccessful attempts to wrestle with relative economic decline and the political scandals of the early 1960s. Tensions emerged within the party on a whole series of social as well as economic issues.[13]

## Affluence

For the New Left, affluence became a metaphor for the inability of socialism to come to terms with the post-war world. The movement was, on the whole, keen to engage with the changed social and economic conditions of this period, sensing the challenge which Labour faced. Indeed, for the most heterodox in the New Left, affluence, like classlessness (see chapter two), necessitated a fundamental reappraisal of socialism. Commentators across the political spectrum wondered whether the Labour Party was irreversibly weakened by the economic and social changes ushered in by the 1950s. The increase in living standards experienced by many working people, the access they gained to a new consumer culture and lifestyle, especially in areas of labour movement strength, and the changing patterns of work – the expansion of white-collar employment and decline of older manufacturing industries – all seemed to work against Labour. Critics asked whether Labour's constituency was being irreversibly depleted and altered. As an influential book which appeared immediately after the 1959 election put it: must Labour lose?[14] How profoundly had affluence altered both the balance of power and conditions of life within British society? How urgently did Labour need to alter its beliefs and culture in the wake of these changes?

These questions lay at the heart of the New Left's agenda, encouraging an important assessment of the implications of social change, not just for the Labour Party, but for the ideology of socialism as a whole. Willingness to pose these questions distinguished this formation, generating some of its most original and important analysis.

Significantly, affluence encouraged a receptivity to a wider range of intellectual influences than were available in the traditional socialist repertoire. J.K.Galbraith's work influenced many, not least his convincing argument that new circumstances required a novel political analysis.[15] Norman MacKenzie suggested that Britain was following the American model of economic development which Galbraith had outlined, arguing that:

> Britain is moving towards a form of People's Capitalism – a more industrial society, in which economic power becomes more concentrated, in which the role of the state and the bureaucracy is enlarged and in which full employment and social welfare make the system acceptable to a majority of the people.[16]

In addition, the New Left played an important role in popularising Galbraith's influential concept of 'private affluence and public squalor'.

Affluence also encouraged an analytical response which mingled economic with ideological and cultural ideas, under the influence of Williams' work in particular (see chapter four). According to Norman MacKenzie, capitalism was now generating a new 'psychology of wants';[17] these were reshaping many of the social aspirations which Labour claimed to represent. In Hall's view, 'consumer capitalism did genuinely – about the middle of the roaring fifties – break through some kind of sound barrier in public consciousness'.[18] This new culture generated a series of conflicts between private interests and public goals which reinforced the ideology of classlessness. The theme of affluence provided a conduit, therefore, to the analysis of deeper, social and cultural changes. Undoubtedly, it elicited much more than ritual condemnation from this formation.

Labour's continued reluctance to engage with the implications of affluence and modernisation frustrated the New Left, though it was compelled to recognise the exceptional nature of Crosland's contemporary arguments (outlined below). On the whole, the Conservatives were pilloried by Labour for their residual hostility to welfare and for unleashing individualism into British social and economic life. Until 1959, Labour Party thinking had failed to move beyond these emphases. Critics in the New

Left increasingly felt that the limitations of the welfare model on which the party relied, and the absence of an alternative to affluence, were paralysing the left. The New Left, on the other hand, was able to challenge the assumptions of conventional economic and political thought from its relatively unemcumbered ideological position. The narrowness of mainstream political discourse was increasingly held responsible for limiting imaginative policy responses and criticised for failing to comprehend social and economic change. Michael Barratt Brown, for instance, questioned the importance of the defence of sterling and the maintenance of the sterling area as mainstays of post-war policy:

> Why does British capital seek investment opportunity overseas? Why does the British government support the international strength of sterling at the cost of stagnation at home? Mr Schonfield believes that it is not in the main a search for higher returns on capital but that it is rather a hangover from a grander past with little thought given to the cost of being a great power in the modern world.[19]

Explanation for pressing economic problems might be sought also through ideological, cultural and political analysis.

New Left critics increasingly deployed their sensitivity to the overlap between the political and the economic in their assessment of mainstream political debate. In the first edition of *ULR*, Hall provided an account of the changing ideas of contemporary conservatism. Whereas 'most socialists would be tempted to say that it is merely the "old Toryism" writ large',[20] he demonstrated that important shifts had taken place within Conservative politics and that these had generated a new series of political tensions: indeed, 'the process by which it remained in business – the process of public theft and private accumulation by which the new Tories snatched up the welfare state and roped in the middle classes – is an unfinished process'. He concluded that the welfare state was not necessarily alien territory for the right in British politics. Labour's political strategy, which depended greatly on defence of this achievement, was, therefore, flawed. Labour was presented by the Conservatives as outdated and sympathetic to bureaucracies, 'for the "peaceful revolution" appeared to have brought only the encroachment of bureaucracy, with its distancing effects upon intelligent and spontaneous participation in the life of the community.'[21]

This perspective encouraged some lively and original writing, especially in *New Left Review* after 1960, which gave greater emphasis to analysing contemporary events than the original New Left journals. More importantly, a distinctive New Left style and methodology were developed in the wake of the political crisis experienced by the left in this period and the defensive responses this elicited from the Labour Party.

## Revisionism in the Labour Party

Crosland provided the major exception to this characterisation of Labour's thinking, especially his highly influential text *The Future of Socialism*, which shaped key aspects of Labour's agenda in the late 1950s. Post-war capitalism had been transformed, he argued, by the Labour government, the growth of the public sector, the apparent elimination of poverty and the 'managerial revolution'. He highlighted the new balance of power and influence within contemporary society. The principal consequence of the expansion of welfare provision and the public sector was a new restraint upon the political and economic power of private business. Many private enterprises had experienced a marked shift in culture and organisation. In particular, a gap had emerged between the ownership and control of British industry and finance. The domination of the individual, large-scale entrepreneur or shareholder had come to an end. Key economic enterprises were now run by non-shareholder managers who were bound by a new corporate ethic – management 'with a human face'.[22] This recognition that the economic system had altered fundamentally necessitated a revolution in Labour's political style and policy commitments. Nationalisation was no longer appropriate as a policy instrument. In fact, stable economic growth offered the most likely avenue for a peaceful transition to socialism, obviating the need for an assault upon existing economic relations. He did, however, stress the continuing significance of welfare, social equality and redistributive taxation as goals for the left.

Whilst Crosland won over significant sections of party opinion to his ideas, the full implications of the revisionist position remained problematic for Labour. His ideas were interpreted by Gaitskell as proof of the need to overhaul the party's 'dated' image, inspiring his unsuccessful attempt to rescind Clause Four of Labour's Constitution – the symbolic commitment to the collective appropriation of the means of production. Despite his defeat on this issue in 1959, Gaitskell oversaw the permeation of revisionist ideas into party policy. Crosland's vision provided the rationale behind *Industry and Society*, Labour's keynote document of this period, which boldly stated that 'the nationalisation programme was designed to make a real contribution to the broader aims of socialism – to social justice, economic security and a new spirit in industry. These expectations ... have been substantially realised.'[23] New criteria were proposed to justify the commitment to nationalisation in specific cases: only firms which were acting contrary to the 'national interest' would be taken into public ownership; whilst private interests would be fully compensated in cases where nationalisation was applied.[24] The frontier between private and public sectors, established from 1945-50, was to be defended. Moreover, the state under Labour was to enter into a new relationship with private enterprise.[25] Large firms, this document suggested, were no longer driven solely by the profit motive, nor did they necessarily generate antagonistic industrial relations. Because of their size, they were more amenable to state planning and direction.

Planning was increasingly invoked as a mechanism whereby the benign state would work in harmony with private enterprise, establishing a 'broad framework within which the creation of new wealth can go smoothly and rapidly ahead and the detailed decisions of industry do not come into conflict with national objectives'.[26] Planning and the national interest were irredeemably conflated, so that in Labour's subsequent programmes, *Plan for Progress* (1958) and *The Nationalised Industries: Success Story* (1958), the plan was presented as the guarantor of national development, standing above the many competing sectional interests within the nation. This perspective deferred serious strategic problems to a later date when Labour would be called on to implement this programme.

The articulation of revisionist themes and their absorption by leading thinkers and policy makers in the Labour Party constituted an important influence upon the New Left's political development. The success of revisionism highlighted the inadequacy of older interpretations of British society. Revisionist ideas also revealed the significance of adjusting to the changed basis and direction of post-war capitalism. Indeed, the distillation of a coherent and intellectually rigorous position within the Labour Party compelled the New Left to devise its own alternatives in these areas. But New Left writers also sought to contest Croslandite ideas, sensing their hold over many on the left. The diversity of New Left perspectives was, at first, evident. Some – Miliband for instance – viewed the hegemony of Crosland's ideas as the latest twist in the long narrative of Labour opportunism: 'Their ideas amount to no more than a plea for Labour' return to the old days before 1918 when the Party did not have a Constitution which held Socialist implications'.[27] Yet, for other observers, these ideas, and their influence upon

Labour Party thought, represented a qualitatively different phase in the party's development, and required a careful response. Hall, for instance, provided a history of the genealogy of these ideological tendencies in the second edition of *New Left Review*. He suggested that Crosland's vision constituted an attempt to bring Labour politics face to face with the new world of British capitalism and to provide an alternative interpretation of Labour's role in a period of crisis about its political identity.[28] More generally, Labour's thinking had not changed entirely: according to Hall, these newer ideas had been grafted on to its more orthodox and traditional culture. The need to understand and combat these trends in the party was reiterated by Anderson's study of social democracy in which he assessed the implications of the Swedish model for Britain. He recalled how Crosland's ideas had outmanoeuvered the traditional left and right in the party, largely due to his readiness to embrace the spirit of modernity within the British economy; this allowed him to present his enemies as insular and backward-looking.[29]

Revisionism inspired the New Left's most concrete intervention in these areas – 'The Insiders', a largely empirical response to *Industry and Society*, which set out to refute the claims that ownership and control has been separated in modern industry and that the managerial revolution had taken place.[30] (This document is outlined in greater detail below.) Its authors (parts were jointly written by Hall, Samuel, Peter Sedgwick and Charles Taylor, others individually penned by Sedgwick, Clive Jenkins, Miliband and Mike Artis) rejected Crosland's vision as an inadequate representation of the contemporary world, which would lead the Labour Party to acquiesce in the continuance of profound social inequalities. These included the gap between private affluence and public squalor, the imbalance of priorities in the calculation of education and welfare state expenditure as compared with defence or advertising spending, as well as the persistence of social poverty amidst the spread of affluence.

Anderson, meanwhile, rejected the idea that opposition to Croslandite propositions should be premised on a conception of capitalism as a 'bipolar system of exploitation' (a logic he perceived as fundamentalist and outdated). He preferred to consider capitalism 'as a social praxis in alienation from all its agents at all levels' – a system where the real decisions had been already taken, away from the 'territory of the average political debate'.[31] Refusing to adapt either to the revisionist reading of social change, where capitalism was quietly disappearing from view, or the fundamentalist perspective, where it remained effectively unchanged, the New Left, by and large, staked out a middle course.

Simultaneously, a hopeful vigil was constantly maintained in this milieu for signs of change in Labour's thinking. In London a dialogue was maintained with revisionist intellectuals and sympathetic Labour figures, some of whom spoke at the London Club. Admittedly, Crosland himself thought little of the New Left's critique, though he considered 'The Insiders' sufficiently serious to merit a reply.[32] There is evidence that this dialogue was occasionally reciprocal, with the party absorbing New Left ideas and language on certain questions. Towards the end of 1960, *New Left Review*'s editorial hopefully suggested that 'the Party has begun to mark the contrasts between "private opulence and public squalor", to learn the catechism of complaints which it must learn, if socialist theory is to deal with the realities of mid-century capitalism'.[33] This merely confirmed the suspicions of some in the New Left that their own arguments had moved too far from established socialist premises. In particular, ex-communists in the *New Reasoner* group remained more sceptical about Labour politics. Significantly, it was in this milieu that Miliband felt most at home, developing his influential critique of the contemporary Labour Party and its historical role in British politics.[34] It was the *ULR* wing of the movement which ventured furthest into this milieu, becoming involved in the battles of 1959-60. As Labour's left failed to mount a successful opposition to the onset of revisionism and ceased to function as an effective source of alternative policy ideas, this difference in attitude became more important.

## Labour's Left

The experiences of the Attlee government were central to the emergence of a left opposition within the Labour Party after the war. Whilst this grouping was motivated principally by foreign policy questions, it also aired an alternative interpretation of domestic developments. Hostility to the slowing down of the government's nationalisation programme combined with disquiet over the introduction of charges in the health service.[35] Within the 'Keep Left' group, which emerged in the parliamentary party in 1947, these disappointments were central. The personality of Nye Bevan, the charismatic and powerful spokesman of this grouping throughout the early 1950s, was instrumental in shaping the nature of this opposition. As Ben Pimlott reveals, much of the factional in-fighting of this decade was determined by the relationship to Bevan of individuals within the parliamentary party.[36] According to Peter Clarke, the party witnessed a three-way split in the 1950s: between Bevanites and Gaitskellites; left and right; and fundamentalists and revisionists.[37]

However heterogeneous its make-up, the left shared a common strategic perspective. Whilst it celebrated Labour's achievements in both moral and practical terms, its advocates hoped to reaffirm the party's commitment to public ownership throughout the economy. Certainly, criticisms were raised of the form in which nationalisation had occurred, yet these were given slight emphasis against the confident assertion of the possibility of further socialist advance. These beliefs begged important questions, however. How was the public sector to be extended so as to enhance rather than inhibit efficiency? How exactly was the public side of the mixed economy to become hegemonic in society? To these questions the Bevanites had few convincing answers. For the most part, the issues were seldom discussed, a testament to the left's undiminished confidence in the policies initiated in the period between 1945-8. These advances, the left believed, had been halted because of the absence of socialist commitment within the party's leadership. Whilst such thinking kept alive the spirit of radical opposition within the party after 1951, it provided an inadequate basis on which to develop a convincing intellectual alternative. The left was as bound by an acceptance of parliament's centrality as its fellow party members and was equally constrained by the imperative of electoral calculation. As Crosland laid out a new interpretation of British society, therefore, the left countered that little had changed in the 1950s. Nationalisation was proposed as a remedy for uneven economic development and the inequalities of capitalism in general. The left increasingly posed as the defenders of the post-war government's heritage against the tides of revisionism in the party.

Bolstered by the development of the Campaign for Nuclear Disarmament, the fortunes of Labour's opposition appeared to be improving from 1959-60. First, it successfully opposed Gaitskell's attempt to remove the party's commitment to public ownership. Subsequently, it won an impressive victory at the Scarborough Conference of 1960, securing a majority in favour of unilateral nuclear disarmament. But these were chimeric victories.[38] On Clause Four, for instance, Gaitskell encountered widespread opposition from traditionalists who retained loyalty to this symbol and its surrounding culture. His abandonment of the role of reconciler of the different factions in the party provided the real explanation of his defeat. The left's insistent and axiomatic defence of Clause Four won few converts to a new interpretation of this commitment. Relying on totemic opposition on points of faith, rather than the articulation of an alternative interpretation of post-war capitalism, the left failed to take advantage of this setback for the revisionist project. The subsequent collapse of these oppositional perspectives within the Labour Party, dramatised by Bevan's renunciation of unilateralism in 1957, carried significant implications for the New Left. It resulted in the absence of any sustained critique of Labour's economic policy and social priorities, which the New Left set out to remedy. In many ways, the collapse of a vibrant opposition in the party legitimated the New Left as one of the few effective voices of protest against the onset of revisionism.

In political and organisational terms, the New Left enjoyed an ambivalent relationship with Labour's left. On many occasions it sought alliances in the trade unions and wider labour movement. Both original New Left journals advertised *Tribune* and associated meetings, whilst the movement's clubs hosted Labour left speakers and provided a haven for radical members of the party. Behind these contacts lay some substantial areas of political convergence, not least a shared hostility to the party's leadership. This sentiment was reinforced by the emergence of the unilateralist issue. As we shall see (in chapter six), the politics of unilateralism were so central to political debate by 1960, and the search for allies on this question so pressing, that these alliances were powerfully reaffirmed. In the crises of 1959-61, the New Left lined up alongside key figures to the left of the party. The *ULR*, London-based wing of the movement was closely involved in the debates that ensued, organising a daily lobby of delegates at the 1961 conference, and producing a satirical newsletter – *This Week*. Mervyn Jones, in his recent recollection of this period, provides a tantalising glimpse of the possibility of a more institutionalised alliance, recalling that he saw himself as a go-between between these two groups.[39]

But the experience of the revisionist controversies served to highlight the limitations of the Labour left's politics for many outside it. The authors of 'The Insiders' had boldly stated that the orthodoxies of a previous generation could not provide the vehicle for socialist renewal in the post-war period: 'The fact that nationalisation of the means of production has traditionally been part of a socialist programme is not enough to justify our retaining it today'.[40] New arguments were needed to advance social and public ownership. Most of all, the fundamental changes which had occurred within capitalism had to be grasped by those interested in socialist renewal. Whilst

Labour's revisionists were eager to put their stamp on these changes, their opponents relied too heavily on a call to faith in the belief that nothing of substance had changed in the post-war world.[41]

New Left political instincts led to the rejection of this brand of politics. References to Labour's left became increasingly critical, especially amongst the younger wing of the movement. *ULR* played an important role in asserting the need for a distinct New Left political vision and culture outside the traditions and structures of labourism. Increasingly, its writers remarked upon the common assumptions behind the different positions within the Labour Party, finding the politics of the left, in particular, curiously debilitating. Characterised as the defenders of party tradition and conscience, the left was socialised into its hostility to the Labour leadership, espousing a rhetoric of socialist mobilisation, yet fetishising the constitutional mechanisms of the party. Miliband's forceful critique of the limitations of 'parliamentary socialism' was influential here.[42] These sentiments were reinforced by the prevalent belief within the New Left that economic concerns could not be separated from the dissemination of alternative values throughout society. The reiteration of formulaic ideas about nationalisation, the New Left believed, obscured the real tasks for socialists in this area. Its thinkers sought a new consensus, based upon an alternative interpretation of society, ethics and the economy. The project of sustaining an independent movement outside the Labour Party was, therefore, tied to the rejection of the Bevanites' outlook. The New Left's celebration of independent activity and mobilisation on various fronts of struggle was premised on a distance from these sections of the labour movement. On these points near unanimity was reached within the New Left, providing a cornerstone of identity for this fragile political formation.

## Wilson in the Ascendant

Whilst the years from 1959-62 were notable for the degree of conflict within Labour's ranks, they also marked the origins of a new phase in its history. This change, culminating in Harold Wilson's accession to the leadership, was evident in the keynote document *Signposts*, produced in 1961. This statement of Labour's domestic policy sharpened earlier revisionist documents in several areas: in particular, it placed greater emphasis on modernisation within the British economy and the key role of science. In addition, it launched an attack upon the 'symptoms of decline' throughout the nation, as the economic boom began to recede.[43] The re-emergence of profound inequalities, associated with the resurgence of private industry and wealth, was highlighted, whilst the government was criticised for its reluctance to develop a strategy to remedy the inefficiency and injustices of large-scale private monopolies. Against the 'growth of new forms of privilege and the rapid concentration of economic power which has taken place since 1951',[44] *Signposts* called for the more efficient 'planning of our national resources'.[45] The 'vast concentrations of economic power' should be made accountable to the national interest.[46] With this radical rhetoric came the hint of a more stringent interpretation of the possibilities of nationalisation and a more restrictive set of regulations within which private monopolies would operate. Whilst these commitments had appeared before within Labour's thought, *Signposts* marked a shift in both the tone and substance of party discourse on these matters.[47]

Wilson's position in the party was aided both by his stress upon internal reconciliation, putting aside the battles of previous years beneath the unifying banners of modernisation and economic expansion, and doctrinal reticence. Ben Pimlott describes Wilson in the 1950s as a 'tribal Bevanite, a tactical Centrist, and an ideological revisionist'.[48] As a political manager, Wilson's touch was initially far lighter than his predecessor. Ironically, he was aided in this process by the latter's opposition to Britain's entry into the Common Market in 1962. This stance proved popular with the majority of the party and won Gaitskell the temporary assent of many on the left. From 1962, Wilson's style and tone strongly influenced Labour's public discourse as the Conservative government was lambasted for its failure to modernise Britain. This emphasis was combined with a far sharper critique of the increasingly evident social disparities within the nation. The populist edge that Wilson injected into Labour Party campaigning was reflected throughout its literature by 1963, the year of his victory over his Gaitskellite rival George Brown in the party's leadership contest. Wilson held out the hope that national economic reconstruction, conducted through central institutions, and scientific advance would revive the flagging British economy. As Pimlott suggests:

> Wilson seemed to bring together – uniquely – Labour idealism, state-of-the-art economics and popular enthusiasm. He led not just a charmed life but one of feverish excitement and charisma. Sparkling at impromptu gatherings, master of the big audience, skilled in the new medium of television, rapier-like in Parliament, he built a formidable alliance of

manual workers, technicians and what would nowadays be called the chattering classes who were briefly persuaded by his vision of a streamlined, meritocratic future.[49]

For many party members he seemed to offer salvation from the political wilderness of the 1950s. From 1963-4 he launched a 'crusade' against the government, appealing to a broad and diverse range of social groups, and exploiting the emergence of a satirical and modernist culture among sections of the intelligentsia.

For the New Left, Wilson represented opportunities and pitfalls. Aspects of his project struck chords with sections of the movement, partially contributing to its demise as an independent formation; yet writers within the milieu were sceptical about his political trajectory from an early stage. Certainly, Labour's public discourse after 1961 suggested that New Left emphases were, in a diluted form, being taken on board. This raises the question of the degree of ideological overlap between the New Left and 'Wilsonism', and has led some commentators to speculate on the potential influence of Wilson over the New Left. An interesting parallel arises here with the relationship between a later comparable project, the ideas associated with the journal *Marxism Today* in the 1980s, and the changing emphases and policy style of the Labour leadership under Neil Kinnock. For some critics, *Marxism Today* legitimated aspects of Labour's revisionism, contributing to a climate in which wholesale rethinking was more acceptable.[50] The parallel looks promising because both of these currents were most effective in their sharp attack upon the orthodoxies of the party's 'old guard'. In both cases, these critiques were imported into the 'modern' agenda of the contemporary leadership. The similarity extends also to the controversy which this political proximity aroused. Wilson's apparent sympathy with certain New Left ideas caused concern within this formation, then and later.[51] Figures close to Wilson developed connections with the New Left, particularly Peter Shore and Barbara Castle, who spoke at New Left meetings and contributed to their publications. Clearly, a shared interest in a more dynamic and modernising politics made such individuals relatively sympathetic to the New Left. Beyond this, there were thematic connections between these camps. From 'The Insiders' onwards, the New Left called for a programme of national economic reconstruction based upon a more rational, centralised and redistributive policy framework. This meant moving beyond older emphases upon nationalisation as the key element within a radical economic strategy.

Sections of the movement, like Wilson, regarded modernisation as a social and economic necessity. The question arises, therefore, whether later critics are right to suggest that Wilson's agenda began to shape New Left ideas.[52] It has been argued that this process occurred in two ways. First, individuals in the London Club were, as we have seen, closely involved in the revisionist debate. This proximity allowed several writers from this milieu to empathise with Wilson's inclusion of modernisation within Labour's staid political repertoire. Some of the younger figures involved in *New Left Review* after 1961 (Anderson, in particular) came to appreciate the 'hegemonic' strategy pursued by Wilson. Second, New Left economists, such as John Hughes and Michael Barratt Brown, were optimistic about the possibility of tilting the Wilsonite policy agenda in a more radical direction.

The question of this relationship is complicated, however, by the story of the New Left's one moment of influence upon Labour's policy formation in the period prior to Wilson's ascendancy to the leadership. In November 1960 work began on a new domestic statement for a submission by the party's Home Policy Committee. The working party to produce this was drawn from across Labour's ideological spectrum. According to David Howell, '*Signposts* ... appears to have begun as a Research Department paper, that placed considerable emphasis on issues then being debated by the New Left, especially the extension of democracy beyond formal political institutions and questions of culture and the mass media'.[53] In March 1961 the working party produced a draft which included references to all these questions. In May it was passed back to the Home Policy Committee and, then, placed before the National Executive Committee. Here, it was rejected and referred to a group of party officers who revised the draft substantially. The remaining references to cultural and kindred topics were removed whilst Hugh Gaitskell, Richard Crossman and Wilson re-wrote key sections on land, transport and education policy. It was this document which emerged as *Signposts*.[54]

Details of the original, New Left-inspired draft appeared in *New Left Review*. The content of this submission illustrates the profound differences that separated the New Left from Labour's thinking, despite the temporary influence of New Left ideas, both before and after Wilson's leadership. This draft emphasised the need to democratise all aspects of British life, including the economy. It included a sharp critique of the hierarchical nature of many contemporary institutions and aspects of life, about which Labour was quiescent or defensive. In the sections of the draft entitled 'Democracy in

Industry', 'Democracy and Minorities' and 'Democracy and Bureaucracy', the importance of establishing a democratic and participatory culture within and beyond industry was asserted. Meanwhile, the rights of individuals as citizens, workers and consumers were expanded in the wake of the encroachment of monopolies and state bureaucracies:

> Paradoxically the very extent of our public services means that the individual is often subject to an arbitrary power. As a patient in hospital, as a resident in an old people's home, when applying for a pension or national assistance, when in dispute with an insurance company or the inland revenue or customs, time and again the individual is placed in a position of dependence... we need to set up effective new organisations to redeem the inferiority of 'us' relative to 'them', to protect the individual citizen's rights against the arbitrary power of organisation, to ensure that the public services really do serve the public.[55]

These sentiments were far too libertarian for Wilson and others at the head of the party, hence their removal from the final version of *Signposts*.

Differences between the New Left and Wilson can also be located in their diverging conceptions of modernisation. For the New Left, this theme was connected, through the concept of community, to the question of which social groups might benefit from this process and how it should be resourced. This was true, for instance, of the incomes policy proposed by writers in this formation (outlined below). Kenneth Alexander, writing in 1961, bemoaned the absence of any appreciation of the connection between the political and economic dimensions of policy in Wilson's perspective, citing the lack of any 'sense of the need to continue a political battle against the centres of economic power if the plan is to work'.[56] For the New Left, modernisation was always counterbalanced by the need to instil grassroots and participatory democracy, as well as the political mobilisation of the subaltern classes. For Wilson and the Labour government after 1964, on the other hand, redirection and regulation of the economy by the state were the main priorities.

Even after 1962, when the first New Left was organisationally moribund, its intellectual project continued in the writings of a number of individuals contemplating the possibility of a Labour victory at the forthcoming election. Several critics continued to deploy the expansive mode of analysis which intellectuals in this movement had developed, intertwining political, cultural and economic insights to interpret and criticise Labour's programme. In 1964 John Hughes explored the possibility of a radical economic strategy for the Labour government in an analysis that incorporated a broad range of social and political themes. Posing the question, 'can a Labour Government combine "management" of the mixed economy with a real shift of social and economic power towards the community?',[57] he anticipated some of the key political themes within the life of this administration. He called for more centralised economic institutions and planning departments, but stressed the need for 'the extension of democratic participation in and control over economic institutions and decisions'.[58] In conclusion, he outlined a more democratic framework for planning, especially at regional and local levels. His essay contained a blunt warning about the dangers of long-term planning without an accompanying shift in the forms of social accountability. More generally, his argument throws into relief the analytical and political evolution of the first New Left's ideas in these areas. His conception of the interrelations between the political and economic and stress upon the importance of organising a popular coalition on the moral, cultural and ideological fronts was partly shaped by the proto-Gramscian conclusions which some within the first New Left had reached. These arguments were not the product of direct engagement with Gramscian ideas but were the outcome of a slow and uneven intellectual evolution throughout these years, a process elaborated below. Under the influence of Williams above all, the New Left sought to transcend orthodox Marxist economism, the politics of labourism and the methodological empiricism of conventional policy analysis. Aspects of this approach prefigured the influential reinterpretation of the development of British society later propounded by Anderson and Nairn, a point reinforced by Willie Thompson's analysis of their ideas:

> The importance of this [Anderson/Nairn] model probably lies less in the contentious details of its content than in the assertion of a strong link between historical development, the forms of state structure, the character of a national culture and the performance of an economy – up to that point regarded by informed commentary as quite separate issues.[59]

A similar analysis to Hughes' was developed by Anderson in 1964, though with a more explicitly theoretical emphasis. In the course of his assessment of the nature and character of the new government, he wielded the Gramscian conception of hegemony:

The present crisis of the governing class allows the Labour Party to split the Conservative bloc, detaching from it specific social groups in the population. First and foremost among these is the 'technical intelligentsia': scientists, technicians, engineers, architects, managers and professional workers, employed in both private and public corporations.[60]

In an imaginative and, at times, sympathetic analysis, he ascribed to 'Wilsonism' the properties of a hegemonic political project, or, in the words of one commentator, 'more coherence than it ever really had'.[61] Wilson had moulded an alliance from groups with differing interests through a distinctive and cohesive moral and political vision. Harnessing the most modern elements within the nation to his condemnation of the aristocratic, decaying and class-ridden society overseen by the Tories, Wilson presented an image of a new Britain and hijacked the discourse of modernity. A range of social identities were celebrated within this outlook: the technician, the skilled worker, the intellectual and the modern manager all figured in this new ideological coalition. The parallel suggested earlier with new left currents in the 1980s is apposite here: Anderson's conception of, and perhaps admiration for, the hegemonic properties of Wilsonism prefigured the analysis of Thatcherism associated especially with Hall.[62] Interestingly, both were criticised for overstressing the coherence of these ideological projects. The similarities between and influence of these analyses, despite obvious differences, suggest that New Left ideas in Britain have been especially influential when articulating a critique of the failure of conventional socialist analysis to represent the political world with sufficient accuracy and conceptual skill. The parallel also reveals the continuing desire within the British intelligentsia for the left to expand its constituencies beyond the traditional labour movement and to harness intermediate social strata – especially those at the sharp end of the technical division of labour – into a broader political coalition. Significantly, some within the later New Left disagreed with Anderson's argument, for instance his erstwhile collaborator Nairn, who did not share this optimistic evaluation: 'the difference of opinion resulted in a sceptical article he wrote on "Wilsonism" being poorly received and, although published, having its ending changed to reflect a more positive assessment'.[63]

Anderson was, in fact, more critical of Wilson than this comment suggests: he was especially sceptical about the latter's purely rhetorical denunciation of older elements within British capital. Such sentiments did not entail a frontal assault on real capitalist power. He also pointed to the weakness of a politics which was so embedded within the framework of the nation state. Despite Wilson's denunciation of the age of empire and Labour's previous subordination to the Atlantic alliance, the party's heightened jingoism and 'complete absence of specific commitments on colonial issues' meant that Labour was likely to play a conservative role within international affairs.[64] Refusing to accept the terms of contemporary political debate and the dominant version of Britain's role in the world, Anderson anticipated some of the difficulties which Wilson's government faced after 1964. But Anderson's appropriation of ideas which developed within the first New Left milieu marked the end of this mode of analysis, as he abandoned the insights of this movement and began his 'importation' of Western Marxist thought. Increasingly contemptuous of British empiricism, he moved away from the low-level approach to theory of the first New Left, relinquishing any sense of hope about the intellectual capabilities of the domestic intelligentsia.

## THE NEW LEFT'S CONTRIBUTION TO SOCIALIST POLITICAL ECONOMY

The first New Left generated a substantial body of writing on political events and long-term trends in both economy and society. Throughout, its writers provided a fresh assessment of a number of themes which had figured prominently in earlier socialist thought, as well as new problems thrown up by post-war capitalism. This analysis underwent a process of evolution as left orthodoxies were contested and the largely unchartered territory of political analysis beyond the traditions of classical Marxism and Fabianism was explored. Falteringly, the New Left moved from instinctive distaste for older orthodoxies to the distillation of an alternative position. This evolution can be measured in its engagement with four themes which recur in its work: (1) the nature of the elite in contemporary society (2) the public sector (3) planning, and (4) the importance of democracy for both workers and consumers.

### Interpreting the Elite in Contemporary Society

The central thesis of 'The Insiders' was that the Labour Party had concentrated so exclusively on the functionless shareholder as the central figure of capitalist organisation that it had neglected the emergence of a corporate elite made up of managers and large investors. This elite had seized the high ground of post-war society. The transformation of capitalism did not entail the disappearance of social and economic inequity. In fact, new inequalities, particular to this stage of corporate capitalism, had emerged. Most of all, New Left writers emphasised the disparities between the public and private sectors of the economy and the resulting imbalance of social resources. New conflicts and inequalities had emerged within these spheres. In the private sector, Labour was too complacent about the large corporations. A new series of alliances, founded on social, cultural and educational privilege, had grown up at the top of British society, between managers, financiers, overseas investors and large-scale shareholders. The contradictions and gradations within this bloc were ignored by Labour, as were the increased social power and influence of this elite. A revolution of a kind had occurred, but had not dissolved the power of large shareholders, directors and managerial executives.[65] The New Left, in fact, redefined the post-war settlement as an uneasy compromise between a new power elite and subaltern groups. Whilst the analysis of this elite in 'The Insiders' was curtailed by its empirical frame of reference, this document prepared the development of a more general critique of the social transformations effected since Labour's defeat in 1951.

'The Insiders' was an equally important benchmark with regard to the public sector. Its authors suggested that whilst the question of nationalisation constituted the most salient policy debate in the party, the form in which public ownership occurred was rarely raised: 'As things stand at present we cannot say that public ownership has meant social control.'[66] The New Left's more sceptical attitude towards nationalisation opened the way for a critique of the public sector in general. Here, the Morrisonian form of nationalisation, the Fabian assumptions behind the welfare state and the defensiveness with which Labour clung to its achievements were perceived as political problems rooted in Labour's past. The authors of 'The Insiders' concluded that nationalisation and state regulation were not necessarily antithetical to the interests of the business community: some firms had been handsomely rewarded through state compensation. The national interest, this document concluded, had to be redefined, not abandoned to the hegemony of large capital.

The belief that a complex, interlocking elite dominated the economy was elaborated in largely empirical terms. The argument rested firmly on the backgrounds of and relationships between 'controllers' and 'insiders' at corporate and political levels. Both 'The Insiders', and its successor 'The Controllers' (written by Michael Barratt Brown) pointed to the role of interlocking directorates, the influence of large-scale shareholders in key British industries and the connections between these important political interests.[67] Yet, this empirical frame of reference grated against some of the broader themes of its analysis. Clive Jenkins' influential study of the composition of the boards of nationalised industries and the survival of hierarchical relationships within them, in *Power at the Top* (1959), was sharply criticised by Kenneth Alexander on exactly this score: Jenkins' analysis left many of the difficult questions about the newly nationalised industries unanswered.[68] These included the precise nature of the relationship between public and private industry, the mechanisms through which corporate power was wielded and the implied homogeneity of the elite in Jenkins' account. Alexander's argument signalled that the New Left was not, on the whole, content to rest its economic case upon the 'facts' which indicated that a new elite had emerged, but sought a more theoretically inclined account of elite domination. Wright Mills' division of the major institutional structures of power in American society into three overlapping elites – the military, corporate-industrial and politico-administrative – provided an important 'map' for this conceptual journey.[69] The composition, functions and effects of this elite now constituted the objects of New Left analysis. This shift was evident in the years after 'The Insiders' was published, but has been obscured by conventional historiography on the New Left, which tends to stress the essential continuity of its analysis. In Samuel's words:

> In 'Out of Apathy' we depicted capitalism as a moribund social order whose race was nearly run – 'last stage capitalism', as we hopefully designated it ... a system in E.P.Thompson's words, 'ripe' and 'overripe' for destruction. In a hierarchical vein we took up arms against Britain's 'ancien regime', its grouse-shooting merchant bankers, its caste-like institutions, its privileged schools. The New Left was convinced that the old ruling class was intact and indeed a great deal of our empirical research – or 'power elite' analysis – was devoted to mapping its contours. Our phraseology was determinedly up to date and sociological: the images which lay behind it were archaic.[70]

Some of this was true of 'The Insiders'. Whilst Marxist emphases on class were replaced by the assertion of a broader division between 'the controllers' and subaltern groups, the vague terms in which this dynamic was developed permitted the retention of a crude and one-dimensional account of elite manipulation and domination.

But these emphases were gradually replaced by new lines of analysis. Understanding the composition of the elite was premised upon a more sophisticated picture of post-war society. Detailed description of corporate life provided an invaluable platform for a critique of the resources available to large economic institutions and their relationship to the broader social environment. New Left writers increasingly stressed the variety and specificity of locations and sites at which power was wielded and contested in the economy, citing, for instance, the private 'giants', the monopolies and the nationalised industries. They also talked more about the micro-dimensions of economic life. The notion that one determinant or variable might provide the peg around which a complete analysis of society and economy could be hung therefore became increasingly improbable for the New Left. Significantly, the CPGB's Sam Aaronovitch's subsequent analysis of the British ruling class ignored this heterodox analysis altogether, reiterating the orthodox Marxist thesis that finance capital continued to dominate the British economic system.[71] Among the New Left, power was rarely perceived as the preserve of one entrenched interest group. Simplistic 'class against class' scenarios were rejected whilst the shifting basis of the corporate and political elites merited an analysis which explained the specific ways in which social power was wielded and might be contested. In certain respects, this pushed these writers towards a pluralist explanation of power, a position adopted by contemporary analysts who viewed Britain as entering a post-capitalist era.[72] Yet, focus upon changes in ownership and control within the British economy, as well as a marked sensitivity to social and economic inequalities, ensured that the New Left's analysis transcended conventional demarcations. Gradually, the tight-knit elite perceived as the enemy by 'The Insiders' was displaced by a more refined and hegemonic conception of the operations of economic and social power.

## Re-evaluating the Public Sector:
## Nationalisation and the Welfare State

A series of strategic questions underlay the agenda of nationalisation for the New Left. What exactly were the functions of nationalisation and the public sector in general? To what extent could alternative forms of social regulation and control be developed? Was nationalisation the only, or most effective, form in which the principles of community control might be advanced?

According to Hughes, in his contemporary analysis of the steel industry, public ownership was intimately connected to questions of democracy within the industries themselves, and also to the mobilisation of opinion behind a broader set of criteria in assessing economic performance. This perspective differed markedly from Labour thinking. Debates had taken place in the party as to the criteria for and timing of nationalisation, yet these arguments left intact 'the terms ... of the mixed economy'.[73]

The critique of the strategic role of nationalisation encouraged these critics to examine the relationship between the public and private sectors of the economy. John Hughes, in particular, identified the role of vendor within the monopoly-dominated private sector which the nationalised industries had been forced to assume. Nationalisation had been beneficial to private interests because of its tendency to reorganise 'under a single management ... the capital, equipment and technology of these industries so that they were using modern technology in an integrated way'.[74] This critique reinforced the disappointment felt by many at Labour's previous failure to reform structural and hierarchical relations within the industries themselves. For the New Left, the struggle to construct an alternative engendered a receptivity to different traditions within the socialist heritage. Hall recalls that:

> G.D.H.Cole was the first socialist whom I ever heard advance from the basis of a more democratic conception of social ownership, a full-scale critique of the bureaucratic forms of 'Morrisonian'-style nationalisation favoured by the 1945 Labour government. This critique has been enormously influential in shaping the attitude of many socialist of my generation towards 'statist' forms of socialism.[75]

The notion of a more dynamic and democratic public sector dictating the terms of the economy was therefore popular within the New Left. Social ownership displaced nationalisation as a political motif within this milieu — an emphases appropriated, in a different context, by the Labour leadership in the early 1980s. Peter Marris, for example, proposed this as a populist counterpoint against the bureaucratic structures of the nationalised industries.[76] Likewise, Hall called for the:

> reapplication of the principle of common ownership to our economic thinking — not as a well-worn shibboleth which must be defended, like Buckingham Palace, because it is there — but because we cannot make a

system which is geared to go forward reverse itself, unless we are prepared to work it ourselves, unless it is responsible to us.[77]

Informed by this perspective, Hughes argued the case for a more socially responsible and regulated transport system – 'a transport policy to fit social needs' – and a more flexible and interactive relationship with unions, local interest groups and communities.[78] This example neatly illustrates the New Left's concern to decentre the principle of common ownership and disperse power throughout the community. New Left thinking was strongly motivated by the desire to liberate common ownership from the orthodoxies which had, in the late 1950s, ensnared it. These critics wished to decentralise political power by socialising and democratising ownership, yet simultaneously hoped to discover more effective levers for macro-economic policy.

The welfare state was also subjected to a distinctive critique in this period, though it proved a more difficult target. Loyalty to this major social advance remained strong. Yet, by the end of the 1950s such a commitment was more problematic. The appearance of an influential body of academic criticism of the extent and delivery of the 'welfare revolution' led to a fundamental reassessment of the agenda.[79] A parallel re-evaluation occurred within the New Left as related debates took place in both original journals. In the *New Reasoner*, Saville's historical assessment of the welfare state generated a sharp series of exchanges, especially his assertion that the welfare state was 'essentially bourgeois' because of its socially palliative effects on working-class aspirations.[80] This view was developed in direct opposition to Crosland's assertion that the welfare provisions of the Attlee government constituted a major social revolution: the welfare state, Saville argued, had scarcely touched the entrenched social relations of British life.

Thompson perceived the significance of some of the points made by his fellow editor as soon as he read the first draft of the article. A vigorous correspondence between the two ensued, in which Thompson suggested that the most urgent strategic concern for the left emerged at the point where Saville's analysis stopped: should socialists seek to extend the principles of welfare into the mixed economy as a first step in a transitional phase between capitalist and socialist society?[81] Moreover, the article fudged the important question of the response socialists should make to the welfare state. Should they reproduce the scepticism with which Marxists had regarded these institutions? Or should socialists highlight the contradictions inherent in maintaining welfare provisions within an economy dominated by the interests of private enterprise? Thompson also questioned the framework of Saville's analysis. The latter had construed this question in binary terms: either the welfare state had solved the problems of social inequality (Crosland's view), or they had not (Saville's own argument). This criticism was echoed by other contributors in the subsequent edition of the *New Reasoner*. In particular, several critics suggested that Saville had underestimated the historical specificity and significance of both the post-war Labour government and the social and economic consequences of the social reforms which had occurred throughout the century. For Dorothy Thompson, Saville's analysis underplayed the significant political advances made by the post-war government after 1945. In her view, the welfare state constituted a socialist achievement.[82]

The New Left, more generally, explored the space between these two perspectives. Increasingly sceptical of the notion that the welfare state had abolished exploitation and inequality as issues of concern, it also avoided the functionalism inherent within Saville's account. The practices and institutions of the welfare state were interpreted as the location of a series of inequalities and power relations which structured the provision of social services. From this perspective, the welfare state, and the health service in particular, were increasingly viewed as a terrain of struggle. This view was closely associated with the critique of welfare which appeared within the Labour Party at this time in a number of reports and studies produced by, among others, Richard Titmuss, James Buchanan, Edward Pilkington, Geoffrey Crowther, Lionel Robbins and William Plowden. New Left writers sympathised with the emphases of some of these critics on the need to redistribute resources more rationally and equitably. Sheila Lynd, in an early edition of *New Left Review*, dissected the power relations at the heart of the medical services within the welfare state. Noting both the encroachment of the bureaucracies of welfare and the tendency to build new hospitals on top of existing and dilapidated structures, she pinpointed levels of expenditure on the health service as a site of further political conflict.[83] In the early years of the New Left's existence, therefore, a body of criticism of the nature of welfare provision emerged. The welfare state had not abolished primary poverty and inequality; citing Richard Titmuss' view that 'we put too much faith in the 1940s in the concept of universality as applied to social security', Dorothy Thompson highlighted numerous ways in which welfare services had to be extended and improved.[84] In particular, she noted the importance of 'local controls and initiatives' in the development of new forms of social service, against prevailing tendencies towards centralisation and official constraint.[85]

Significantly, this agenda did not capture the attention of the movement for a prolonged period. The tradition of loyalty to the achievements of the post-war Labour government, especially in the wake of Tory reluctance to maintain levels of public expenditure, militated against intellectual work in this area. Yet, even here, dissent from labourist sentiment was evident. According to Hall, 'we were right to criticise the forms in which welfare is delivered. That is not to say that we weren't willing to defend the welfare state'.[86] The New Left instinctively identified the weaknesses of Labour's vision of welfare, suggesting it was bland in tone and undemocratic in aspiration. Indeed, the sensitivity displayed by these critics to contemporary debates about the importance of planning flowed from its reassessment of the welfare state and the public sector: future social advance could not be predicated on the construction of public bureaucracies or left to state management. It was in civil society, rather than the state, that social provision had to be realised – from below, not above. The public sector, therefore, constituted an arena which needed democratisation as urgently as its private counterpart.

## The Case for Planning

Planning was integral to Labour's political outlook after 1958, combining the themes of economic expansion and the separation of national objectives from those of particular interest groups. These ideas provided a strong basis for opposition to the Conservatives, especially when allied with a celebration of technological and scientific development. But these sentiments also left important questions unresolved. What would happen if the various partners within the nation did not concur in their estimation of the national interest? How would such conflicts be regulated and decided? To some extent, such problems were impossible to foresee from the relatively harmonious decade of affluence, though the experience of the Attlee government alerted some in the party to the difficulty of securing national consensus. Difficulties also lay ahead regarding the agency to carry out the plan. Which parts of the state were to plan for growth and equality? How were such decisions to be taken and implemented? From where would the initiative in policy terms originate on key economic and political questions? Whilst concrete answers to these questions were not forthcoming during this period, it was clear that Labour intended to continue its post-war record of implementing control from above, by expanding the capacities and institutions of the central state. From this perspective, the greatest obstacle to a more humane economy was the erosion of responsibility and direction from the central state.

This outlook conflated the belief in the ultimate irrationality of both the private sector and the interests of sectional groups, with the notion that planning and central control were inseparable. As the social and economic problems left over from the decade of affluence became more evident, the notion of the rationality of the plan became entrenched in Labour's thought. The interests of sections of the community were, accordingly, less rational than those of the state. Planned expansion for social equality would be the product of the non-partisan sections of the community and would be overseen by neutral experts.[87] The centrepiece of this vision was the central state. As Labour's rhetoric became more radical in its redistributive commitments from *Signposts* onwards, it became more emphatic in its call for national institutions for development and investment. Planning had come to mean rationally organised uniformity from above. The value-free state was to be directed by the party of the new consensus. Labour's view of the state was essentially conservative: it ignored calls for institutional reconstruction or reform and for greater local autonomy. In many ways, this conception of planning represented a potent and novel articulation of older traditions in the labour movement. Combining Fabian faith in the neutral state and the increasingly pervasive theme of modernisation, the plan unleashed a new set of arguments in favour of central institutions. Whilst a radical and redistributive edge was also involved, this view carried a disciplinarian side to it. Those opposed to the statist logic of the plan might find themselves enemies or opponents of modernisation and progress. The state's key institutions, managed by leading sections within the party, were bound to come to the fore in disciplining as well as directing the nation. Paradoxically, this might be done 'on the nation's behalf'. As the boom conditions of the 1950s slowed, such tendencies came more readily to the surface of British politics.

For some commentators, the first New Left represented a more radical version of the same thrust towards the modernising, central state: this was evident, for instance, in the advocacy of an incomes policy by some of its leading economists. According to Samuel:

> *A Socialist Wages Plan*, a pamphlet which we published jointly with *The New Reasoner* in the run-up to the merger, was even more ambitious,

proposing a national audit where differentials and relativities could be settled, the needs of the low-paid answered and welfare norms imposed. 'Bureaucratic utopianism' according to one of its critics (Peter Sedgwick) and 'a constructive policy for ... a period of planned economic expansion' according to its friends, this was to be our most influential contribution to Labour Party thought.[88]

Yet, despite similarities with the Wilson government's subsequent practice, this programme actually brought new dimensions to the incomes policy debate. Its authors, Hughes and Alexander, set out a programme of price stabilisation and controls on private enterprise by means of 'a more co-ordinated approach to wage determination on the part of the unions, the use of more rational criteria ... [which would] therefore reduce the pressure of social wage competition'.[89] Labour, they argued, needed an integrated strategy for dealing with trade union wage demands. This should recognise the social as well as economic aspirations of many working people. The main thrust of the incomes policy which they outlined was the development of a political programme through which the unions and Labour could be brought into agreement as a platform for further political and economic advances. In one sense, Samuel's assessment is accurate: they were concerned with the regulation of demands from below. But the New Left's commitment to community shaped their views here: for both, the mobilisation of subaltern groups was an essential counterpoint to an incomes policy operating on a national level. Hughes, in a later article, argued that 'if it comes to a confrontation, a Labour government is in a strong position to appeal to democratic principles against monopoly power'.[90] Their incomes policy constituted a political strategy to offset the drift within the mixed economy towards the restriction of wages in situations of duress, providing a forum where a future Labour government would have to attend to union demands.[91] This, in fact, constituted the antithesis of the incomes policy instituted by the government after 1964.

Certainly, the New Left argued for a more rational and planned distribution of economic resources, from an early stage. Its commitment to this goal was, however, distinguished by the political context in which planning was placed. Planning was part of a broader series of political and ideological manoeuvres. It was certainly not a substitute for political mobilisation. In fact, planning was connected to a number of important questions within the political thought of the New Left. How was the plan to be implemented? Who was to put it into practice? How was it to relate to regional, social and occupational groups? This movement's instinctive empathy for the spontaneous dimensions of political life always militated against an overemphasis upon centralised control. Indeed, much of its reaction against the corporatist focus of the Wilson government was informed by this perspective. Commentators such as Hughes increasingly concerned themselves with the possibility of a planning method which devolved power and decision-making at different levels within the national community, arguing that 'a representative basis for public opinion at regional level is equally important for the labour movement to press for; we do not want a bureaucratic structure of decision-making. The aim is to decentralise as well as to develop the economy.'[92] In the same article he asserted the importance of different levels of planning: 'At the regional level a serious attempt has to be made to interrelate industrial location and development, the extension of vital public services (transport, parks, economy, etc) and social investment in urban construction.'[93]

The Wilsonite emphasis on the plan was, therefore, interrogated by the New Left. According to Malcolm MacEwen, 'planning is still in its infancy. We still do not know how to do it at all constructively, flexibly or democratically.'[94] These critical points were commonplace within New Left writing and stemmed from the belief that statist definitions of socialism were increasingly outdated and discredited. It was in civil society that the ground for a radical political alternative was to be found. Of this, nearly all sections of the movement were sure: 'As opposed to Labour orthodoxy we called for a new kind of politics; one which drew strength from movements outside the framework of the traditional parties and took as its starting point the spirit of growth.'[95] Contrary to Samuel's argument, therefore, there emerged a body of analysis which sensed the dangers inherent in Wilson's politics. In particular, this movement's critics raised the question of which views were installed in power through the paternal state. Whilst Wilson celebrated the technological possibilities of modernisation, these radical critics juxtaposed planning with the themes of community and alienation. Even if, as Charles Taylor has recently argued, New Left ideas were 'too-simple (sic)' in this area,[96] a decisive break was registered from orthodox Labour thinking. Steering clear of the discourse of expert planning from above, the New Left attempted to place humane and democratic modernisation on the agenda.

Ultimately, however, this critique remained marginal within the broader labour movement. Indeed, within the New Left, planning implicitly touched on tensions about the movement's identity. Were New Left devotees modernists or radical democrats? Did the desire to plan and reallocate from above involve the denial of the significance of movement and ideas from below? Was there an alternative, more democratic way of extending the public sector into the economy?

## Democratising the Economy: Workers and Consumers

The New Left set out to democratise the agenda at the heart of British socialism in a number of areas in which the left had hitherto shown little interest. Even on questions where socialism had put down strong roots, the New Left provided an unconventional and challenging voice to contemporary debate. This led it, for instance, to transform traditional arguments in favour of industrial democracy. Admittedly, this question did not figure high on its theoretical or practical agenda. The relatively quiet industrial and economic conditions of the later 1950s explain the low profile of this issue, in particular the absence of a comparable series of industrial conflicts to those which took place in the late 1960s.[97]

Industrial democracy was problematic anyway because of its centrality to orthodox socialist thought. This goal had enjoyed a lengthy pedigree on the left, featuring in the programme of the Communist Party since its formation in the form of its repeated advocacy of workers' control.[98] Among the New Left, however, calls for a democratised workplace arose from the commitment to the abolition of alienation, belief in democratic advance across civil society and critique of the Morrisonian structures of the nationalised industries. In particular, New Left thinkers offered a different understanding of this principle to that which prevailed within older strands of socialist thought which emphasised the need to centralise power in the economy and the primary role of the industrial sphere. For some in this movement, however, a commitment to industrial democracy undoubtedly provided a bridge to an older political outlook.

The demand for a more plural and democratic culture was perceived by the New Left as a complex process, traces of which could be found in the demands of trade unions as well as, for instance, community associations. Simultaneously, the need to broaden the political outlook of the unions was explicitly addressed. According to Taylor:

> something recognisably like a socialist society can only come about if at
> the same time and well before the political changes are undertaken there

are, for instance, movements of workers demanding a say in the decisions which affect their lives, immediately perhaps on a local level, ultimately on the level of the whole industry if there are movements of people demanding socialist policies in local government and so on.[99]

The refusal to foreground industrial struggles in a dogmatic fashion is evident here. So, too, is the attempt to overcome traditional demarcations between industrial and political questions. This perspective informed the movement's critique of pre-existing models of industrial democracy. The former communist Denis Butt, for instance, rejected the axiomatic fashion in which industrial democracy had been proposed. Describing the organisational structures of the new capitalist enterprises, he concluded that it was necessary to alter both the internal organisation of workplaces and industries and the division between industrial and social concerns.[100] This emphasis anticipated some of the key themes of the next Labour government, when the party found itself unable to maintain the separation, which had gone unchallenged throughout the 1950s, between the industrial and political wings of the labour movement. According to Hughes, assessing the prospects of the incoming Wilson government, the shift to joint and shared decisions at all levels of industry was critical (a more radical demand than the proposals for worker-directors made in 'The Insiders'). These changes were the prerequisites of further social advance.[101] As became clear later in the decade, such an assessment would have been a useful antidote to the centralism which characterised this administration. By 1961 the ideas articulated by Hughes had become commonplace throughout New Left writing as industrial questions returned to the political agenda. *Signposts* was, according to William Norman, open to criticism because 'the more difficult problem of how to ensure democratic control of state bureaucracies is ignored, together with the role of trades unions and workers' control ...'[102]

The rhetoric of industrial democracy was accompanied by a more complex assessment of the political case for such demands. This approach allowed for a greater emphasis on practicality and the need to engage with the particular contexts facing trade unionists. Analytically, this meant a rejection of workers' control as an article of socialist faith. New Left writing in this area was dominated by two impulses: the desire to provide an accurate assessment of the politics of contemporary trade unions in Britain and more speculative consideration of the impact of the culture and structures of modern technology and the industrial process more generally. This latter emphasis paralleled the theoretical reflections of a number of continental theorists — Gorz in particular. Above all, the first New Left began to re-examine the implications of workers' participation in the working environment. Jenkins had suggested that the demand for democracy could be met by a system of power-sharing and joint consultation at more levels within the nationalised industries.[103] Against this view, Alexander (in his review of Jenkins' book) proposed a more sophisticated notion of industrial democracy, isolating apathy and the authoritarian context of work in the newer industries as problems which had to be faced by those who supported workers' control. Exploring the interrelations between the worlds of industry and society more generally, he suggested that 'it is probably anti-marxist but it makes sense to me that "alienation" has flourished in other soils than that of either the ownership of the means of production or the administrative and managerial structure ... of firms and work-places'.[104] The tendency to equate socialism with the common ownership of the means of production was effectively challenged by such thinking: industrial democracy was connected to the notion of the democratisation of social and civil life.

One of the criticisms made of traditional socialist discourse by the New Left was its restricted presentation of social behaviour and identity. The movement's writers frequently explored the way in which communities of different kinds were affected by economic and social power; the consumer constituted one such community of interest. Concern for the consumer, however, represented more than the recognition of a new and emerging interest group within society. Anxieties about contemporary patterns of consumption were linked to deep-rooted and important features of contemporary society, an argument controversially taken up by *Marxism Today* in the 1980s. It would, though, be misleading to overemphasise the speed and extent of this recognition in this earlier period. Jenkins' support for the representation of consumer groups on the boards of nationalised industries was unusual on the left.[105] Whilst radical writers nodded in the direction of consumer protection groups in their criticism of the monopolistic tendencies in various sectors of the economy, few made such concerns central. In fact, there was little tradition of interest in the activity of consumption on the British left. The predominant focus of both Labour and communist economic thought had been the relations of production. Indeed, the political cultures of both manifested a shared emphasis on the primary agent of political transformation — the male (usually blue-collar) worker. How wages were spent and time was organised outside the workplace had been unimportant in mainstream trade union and Labour circles.

Yet countertraditions did exist in this area. For the Communist Party, involvement with the post-war squatters movement signalled the importance of political issues beyond the workplace.[106] This tradition, in fact, stretched back to the broader conception of political struggle developed during the Popular Front of the 1930s. For Labour, political opportunities arose from the government's discomfort as Conservative economic policies failed to hold up the prosperity of the previous decade. In a party pamphlet published in 1961, *Fair Deal for the Shopper*, the consumer (here assumed to be female) was characterised as the victim of selfish monopolistic practices. She was 'widely exploited' and subject to 'deception, false advertising, misleading claims for products, sales of unsafe and poor quality goods, dishonest service and other malpractices...'. A system of 'consumer welfare' under the influence of a national, centralised 'Consumer Council' would be set up for her protection.[107] Labour's response to this agenda involved the recognition of genuine discontent and anxiety on such issues – the results of monopolies controlling pricing arrangements and misinformation by advertisers. Its remedy was increased state regulation and administration, suggesting in the same pamphlet that 'there is a strong case for bringing into a new Department of State those powers and administrative duties that can be better exercised by a new authority primarily concerned with consumers' interests'.[108] These ideas were the product of both old and new emphases. Most obviously, the tradition of welfare provision continued to determine Labour's approach to social questions. Simultaneously, though, its recognition of the new political conditions of the early 1960s – symbolised here by its attention to consumption – was part of the shift in Labour politics and image which Wilson orchestrated. The extent of this shift is evident from the distance which the party had achieved from the strictures of austerity which dominated the Attlee government's increasingly desperate attempts to hold the economy together in the late 1940s.[109]

But the paternalist core of Labour's vision, exemplified in its response to these apparently new constituencies, remained intact. This paternalism was deeply gendered: one of Labour's few references to women's interests and needs occurred in its recognition of the salience of consumption in the post-war world. Here, Labour unthinkingly endorsed the conventional belief that consumption – part of the feminised private sphere – was disrupting customary relationships. Consumption symbolised the complex and contradictory relationship between women and the political and social worlds dominated by men.

The New Left's interest in the question of consumption was, therefore, unconventional in a number of ways, and was inspired by the enthusiasm of its younger members to engage with the complexity of the social world. Yet, it did not pursue its interests here in any depth: the absence of explicit discussion about gender and consumption is notable, despite interesting exceptions such as Nicholas Walter's survey of women's magazines in the last issue of *ULR*.[110] To some extent, this was caused by the tendency to subsume consumption under the category of culture. In the work of the cultural modernists in New Left circles, the advent of the consumer of mass market goods was viewed as a by-product of the conservative effects of affluence and 'consumer capitalism'. The consumer, according to Hall, was:

> A bland half-thing of a *man* [my emphasis] peering nervously at the frontiers of consumption and taste. That he makes with his skill, masters the machine with his craft, leaves and adapts to the applied techniques of science, manages with his mind, experiences with his senses, and suffers with the rest of us, is incidental to the routines of consumer capitalism.[111]

The consumer was irredeemably alienated and was implicitly counter-opposed to the rational and liberated socialist subject. This view tended to generate hostility to the notion of consumption as an arena of political and social concern.

Simultaneously, however, the New Left developed a different response to this question. Not all of its writers dismissed the arena of consumption as one of irredeemable and undifferentiated alienation. Williams recognised the importance of this agenda to many who were unrepresented by workerist conceptions of socialism and expressed support for the associations which had emerged in defence of consumer interests.[112] This sentiment connected with an equally powerful New Left commitment – opposition to the increasingly monopolistic trends in key areas of the welfare economy. 'The Insiders' was especially critical of the drift towards oligopoly, cartelisation and the 'tyranny of size' within sections of the manufacturing and service economies. The big corporations were imposing their definition of the national interest. Against the corporations and their managers, the New Left argued for a broad and popular coalition. For writers such as Jenkins and Hughes, the consumer represented social groups which had to be won to a broader oppositional programme against the bureaucratisation of the public sector and economic injustices within society as a whole. This perspective provided an important supplement to the concern for workers within the hierarchical structures of nationalised industries.

Behind these different approaches to this question lay an important development which makes this agenda more significant in hindsight. This consisted of cultural and social changes of which consumption was a part. Here, the debate around classlessness (outlined in chapter two) was signified by the more innocent question of consumption. If consumption was helping to alter the map of contemporary social and political allegiances, as was argued in the 1950s (though this thesis was challenged by John Goldthorpe and David Lockwood),[113] then it had to be addressed as an area in which political and economic identities might be made or altered. In fact, this process did not unfold as many commentators predicted at the time. The availability of a new range of consumer goods did not produce an axiomatic group of Conservative voters. In the longer term, however, the spread of consumerism and associated changes in working-class lifestyles 'disarticulated many traditional cultural attitudes and social hierarchies, and this had consequences for politics, the constituencies for change and the institutions and agendas of the left'.[114] The cultures of individualism and consumerism helped erode the basis on which politics had been conventionally conducted.

Whilst the first New Left did not develop this agenda in a sustained fashion, the attempt to engage with and 'sketch the meanings of these rapidly shifting contours of change'[115] involved a deeper appreciation of the connections between contemporary culture and politics. This differed from the more short-term focus with which Labour tended to approach these issues. For those who wanted to make a complete break from statist and workerist models of socialism, the field of consumption provided a potential site for democratic mobilisation and conflict, alongside more traditional arenas of political protest. Some of the key political themes of later years were anticipated here, for instance the sensitivity in Jenkins' analysis to potential divisions between producers, in the form of trade unions, and consumers. Ultimately, it was to Labour's disadvantage that it ignored the warnings thrown up by New Left work.

## MODERNISM AND AGENCY

These intellectual advances were carried into later struggles and events by many who had participated in the New Left. Important political spaces had been opened by its analytical exploration outside the discourses of labourism and communism. In particular, the New Left rediscovered the more holistic conception of economic and social life which earlier socialist traditions had developed. Simultaneously, it added a new dimension to contemporary debate with its emphases on the ideological and political underpinnings of economic changes, a position which bore similarities to Gramscian ideas and other strands within Western Marxism. Within this framework, modernism – both as an aesthetic and a philosophy – played a significant role. Two dimensions to modernism can be specified here. First, contemporaries welcomed the importation of the ordered styles of modernist culture and aesthetics into economics and political thinking. Modernism, in this sense, signified the desire to overturn the old, 'irrational' order throughout political life, a theme powerfully developed by Wilson in 1963-4. Second, it also inspired the attempt to develop a politics which was grounded in the conditions of the present. Some New Left ideologues saw the need to harness contemporary trends to a different set of social and political foundations, rather than reading contemporary society from the prior commitments of older socialist orthodoxies.

Whilst these two interpretations of modernism were often complementary, this was not always the case. The second sense led the New Left to distinguish itself from orthodox socialists in its more sensitive response to the erosion and fragmentation of pre-existing collectivities. The constituencies which were to be mobilised against 'The Insiders' had to be addressed more specifically. In addition, writers in this milieu tried to expand the left's conception of the political field, moving away from the idea of mobilising a single, coherent class to emphasise the process by which a bloc of social forces was forged and its political hegemony secured. This more expansive notion of the constituencies for socialism carried a number of strategic and political implications. As Colin Mercer and Bill Schwarz have pointed out in their discussion of Thompson's populist rhetoric:

> In this context, the notion of 'the people' represents a more expansive category than the proletariat. It rests on a sociological basis (the need for alliances with intermediate social sections) but also has a political and ideological dimension pointing to those forms of oppression not directly rooted in class forms of exploitation.[116]

Expansiveness, however, could well result in strategic vagueness and the dilution of political commitments – a criticism repeated against later calls for a coalitional approach to political mobilisation. In the case of the first

New Left, this approach stemmed from its opposition to the provision of bureaucratic or uniform solutions from above. Modernism was deployed to express two aspects of the New Left agenda: its belief in the creative potential within society which had been frustrated by contemporary capitalism, and its commitment to a deeper culture of political participation. Certainly, this modernism was not shared by all parts of this movement. As we have seen, some were more interested in returning to the past as a way of imagining the future. Thompson, in particular, stressed the importance of rediscovering an apparently coherent and accessible radical tradition.

This emphasis upon a broader and more diverse set of constituencies also stemmed from the New Left's ambivalence about the agency for socialist transformation. The assumption that the industrial working class provided the advanced guard of socialist mobilisation was called into question by this movement on a number of fronts. Yet, unlike within the New Left in the United States, this theme was never explicitly negotiated. The absence of this debate was the result of the proximity of many in the New Left to Marxist ideas in their theory and labour movement traditions in their politics, though the classlessness debate touched upon this question (see chapter two). In fact, it was an outsider, C. Wright Mills, who broached this issue in a direct way, questioning the strategic primacy allotted to the industrial working class by the majority of the British movement in his celebrated 'Letter to the New Left' (1960):

> What I do not quite understand about some new left writers is why they
> cling so mightily to 'the working class' of the advanced capitalist societies
> as the historic agency, or even as the most important agency in the face
> of the really impressive historical evidence that now stands against this
> expectation. Such a labour metaphysic, I think, is a legacy from Victorian
> Marxism that is now quite unrealistic.[117]

Whilst this theme was not explicitly addressed in British New Left writing, the logic of some parts of the movement's politics supported his argument. The sympathy evoked within this milieu for other movements which had emerged outside the orbit of the labour movement, as well as concern for the interests of specific social groups, suggested that the New Left's political instincts were more revisionist than its public statements. Clearly, not everyone involved shared these emphases. In particular, Thompson held to a conception of political struggle which harked back to older traditions, in his case Communist Party strategy. Yet his outlook also displayed a deliberate ambivalence about agency, the product of his reliance on the language of cross-class mobilisation. 'The people against the monopolists' was one of his favourite New Left rallying cries – a throwback to the rhetoric of the Popular Front.[118] Ironically, this perspective possessed sufficient similarities, despite its different underlying trajectory, to the more pluralist concerns of the London New Left milieu, to prevent more wide-ranging debate in these areas.

Nevertheless, tensions can be detected in New Left praxis around this issue. Indeed, Anderson's later criticism of the populism of the New Left stems from a perceptive assessment of its reliance on a vague conception of agency. But his criticism is, in some ways, misplaced. The New Left engaged with the complex patterns of contemporary social change, interrogating the central assumptions and arguments of socialism. Certainly, this movement sometimes invoked 'the people' in a simplistic fashion. Yet, this tentative attempt to envisage a more broadly based and flexible coalition of forces foreshadowed the discoveries of later political generations. The movements for workers' control which emerged in the 1970s borrowed from the breadth of New Left interpretations of industrial democracy. Furthermore, the coalitional approach of New Left politics reappeared in some of the socialist municipal experiments of the 1980s.[119] Here, the idea of exploring new points of antagonism and addressing a plurality of interests within community life was partly a legacy of this movement. Reducing these aspects of New Left thought to 'populism' misrepresents the precise nature and subsequent significance of its revisionism on these questions.

The political and economic thinking of the first New Left advanced considerably throughout its lifetime, although its later critics have rarely acknowledged this. The willingness to consider economic and political problems as interrelated generated new ideas about political life. Accordingly, it became common for ritualistic denunciation of capitalism to be replaced by more subtle and astute analysis of the polity, economy and balance of forces within society as a whole. These observations can be illustrated with reference to one of the first New Left's most concrete legacies, the *May Day Manifesto*, produced in 1967-8, under the influence of the three central figures of this earlier movement – Hall, Thompson and Williams.

## THE MAY DAY MANIFESTO

The production of this manifesto after three years of the Wilson government brought together, once more, the leading figures of the first New Left. Yet, whilst it was intended as the starting point for a new initiative in British politics, this text ended up as a rather isolated critique of the direction taken by the Labour government, and the development of British capitalism more generally. Later commentators have omitted to consider the ideas of this earlier political formation as the key to understanding this document. Outside this context the document seems uneven and incoherent.[120] In fact, the Manifesto reveals the shift which New Left political analysis underwent between 1956 and 1962, by which time a roughly coherent set of ideas had been distilled. These opened some New Left figures to the insights of the Western Marxist tradition, which was becoming increasingly available in this period. Here, the division between the early and late New Lefts is more complex than is usually presented. The Manifesto was the work of individuals associated with the first New Left generation, even though this movement had expired as a meaningful force. But a process of osmosis between the two groups had occurred, to some degree at least. The theoretical programme pursued in *New Left Review* after 1962 undoubtedly affected figures from this earlier generation, especially Hall and Williams. The uneasy combination of old New Left ideas and new theoretical influences explains much of the eclecticism and unevenness of this text.

Significantly, Gramsci's concept of hegemony had, by 1967, been introduced into New Left debates, for instance in Anderson's and Robin Blackburn's introduction to the influential collection, *Towards Socialism* (1965). This concept was also deployed in Anderson's 'Origins of the Present Crisis', which also appeared in this collection. In this he set out his influential thesis about the 'corporate' nature of working-class consciousness in Britain. In particular, he developed his and Nairn's interpretation of the compromises effected between the aristocracy and bourgeoisie in English political history from the eighteenth century, bequeathing a hybrid elite which dominated and shaped British society. Whilst the implications of this re-interpretation of British history reverberated on the intellectual left, another contribution to *Towards Socialism* – Robin Blackburn's essay 'The new capitalism' – was equally important in translating key ideas from the continental Marxist traditions in a British context. Blackburn charted the shift in the forms of capitalist operation in the 1960s, highlighting the widespread use of more 'rational' methods of accumulation, the increased role of the state in the economy and the 'modification of the national economic framework' under pressure from international economic forces.[121] He applied to Britain the central concepts of continental theorists such as Gorz (who also appeared in this collection),[122] Sartre and Lefevbre, all endeavouring to theorise the nature of late capitalism.

These disparate ideas were important in providing theoretical guidance and inspiration for some of the analysis in the Manifesto, though its argument was self-consciously made in an idiom that recalled the writing of the original New Left journals. The centrepiece of this document was its description of the 'new capitalism' that reigned in Britain: a successful accumulation strategy required a form of planning which would enhance the interests of the handful of large industrial corporations, because these were unable to operate profitably unless the 'size, nature and operating conditions of future markets can be assessed and assured'.[123] The state played a central role in this system, planning ahead and ensuring popular consent. In this scenario, the Labour Party played the crucial role of co-opting the working classes through its hold over the trade union leadership: Wilson's failure to deliver social advance and radical economic measures were, thus, explained by long-term structural factors. Some important early New Left themes recurred within this analysis, especially in the Manifesto's stress upon the reappearance of both public squalor and private affluence as inequalities in health provision, education and housing were condemned.[124] Significantly, the Manifesto also retained the old New Left's emphasis upon the malevolent role of the 'controllers' at the head of the economy, the advertisers who distorted social priorities and responsibilities, and the failure of nerve and commitment manifested in the government's policy in the fields of culture and communications.

In other areas, however, the Manifesto marked a subtle shift away from the first New Left's thinking. The sense of proximity to Wilson's project, which was noted earlier, was now interpreted as little more than a trick to secure legitimacy across the spectrum of left opinion: his were an 'alien and thwarting ... manipulative politics ... which has taken our meanings and changed them, taken our causes and used them; which seems our creation, yet now stands against us, as the agent of the priorities of money and power'.[125] In addition, a critical distance was established from the rhetoric of modernisation deployed by Wilson. This was now viewed as an extension of the new technological imperatives at the heart of contemporary capitalism. These encouraged an increasingly centralist tendency in policy formation, leading the Manifesto's authors to return to the localism and community orientation embedded within early New Left politics, so that 'the starting point, then, is where people are living. Not the abstract condition of a party or a government or a country, but the condition of life of the majority of ordinary people'.[126]

In conclusion, the authors celebrated the prospects of a genuinely radical economic programme for Britain. This would involve, among other measures, a shift towards a more democratic political culture, the creation of new institutions to make national decisions about production and investment, together with higher taxation and import quotas. The confidence of these radicals in the possibility of substantial advance towards socialism by a single government was undimmed. Significantly, much of this vision reappeared in the guise of the alternative economic strategy proposed by Labour's left in the mid-1970s, a go-it-alone programme for British socialism in the teeth of domestic dissent and international economic pressure. An important connection between these ideas and subsequent Labour politics was provided by Hughes, one of the authors of the party's 1973 statement opposing entry to the EEC. In some ways, therefore, the Manifesto represented a retreat from the critical ideas of the earlier New Left, whose writers questioned the merits of many of the assumptions behind such proposals.

But the Manifesto was also the product of its tempestuous political context. The extent of disillusion with Wilson was, for some, exacerbated by the hopes generated by his political ambiguity and radical rhetoric. The emotional involvement with the incoming Labour government and subsequent disappointment were symbolised by Williams' resignation from the Arts Council during this period. It is equally important to appreciate the eclectic nature of this text: the influences of its various authors was marked, though this was less the case with the second edition produced in 1968 and edited more tightly by Williams. Whilst the traces of continental Marxist theory were present, as illustrated above, the Manifesto also marked a return to an explicitly humanist language, a tendency ensured by the participation of Edward and Dorothy Thompson, Royden Harrison and Saville. The Manifesto may, as Michael Rustin suggests, have represented an attempt to 'synthesise' the early New Left's agenda 'into a unified programme',[127] yet, its content merely highlighted the various paths which emerged from the different and sometimes incommensurable agendas at the heart of the first New Left.

Towards the end of the text, *ULR*'s sensitivity to different social groups reappeared in the celebration of the new struggles of the 1960s, emphasising the role of students and black youth.[128] Calling for a realignment of the left in a coalition of single-issue groups, political campaigns and autonomous, local Manifesto cells, the authors echoed the politics of 1956-62. By the following year, 1968, a new agenda was in the offing, taking autonomy and radicalism far beyond the reaches of this analysis. Not surprisingly therefore, the Manifesto failed as a political movement: following a National Convention attended by six hundred activists, this project fell apart as its ultra-left rivals moved in and political radicalism moved into a more libertarian and countercultural groove.

Appreciating the complex intellectual history of this document does not preclude a critical analysis of its content. As several commentators have suggested, its interpretation of Wilson provided the dominant view on the radical and Marxist left for the next twenty years.[129] The crudity of much of its analysis, its fetishistic emphasis upon Wilson's political betrayal and its incomplete synthesis of different intellectual currents are evident. Yet, within the history of the New Left as a political and intellectual formation, the document is revealing. It illustrates the depth of the divisions which underlay the first New Left, illuminates the openness to theory which the political analysis of this movement encouraged among some of its participants, and challenges the simple notion that the ideas of the first New Left were completely divorced from its political successors.

## CONCLUSIONS

The New Left generated some important critical ideas on a number of questions which the political economy of socialism needed to face in the post-war era. Its critique of the drift towards state expansion and regulation, alongside the methodological advances registered in its work, stand out as the most important contributions its writers made in this area. With hindsight, its insights into the limitations of Labour's political vision were particularly prescient. New Left analysis illustrates the frailty of Keynesian political economy in Britain in numerous ways and anticipates the more developed criticism of the weaknesses in the dominant government philosophy of this period identified by later critics, such as David Marquand.[130] His suggestion that it was neo-liberals and radical socialists in the 1970s who offered more coherent answers to the problems this system encountered might be extended to incorporate earlier critical voices.

But the limitations and weaknesses of New Left ideas in this area are also important. Despite its commitment to the construction of a new economic and moral order, this formation was patently incapable of achieving such a goal, leaving it reliant upon (and increasingly desperate for) a change of heart by Labour. Furthermore, some major contradictions bedevilled its political and economic analysis – a body of ideas which remained a long way from constituting a cogent political economy. The New Left's agenda was riven by the tension at the heart of its identity between decentralisation and the empowerment of communities, on the one hand, and the desire for more effective and rational macro-policy, on the other. This split was never transcended, generating the distinctive and dialectical perspective which New Left writers often adopted, yet preventing the development of a coherent, analytical alternative. Indeed, this tension accounts for some of the weaknesses of New Left ideas. The lack of any serious reflection upon the state in these years is striking. To some degree, the political context explains why this was not a contemporary concern: the state played a far more interventionist political role from the late 1960s. Yet, given the New Left's commitment to map the changing basis of post-war society, this project might well have involved a more concerted challenge to the hegemony of both liberal pluralist and one-dimensional Marxist accounts of the state. The New Left's emphasis on community organisation, civil society and spontaneity distracted it from this enterprise. Simultaneously, the project of developing a more radical policy framework for a reforming Labour government, pursued by Hughes and Barratt Brown among others, relied heavily upon traditional Labour assumptions about the neutrality and malleability of state institutions. Significantly, former participants in this milieu were often ill-equipped for the dramatic resurgence of interest in the state in the 1970s, culminating in a debate which was dominated by the theoretical perspectives imported by the later New Left. Miliband's work constitutes an important exception, resulting in a significant and influential debate with the theorist Nicos Poulantzas.[131]

Despite these inadequacies, however, commentators on the New Left are wrong to reproduce the critique mounted by its successors. The methodological shift in the political analysis of writers in the first New Left made sections of the radical intelligentsia particularly receptive to Gramsci's ideas. David Forgacs' notion of the brokerage role for these concepts played by Williams' and Thompson's contemporary work can be expanded to include the political analysis of this formation. Whilst this was sometimes crude and always undertheorised, it undoubtedly opened readers of New Left journals to the project of expanding and refining socialist conceptions of power and elite domination. In this sense, the conventional distinction between the 'populist' and 'culturalist' first New Left and its theoretical and hardheaded New Left offspring, requires substantial revision.

NOTES

1   W.Thompson, 'Tom Nairn and the Crisis of the British State', *op cit*, pp308-9; see also G.Foote, *The Labour Party's Political Thought: A History*, Croom Helm, London 1986, pp287-307.

2   This is articulated most fully by Anderson in *Arguments within English Marxism,op cit.*

3   D.Stafford, *op cit*; Samuel, *op cit.*

4   Chun repeats this criticism, *op cit*, pp29, 50 and 53.

5   An exception here is Bamford, *op cit.*

6   Antecedents for post-war revisionism can be traced to the ideas of some Labour intellectuals and policy makers in the 1930s; B.Pimlott, *Labour and the Left in the 1930s*, Cambridge University Press, Cambridge 1977, p201.

7   N.Harris, *Competition and Corporate Society: British Conservatives, the State and Industry, 1956-1964*, Methuen, London 1972.

8   For a review of the extensive debate about the 'consensus' of this period, see D.Kavanagh, 'The Postwar Consensus', *Twentieth Century British History*, 3, 2, 1992, pp175-90.

9   Hall *et al*, 'Living with the Crisis', in Hall, *The Hard Road to Renewal: Thatcherism and the Crisis of the Left*, Verso, London 1988, pp19-37, p30.

10  B.Jessop, 'The Transformation of the British State', in R.Scase (ed), *The State in Western Europe*, Croom Helm, London 1980, pp23-93; J.Dow, *The Management of the British Economy 1945-1960*, Cambridge University Press, Cambridge 1964.

11  For a review of different interpretations of Britain's economic decline, see A.Sked, *Britain's Decline*, Blackwell, Oxford 1987.

12  A.Gamble, *The Conservative Nation*, Routledge, London 1974, pp74-8.

13  *Ibid*, pp78-86.

14  Abrams and Rose, *op cit.*

15  J.K.Galbraith, *The Affluent Society*, Hamilton, London 1958.

16  Norman MacKenzie, 'The Economics of Prosperity', *ULR*, 5, 1958, pp62-5, p63.

17  *Ibid*, p63.

18  Hall, 'The Supply of Demand', *op cit*, p74.

19  M.Barratt Brown, 'British Economic Policy since the War', *ULR*, 4, 1958, pp36-44, p40.

20  Hall, 'The New Conservatism and the Old', *ULR*, 1, 1957, pp21-4, p21.

21  *Ibid*, p23.

22  Crosland, *The Future of Socialism*, *op cit*, p7.

23  *Industry and Society*, Labour Party, 1957, p8.

24  *Ibid*, p47.

25  *Ibid*, p13.

26  *Plan for Progress*, Labour Party, 1958, p9.

27  Miliband, 'The Sickness of Labourism', *New Left Review*, 1, 1960, pp5-9, p6.

28  Hall, 'Crosland Territory', *New Left Review*, 2, 1960, pp2-4.

29  Anderson, 'Mr Crosland's Dreamland', part one, *op cit.*

30  'The Insiders', *ULR*, 3, 1958, ppi-ii, 25-64, iii-iv.

31  Anderson, 'Mr Crosland's Dreamland, part one', *op cit*, p10.

32 Crosland, *The Conservative Enemy: A Programme of radical reform for the 1960s*, Cape, London 1962, pp7, 16, 92-6.

33 Editorial, 'Scarborough and Beyond', *New Left Review*, 6, 1960, pp2-7, p3.

34 Miliband, *Parliamentary Socialism: a study in the politics of Labour*, Allen and Unwin, London 1961.

35 J.Schneer, *Labour's Conscience; the Labour left, 1945-51*, Unwin Hyman, Boston, London 1988.

36 B.Pimlott, *Harold Wilson*, Harper Collins, London 1992, p175.

37 Cited in Pimlott, *ibid*, p218.

38 For a detailed consideration of these struggles, see L.Minkin, *The Labour Party Conference: A Study in the Politics of Intra-Party Democracy*, Allen Lane, London 1978.

39 M.Jones, *op cit*, p141.

40 'The Insiders', *op cit*, p25.

41 *Ibid*, p25.

42 Miliband, *Parliamentary Socialism*, *op cit*.

43 *Signposts for the Sixties*, Labour Party, 1961, p8.

44 *Ibid*, p9.

45 *Ibid*, p12.

46 *Ibid*, pp17-18.

47 This was apparent too in the conference debate on *Signposts*, Labour Party Conference Reports, Report of Sixtieth Annual Conference, 1961, p103.

48 Pimlott, *op cit*, p218.

49 Pimlott, 'Hyping Harold', *Independent on Sunday*, 26 September 1993, pp34-5, p34.

50 Saville, 'Marxism Today: An Anatomy', *Socialist Register*, 1990, pp35-59.

51 W.Thompson, 'Tom Nairn and the Crisis of the British State', *op cit*, p312.

52 See, for instance, I.Birchall, 'The Autonomy of Theory: A short history of New Left Review', *International Socialism*, 2, 10, pp51-91, pp61-5.

53 Howell, *op cit*, p231.

54 For an 'inside' account of the production of this document, see J.Morgan (ed), *The Backbench Diaries of Richard Crossman*, Hamilton, Cape, London 1981, pp941-5, 946-7 and 952-5.

55 Anon, 'Missing Signposts', *New Left Review*, 12, 1961, pp9-10, p9.

56 K.Alexander, 'Premier Wilson's Plan?', *New Left Review*, 9, 1961, pp53-6, p56.

57 J.Hughes, 'An Economic Policy for Labour', *New Left Review*, 24, 1963, pp5-32, p7.

58 *Ibid*, p12.

59 W.Thompson, 'Tom Nairn and the Crisis of the British State', *op cit*, p311.

60 Anderson, 'Critique of Wilsonism', *New Left Review*, 27, 1964, pp3-27, p4.

61 Pimlott, *Harold Wilson*, *op cit*, p273.

62 See the articles collected in Hall, *The Hard Road to Renewal*, *op cit*.

63 W.Thompson, 'Tom Nairn and the Crisis of the British State', *op cit*, p312.

64 Anderson, 'Critique of Wilsonism', *op cit*, p19.

65 See especially M.Barratt Brown, 'The Controllers', *ULR*, 5, 1958, pp53-61; 'The Controllers II', *ULR*, 6, 1959, pp38-41; 'The Controllers III', *ULR*, 7, 1959, pp43-9.

66 'The Insiders', *op cit*, p25.

67 Barratt Brown, 'The Controllers – I, II and III', *op cit*.

68 Alexander, 'Public Bosses', *New Reasoner*, 9, 1959, pp127-9.

69 C.Wright Mills, *The Power Elite*, Oxford University Press, Oxford 1959.

70 Samuel, 'Born-again Socialism', *op cit*, pp46-7.

71 Aaronovitch, *The Ruling Class: a study of British finance capital*, Lawrence and Wishart, London 1961.

72 J.Westergaard and H.Resler, *Class in a Capitalist Society: a study in contemporary Britain*, Heinemann Educational, London 1975.

73 Norman, *op cit*, p46.

74 J.Hughes, 'New Left Economic Policy', in Archer, *et al*, *op cit*, pp95-103, pp101-2.

75 Hall, 'The 'First' New Left', *op cit*, p15.

76 P.Morris, 'Apathy: A Case to Answer', *New Left Review*, 4, 1961, pp6-7, p6.

77 Hall, 'Crosland Territory', *op cit*, p4.

78 Hughes, 'Three Studies in the Welfare State: 1. Railways and the Transport Muddle', *New Left Review*, 3, 1960, pp19-21.

79 See especially R.Titmuss, *Essays on the Welfare State*, Unwin, London 1958; R.Titmuss and B.Abel-Smith, *The Cost of the National Health Service in England and Wales*, Cambridge University Press, Cambridge 1956.

80 Saville, 'The Welfare State', *op cit*, p20.

81 Thompson, letter to Saville, n.d. (end of 1957?), 'New Reasoner 1959-63' file, Saville papers.

82 S.Hatch and D.Thompson, 'Discussion', *New Reasoner*, 4, 1958, pp124-5 (Hatch), pp125-30 (Thompson).

83 S.Lynd, 'Three Studies in the Welfare State. 2. The Health Service Revisited', *New Left Review*, 3, 1960, pp21-6; see also M.Jeffries, 'Health and Social Class – One', *New Left Review*, 4, 1960, pp39-42.

84 D.Thompson, 'Farewell to the Welfare State', *New Left Review*, 4, 1961, pp39-42, p41.

85 *Ibid*, p41.

86 Hall, in 'Conference Scrapbook', in Archer *et al*, *op cit*, pp129-42, p132.

87 *Signposts*, *op cit*, p7.

88 Samuel, 'Born-again Socialism', *op cit*, p49.

89 Hughes and Alexander, 'A Reply to Critics', *New Reasoner*, 10, 1959, pp92-106, p98.

90 Hughes, 'An Economic Policy for Labour', *New Left Review*, 24, 1963, pp5-32, p8

91 Hughes, 'New Left Economic Policy', *op cit*, pp101-2.

92 *Ibid*, p36.

93 *Ibid*, p15

94 M.MacEwen, 'Planning or Prediction?', *New Left Review*, 22, 1963, pp66-74, p69.

95 Samuel, 'Born-again Socialism', *op cit*, p44.

96 Taylor, in 'Then and Now: A Re-evaluation of the New Left', in Archer, *et al*, *op cit*, pp143-70, p146.

97 See L.Panitch, *Social Democracy and Industrial Militancy: the Labour Party, the Trade Unions and incomes policy, 1945-1974*, Cambridge University Press, Cambridge 1974.

98 J.Hinton and R.Hyman, *The Early Industrial Politics of the Communist Party*, Pluto, London 1979.

99 Taylor, 'Changes of Quality', *New Left Review*, 4, 1960, pp3-5, p5.

100 D.Butt, 'Workers' Control', *New Left Review*, 10, 1961, pp24-33.

101 Hughes, 'An Economic Policy for Labour', *op cit*, p12.

102 Norman, 'Signposts for the Sixties', *New Left Review*, 11, 1961, pp41-9, p41.

103 C.Jenkins, *Power at the Top*, McGibbon and Kee, London 1959, p277.

104 Alexander, 'Public Bosses', *op cit*, p129.

105 Jenkins, *Power at the Top*, *op cit*.

106 J.Hinton, 'Self-help and Socialism – the Squatters' Movement of 1946', *History*

*Workshop*, 25, 1988, pp100-26.

107 *Fair Deal for the Shopper*, Labour Party, October 1961, p6.

108 *Ibid*, p21.

109 F.Mort, 'The Politics of Consumption', in S.Hall and M.Jacques (eds), *New Times: The Changing Face of Politics in the 1990s*, Lawrence and Wishart, London 1990, pp21-47.

110 N.Walter, 'Men Only', *ULR*, 7, 1959, pp54-6.

111 Hall, 'The Supply of demand', *op cit*, p71.

112 Williams, *The Long Revolution, op cit*, pp296-8.

113 J.Goldthorpe and D.Lockwood, 'Affluence and the British Class Structure', *Sociological Review*, 11, 2, 1963, pp133-63.

114 Hall, 'The "First" New Left', *op cit*, p24.

115 *Ibid*, p25.

116 C.Mercer and B.Schwarz, 'Popular Politics and Marxist Theory in Britain. The History Men', in C.Mercer and W.Schwarz (eds), *Silver Linings: Some Strategies for the Eighties*, Communist University of London, Lawrence and Wishart, London 1981, pp143-166, p145.

117 C.Wright Mills, 'Letter to the New Left', *New Left Review*, 5, 1960, pp18-23, p22.

118 Anderson, *Arguments within English Marxism, op cit*, p196.

119 Boddy and Fudge, *op cit*.

120 For a somewhat caricatural discussion of the Manifesto, see N.Tiratsoo, 'Labour and its critics: the case of the May Day Manifesto Group', in R.Coopey, S.Fielding and N.Tiratsoo (eds), *The Wilson Governments 1964-1970*, Pinter, London, New York 1993, pp163-83.

121 Blackburn, 'The new capitalism', in Anderson and Blackburn (eds), *Towards Socialism*, Cornell University Press, Ithaca, New York 1965, pp114-45, p131.

122 A.Gorz, 'Work and Consumption', in Anderson and Blackburn (eds), *Towards Socialism, op cit*, pp317-53.

123 H.Barnes, 'The New Left, the Consensus and the Intelligentsia', *Political Studies*, 16, 1968, pp105-8, p106.

124 R.Williams (ed), *May Day Manifesto 1968*, Penguin, Harmondsworth 1968, pp30-35.

125 *Ibid*, p14.

126 *Ibid*, p17.

127 Rustin, 'The New Left and the Present Crisis', *op cit*, p69,

128 *May Day Manifesto, op cit*, pp165-8.

129 Tiratsoo, *op cit*.

130 D. Marquand, *The Unprincipled Society: new ideals and old politics*, Fontana, London 1988.

131 N.Poulantzas, 'The Problem of the Capitalist State', *New Left Review*, 58, 1969, pp67-78; Miliband, 'Reply to Nicos Poulantzas', *New Left Review*, 59, 1970, pp53-60; 'Poulantzas and the Capitalist State', *New Left Review*, 82, 1973, pp83-93.

# CHAPTER SIX

# 'Neither Washington nor Moscow': Positive Neutralism and the Peace Movement

The New Left was as much the product of international developments as domestic ones. The Soviet invasion of Hungary threw the international implications of Stalinism into relief, raising a number of profound moral and political anxieties for communists worldwide. The failed Suez expedition of the same year dramatised the uncertainties now facing Britain as it gave up its longstanding imperial role but was unwilling to relinquish the cultural and ideological 'baggage' of empire. Suez also highlighted the extent to which conventional approaches to foreign policy were increasingly out of kilter with new international realities, symbolising the passing of the old international order and the arrival of a new state of affairs in which Britain's pre-eminence was greatly reduced. Together with the peace movement which grew in these years, the emergence of the New Left was a manifestation of this uncertainty about the direction of the nation and the incapacity of older orthodoxies to provide a meaningful and realistic role for Britain. The New Left consequently broke from conventional socialist arguments not just in its treatment of British society and politics, but also in its approach to foreign policy questions.

This break was enabled by its adoption of a new principle in international relations – positive neutralism. Below I discuss the implications of positive neutralism, and the connections between it and the burgeoning interest in the 'third world' evident within the movement. Important differences of emphasis and argument characterised New Left ideas on international issues and also on the question of national identity. This is illustrated by examination of the approach to the question of West European integration adopted by leading figures in the movement. Finally, I examine the New Left's relationship with the peace movement, exploring similarities between these currents, as well as some tensions between them. Unlike its heirs, the first New Left empathised strongly with the peace movement's attempt to develop a new kind of politics, which foreshadowed the impact of a number of subsequent radical campaigns and movements in Britain.

## THE INTERNATIONAL CONTEXT

Like its counterparts throughout Western Europe, the British New Left emerged from a substantial reconfiguration of the prevailing pattern of international affairs. Following the ending of the Second World War, new developments began to reshape the terrain of international politics and raise difficult questions about the political culture and identity of Britain. The development of the Cold War in the late 1940s placed a tremendous constraint on the internal political life of many countries and locked international relations into a frozen, apparently immutable pattern. On the Western side, this led to the formation of NATO – the Western military alliance, in which Britain's Labour government played a leading role. The Cold War provided the backdrop to the national and international events of the next three decades. Above all, it legitimated the continuation of the technological developments which had already enabled the production and use of atomic weapons by the United States. But now, other powers, especially the Soviet Union, possessed the capability to construct their own nuclear weapons. These developments created the conditions in which the 'arms race' of the 1950s flourished.

Nuclear weapons became a controversial and widely feared part of the new diplomatic landscape, conjuring up the horrifying possibility of their use in a military conflict between the superpowers. These developments carried a differential impact depending on national context. In Britain, the onset of the Cold War was entangled with problems engendered by the country's declining role as an imperial power. In the immediate post-war period, Britain's withdrawal from formal imperial ties began in earnest, though not without short-term political difficulties and long-term implications. Decolonisation generated some profound questions for the political elite: how could Britain retain her former status as a front-rank power? what kind of international role would she play in future? These questions were increasingly bound up with anxieties about the capacity of British political institutions to command popular allegiance;[1] and, from the late 1960s onwards, with concerns about the nation's economic performance.[2] All of these issues were thrown into relief by moves, from the mid-1950s onwards, towards closer economic co-operation between the powers of Western Europe. Sections of the political elite began to reconsider their attitude towards Britain's present and future interests.

## FOREIGN POLICY AND BRITISH SOCIALISM

In this new and troubled international context, two dominant traditions prevailed on the left. Within the Labour Party, foreign policy thinking was dominated by the Atlanticism of the right. Ernest Bevin, Labour's post-war Foreign Secretary, played an instrumental role in the formation of NATO and orchestrated an indigenous version of the more virulent anti-communist campaign launched in the United States by Senator McCarthy.[3] Throughout the labour movement, a pronounced hostility to communism legitimated a generally uncritical support for the United States in the Cold War, leading to Labour's acquiescence to the policy of sheltering under the United States' nuclear umbrella and providing British bases for American troops and weapons. For the most part, Labour supported multilateral nuclear disarmament, defending a detente-based strategy which might lead to superpower agreement. In 1959, for instance, Labour floated the idea of a 'non-nuclear club', in the hope that lesser nations might indirectly pressurise the two major powers through a drive towards collective disarmament. The prevailing belief in the party was that Britain could do little on its own to facilitate this process. As the decade progressed however, and the emergence of a lively movement against nuclear weapons gathered pace, a substantial body of party and trade union opinion gave their support to an alternative policy – the idea of unilateral nuclear disarmament by Britain.

An aggressive allegiance to the Atlantic alliance resulted too from the continuation of strongly nationalist traditions within Labour's outlook.[4] Support for the United States was one way of preserving a British presence at the 'top table' of international relations. This concern was all the more pertinent in the context of the disengagement from empire which began in earnest in this period and the questions this raised about Britain's strategic and foreign policy interests. As John Callaghan has demonstrated, Labour's political culture was infused with an imperialist ethos. This was manifested during the post-war Labour governments by attempts to shift imperial policy in the direction of less formal governance, but more ruthless, 'informal' economic appropriation.[5] Despite the rhetoric of opposition to empire and support for the Commonwealth which was frequently enunciated by Labour's front bench in the 1950s, as well as the existence of alternative traditions on foreign policy questions within its ranks, Labour said little about the conflicts which occurred during this period in regions still under British rule, nor, indeed, about the documented atrocities committed by the crown's troops in these countries.

This perspective co-existed within the Labour Party, and beyond its ranks, with an entirely different approach to these questions. This second, minority perspective emerged from the understanding of Western imperialism which had been developed within the traditions of Marxism-Leninism. These had generated an influential, though sometimes ambiguous, set of ideas concerning the conditions under which capitalism could be overthrown,[6] and the nature of anti-imperialist struggles in colonised countries. Despite the support which communism enunciated for colonial liberation and national self-determination, and the contribution to anti-imperialist struggles which many communists made,[7] orthodox Marxism-Leninism bequeathed a particularly rigid and often dogmatic approach to the question of liberation from colonial rule; the expression of solidarity with such struggles was irredeemably conflated with support for the Soviet Union.

There was some support for this position in the Labour Party, but the 'anti-imperialist' position was mainly evident inside the CPGB, and, through its influence, in the wider – though still marginal – anti-colonial movement. On foreign policy questions, the British party followed the USSR's line closely, acquiescing in the strengthening of Soviet influence throughout Eastern Europe in the late 1940s and allowing Moscow to shape a great deal of its policy thinking. On the left of the Labour Party, pro-Soviet feeling was also in evidence immediately after the second world war, but it was quickly marginalised. Thus the polarisation of the Cold War was mirrored in the labour movement. There was little room for manoeuvre between Atlanticism and the pro-Soviet position, although pacifism, Quakerism and Christian brands of socialism all generated dissent from Labour's official positions on foreign policy questions in this period.[8] Some Labour MPs even talked of the possibility of pursuing a 'third way' between the two blocs, though this notion was given a heavily nationalist tinge: Britain should be providing moral leadership to the rest of the world in the creation of a dealigned third bloc.

This last position anticipated the early New Left's project in this area, though the implications of this idea were barely registered until the movement developed. The New Left's distinctiveness on international questions arose from the 'break' it efected from the prevailing traditions described above. It sought to transcend the binary logic at the heart of the Cold War and to explore the intellectual and political implications of a 'third course' in international affairs; this led the movement's intellectuals to reflect critically on the nature of British identity and to address some of the new issues which were now challenging the consensus on foreign policy questions within mainstream British political life, notably the impact of nationalist movements in the colonies, the importance of the 'third world', and the implications of West European integration.

## POSITIVE NEUTRALISM

The first New Left looked towards a radical change in the prevailing pattern of international relations, seeking the creation of a space beyond the two camps polarised by the Cold War. This project was expressed in the movement's commitment to the principle of positive neutralism – an idea which combined support for the possibility of neutrality within the Cold War with the prospect of the formation of a third, non-aligned bloc. This second commitment generated within the movement a close interest in the newly emerging 'third world'; primarily as a source of support for the non-aligned movement, but increasingly as a complex and poorly understood area of the world which had been viewed too frequently from an unthinkingly European perspective.

As New Left thinkers repeatedly suggested, the politics of the blocs were reproduced by and reinforced a prevailing sense of passivity and apathy, not only within particular nation states but also throughout the world political system. Positive neutralism meant breaking with the mindset as well as the reality of 'two camp' politics. The New Left therefore stressed the ideological impact of the Cold War, challenging the binary logic which bore down upon dissent and independent thinking and had saturated the culture and conventions of political life in both West and East. In practical terms, the New Left therefore welcomed Yugoslavia's expulsion from the Soviet bloc, the neutrality pursued by India, and the Bandung agreement of 1955 between neutral 'third world' countries. Meetings between non-aligned nations were formalised by the Belgrade conference of 1961. The New Left, meanwhile, sent representatives to several major conferences which aimed to link the independence movements across Africa.[9] The *New Reasoner*, in particular, championed expressions of dissent throughout the Eastern bloc. As Anderson recalls:

> The *New Reasoner* maintained from 1957 to 1959 a record of socialist documentation on Eastern Europe and the USSR without equal on the Left in any country. No issue was complete without articles on or translations from the Communist world. Among these were the essays by Thompson himself to which he refers – eloquent Western equivalents of the Eastern manifestoes of the time – and poems and stories by Dery, Yashin, Hikmet, Wazyk, Ilye, Woroszylki, Brecht and others.[10]

Writers in the *New Reasoner* spelled out the consequences of the Cold War within the Soviet bloc, noting how it helped the communist leadership conflate internal dissent within Eastern Europe with the machinations of the imperialist enemies.[11] Likewise, the autonomy of other communist parties had been seriously undermined by such thinking, leaving them silent in the face of oppression within Eastern Europe as well as the Soviet Union's participation in the arms race. The New Left was equally critical of the West in the Cold War, criticising the political and economic constraints on domestic policy which the Western military alliance enforced. The pervasiveness of assumptions about Western security merged with an unspoken political consensus about British foreign policy and national interests, leading Thompson to observe that:

> allegiance to NATO is part of that religious area behind the Establishment which one may not question. It seemed self-evident to editors, commentators and most politicians that if only it was pointed out that a unilateral initiative might endanger NATO, then our heresy would be extinguished overnight.[12]

Traditional assumptions about imperial grandeur and English exclusivity, the New Left argued, were intermingled with this new 'realpolitik'; consequently, political debate was ordered in a way which kept significant and troubling questions off the national political agenda.

Advocating positive neutralism thus enabled the New Left to maintain a simultaneous critique of both sides in the Cold War; it also informed the development of a novel and subsequently influential conception of international relations in the post-war world. This outlook was the direct counterpart of the domestic project pursued by the movement: the point was to define a 'third way' beyond older socialist traditions in the field of oversea affairs. But exploring the political space between the two camps was an onerous project, given the antinomian logic of the Cold War. The New Left provided an alternative framework for the conduct of foreign policy, and hoped to demystify the assumptions underlying the continuation of the Cold War: repudiating the notion of the immediate threat of Soviet invasion; questioning the military and strategic terms in which foreign policy debate was often cast; and challenging the stultifying effect of superpower antagonism on contemporary politics.[13] The movement keenly explored new political directions out of the contemporary stalemate, proposing (somewhat idealistically) a programme of disarmament targets and meetings for individual countries – Britain in particular – and the superpowers. These steps would ultimately lead to a more flexible, sensitive and democratic world order. A serious interest in the prospects of superpower detente at the highest level was maintained throughout the movement's life. Whilst the torpid atmosphere of developments in this sphere was constantly bemoaned, New Left writers were keen to cite any possibility of breakthrough as evidence that a shift in the culture of superpower relations could prove as significant as formal negotiations themselves.[14]

Positive neutralism also enabled the New Left to make a distinctive contribution to British radicalism in the connection it forged between solidarity for newly emerging post-colonial nations and the importance of agency in both moral and political senses. Just as Thompson had struggled in theoretical terms to return agency to the agenda of socialism, so the New Left, more generally, argued that these nations could make a difference to global politics by voluntarily coming together in a neutral bloc, and forcing a major rupture within the prevailing bloc system. New Left writers therefore called for a shift in Britain's pattern of trade, seeking economic exchanges with non-aligned countries, especially in the 'third world'. These contacts would be institutionalised through 'planned international trade exchanges between like-minded states',[15] allowing space both for the autonomous development of recently decolonised nations, and undermining the economic and political imperatives of the bloc system. These countries should be allowed to develop in their own way – not subordinated to the dictates of a pre-ordained model of economic development, and given space to draw upon indigenous traditions of struggle and co-operation. Positive neutralism therefore provided an influential, alternative understanding of anti-colonialism to that enunciated by the Communist International and by orthodox Marxists more generally. It constitutes one source for the idea of providing 'aid' to third world countries in order to help their autonomous long-term development, which has been central to the work of groups such as Oxfam, as well as bodies like the Third World Information Network.[16]

The influence of this approach to international affairs upon many of the individuals involved in this movement was profound. Thompson, for instance, maintained this perspective throughout his subsequent political career, arguing in 1991 that the non-aligned movement helped undermine the bipolar bloc system and, thus, anticipated international relations in the post-Cold War era.[17] Interestingly, this claim has been heavily criticised by, among others, commentators associated with the later New Left, for whom positive neutralism was a flawed, populist response to harsh international realities. Fred Halliday, in a recent contribution to the debate about the end of the Cold War, puts this view most forcefully:

> The term 'nonaligned' which he [Thompson] uses is not quite as solid as might appear: what is striking about the 'nonaligned movement' is that it has found only a marginal support in Europe (Yugoslavia, Malta, Cyprus) and the majority of European neutrals preferred an atomized, low-key, approach to international issues, not the constitution of a third bloc. All these countries were, moreover, in political and socio-economic terms not 'third' at all, but estranged members of one or other bloc.[18]

His argument is indicative of the continuing strength of the 'realist' approach to bloc politics which the New Left opposed. In reply, Thompson reiterated his faith in the importance of national agency in international affairs, in opposition to the deployment of the language and assumptions of systemic approaches to international relations:

> He [Halliday] insists on reducing all analysis to 'two camps' thinking – capitalism versus not-capitalism or 'Communism', as 'systems' – and refuses absolutely to explore the possibility of 'third ways'. They are ruled out of court categorically. This is an old habit of the editors and contributors who have conducted New Left Review so tenaciously since the early 1960s. Whilst they are willing to employ copiously the somewhat empty (and in my view culturally relativist) term 'the Third World', the very possibility of a 'third way' – or a fourth or a fifth – or, indeed, of a reopening field of possibility, in which new variants of social formation and new combinations of old and newer modes of production might be expected to arise, is ruled out of order as a categoric impossibility.[19]

The continuing purchase for Thompson of the 'third way' project of the late 1950s is apparent in this later argument of the 1990s.

Within the first New Left too, some important differences emerged around the question of neutralism. In particular, the connection between a 'third way' in international affairs and the 'third world' became a contentious issue in this period, as well as in subsequent years. Undoubtedly the New Left moved beyond the traditions of communist anti-colonialism in its solidarity with different kinds of liberation movements in the non-developed world, as well as through its recognition that the balance of forces within the international order was changing. But staking out this new terrain, and developing an adequate political and theoretical understanding of world affairs, and the nature of 'third world' politics in particular, proved far more difficult.

For some, especially in the younger generation, the implications of this engagement with the 'third world' were profound. Imperialism had been used by the old left to connote the formal, political relationships between Western colonial powers and former colonies, or as a political 'swear word' to use indiscriminately against the policies of Western nations. Some New Left radicals began to conceive of imperialism as a more extensive and complex set of processes, a pattern of values and cultures which were deeply embedded in Western societies, and, indeed, to talk of the persistence of 'neo-colonialism'. This generated a more critical standpoint towards European culture, particularly its representations of race and economic development. Peter Worsley, in his critique of the racism of a leading 'progressive', Albert Schweitzer, pointed to the depth and pervasiveness of such ideas.[20] Racism was here conceived not so much as an individual, moral issue, the characteristic of 'extremists', but as a systematic, cultural phenomenon, deeply embedded within British society, which liberals and even socialists could manifest. Writers in this milieu therefore began to analyse the indirect as well as brutally immediate results of imperialism. In the case of Algeria, for instance, space was given in the journals to recording French atrocities as well as to serious analysis of the indigenous opposition.[21] The New Left also wielded its cultural analysis to decode and condemn the survival of less obvious but important forms of imperialism. As Harry Hanson argued, 'under the influence of neo-Lawrentian conceptions of how to deal with Arabs, 'we' have already done so much damage that the prospects of repairing it in the near future, even by a complete reversal of policy, are slight'.[22] Such arguments had an important long-term impact on the political and intellectual re-evaluation of British culture and identity among the radical intelligentsia in subsequent decades.

The 'euro-centrism' of the old left was powerfully challenged in this analysis, whilst the politics of the developing world became far more salient within New Left discourse. Anti-colonialism and neutralism were interdependent commitments in this milieu, yet differing tendencies could be discerned within the New Left's thinking about these agendas. A close interest in the politics of 'developing' countries became apparent within the *ULR* milieu, though this sometimes resembled a pious ideal rather than a real commitment: its opening editorial declared that 'a journal of the left must give special attention to the colonial and ex-colonial world. We apologise for the inadequate space given in this issue to the problems of colonial liberation movements. In future issues we shall try to remedy this.'[23] For the *New Reasoner* too, anti-colonialism was central and resulted in articles on Kenya and Cyprus, for example. The sentiments expressed in these showed elements of continuity with the traditions of communist anti-colonialism, whereas for the younger generations in the movement, 'third world' politics involved a clearer break with older ideas. Here the seeds of future discord were sown: Thompson, as is clear from the above quotation, was sceptical about the term 'third world' from an early stage. He rejected what he perceived as the drift from universal moral principles bound up in the cultural relativism which 'third worldism' legitimated amongst some strands of the later New Left.

Engagement with the 'third world' was a feature of the politics of the earlier New Left too, and had some important theoretical implications. The assumptions of orthodox political and economic analysis, especially of a Marxist kind, were called into question by writers such as John Rex and Stuart Hall in a number of ways. They challenged the idea that 'third world' countries were backward versions of European societies. This emphasis challenged the correlation between levels of economic development and political progress embedded within orthodox Marxist accounts of the obstacles to socialism caused by economic backwardness. Recognition of the 'third world' necessitated, for some, the reorientation of socialist thought: concentration upon class divisions within the metropolitan nations of the West, it was argued, obscured a more fundamental inequality – between the affluent West and its poor, 'undeveloped' counterpart. This theme was developed in a number of directions by the later New Left. An important bridge between these intellectual developments was supplied by Peter

Worsley, who produced his influential and distinctive study, *The Third World*, in 1964. His sympathetic assessment of politics in the developing world culminated in the following characterisation of the world order of the 1960s:

> Between their society of hoes and goats, and the Euro-American world of space-rockets and blast furnaces, there is a Grand Canyon full of bitterness and mutual mistrusts. This is the great 'alienation' of the twentieth century, to them far more vicious and dehumanising than any gulf between worker and bourgeois in capitalist society.[24]

Significantly, Peter Worsley connected this perspective with the politics of the early New Left: positive neutralism, he argued, provided the most meaningful strategy for these nations to make an impact on international affairs. Interestingly, in the book's acknowledgments he nodded in the direction of both the first New Left — thanking Thompson, Saville and Michael Barratt-Brown — as well as the new generation, citing 'Perry Anderson and his "equipe".'[25] Clearly, the 'third world' was firmly established on the political agenda of the first New Left before its demise.

This became a relatively fertile arena for theoretical elaboration and appropriation. It was not only in the largely English orientated discussions on class, humanism and culture that the first New Left instigated a process of revision and rethinking. Writers such as John Rex and Basil Davidson found room in *ULR* for their analyses of the politics of 'developing' societies, which had been inadequately rendered in conventional socialist discourse. Both agreed that the analytical framework which had been 'exported' by the Western left for the interpretation of national or pan-Africanist liberation movements was flawed, though their reading of these situations differed greatly. The main target of this critique was an overly reductionist Marxism. Just as Hall and Williams were arguing for a more expansive interpretation of socialism in the realms of culture and ideology, Rex approached the 'third world' likewise: 'I do not want to deny, in any way, that capitalist exploitation in Africa is a fact... But I do want to insist that there are other factors besides this which have as profound an effect on people's lives and which are no less essential for an understanding of their political motivation.'[26] This meant that the specificities of culture and race in these situations had to be theorised far more rigorously by the left. Rex went on to argue for a new analytical framework to interpret political formations in these contexts. Socialists of varying hues (from Fabians to Trotskyites) were unable to engage with the realities of politics in the developing world, responding to the national liberation movements with suspicion, 'because the lively African political movements are so unlike what the prayer book says revolutionary movements should be like'.[27] The ground was therefore prepared for the reformulation of some of the canons of Marxist thought from a 'third world' perspective, encouraging the assessment of new models of development and revolution, even though they had arisen outside the European context. Rex's development of the sociological tradition of ethnic studies was prefigured in this aspect of the early New Left's theoretical practice. He subsequently proceeded to challenge classical Marxist interpretations of race and ethnicity, in contexts such as the Caribbean, in his examination of the specificity of capitalist development, the complexity of the relations of production beyond the owner/non-owner division, and the importance of social relations outside production.[28] Basil Davidson, meanwhile, found the first New Left amenable to his influential reading of African history (*Old Africa Rediscovered* was published in 1959) and vocal support for liberation movements across the continent.[29]

The coherence of the New Left's ideas on these questions should not be overstated: Hall's sympathetic critique of Rex's 'left Weberianism' in 1980 illustrates the differences which persisted alongside the commitment to the reformulation of Marxism in these areas.[30] Yet, the work of both, alongside that of Basil Davidson and Peter Worsley, illustrates the fruitful nature of the early New Left's transcendence of previous assumptions about race, ethnicity and development.

## CUBA

One immediate consequence of this engagement with the politics of colonial struggles was the questioning of traditional emphases upon the primacy of European models, to which the less 'developed' world should aspire. Younger members of the London milieu were particularly excited by the revolution led by Fidel Castro in Cuba. From 1961-3, Anderson, Hall, Robin Blackburn and Norman Fruchter explored the possibility of an alternative model of revolution on the basis of the Cuban experience.[31] Several features of this revolution were particularly appealing. It had erupted autonomously, without external superpower involvement; as many contemporary accounts attested, Castro had worked with the revolutionary classes particular to Cuba – the peasantry in alliance with fractions of the working and lower middle classes from the cities. Furthermore, he attempted, at least initially, to steer a course between the two superpowers in terms of the revolution's political affiliation. Indeed, the ideological eclecticism which had inspired the revolution was heralded by New Left ideologues. So, too, was the humanistic discourse which Castro mobilised to underscore the popular coalition which he had orchestrated against the old regime. *New Left Review* approvingly cited his claim that 'standing between the two political and economic ideologies or positions being debated in the world, we are holding our own positions. We have named it humanism, because its methods are humanistic, because we want to rid man of all fears, directives or dogmatisms'.[32] It was even suggested that Castro had transcended the limitations of representative models of democracy with his more direct understanding of popular consent. Such claims were, however, regarded with scepticism and concern by more cautious observers of the Cuban revolution.[33]

Above all, Cuban developments dramatically fused two concerns in this milieu: the growing sense of the importance of events in the 'third world', as well as the desire for a romantic and inspiring revolution which did not follow the tainted Soviet model. Cuba provided an important reference point for younger activists who did not share the disillusion and political exhaustion of some of their older compatriots by 1962. Indeed, its popularity marks a shift to the left among some of the younger sections of the first New Left, leading to the more explicit internationalism of the later New Left. Certainly, no political event in Europe could have elicited the following eulogy from Anderson and Robin Blackburn: 'Neither pure under-developed nor industrial society, neither simple neutralism nor Communism, neither parliamentarism nor autarky, Cuba seems to emerge beyond these classifications as a fresh invention of man in society'.[34]

## THE POLITICS OF NATIONHOOD

Despite the commitment of all sections of the movement to the values of positive neutralism, different emphases rapidly became apparent on international questions. In addition, for some in the younger generation, the question of national identity became more troubling in this period – an indirect consequence of the breaks registered by New Left ideas on international matters. In fact, the internationalism of this milieu was always connected to subterranean tensions about national identity and politics. Though the latter were rarely articulated openly, they formed a small part of the movement's intellectual practice. Without overstressing the importance of this issue – it received very little public attention – it is possible, with the benefit of hindsight, to perceive the origins of subsequent tensions around the question of national identity underlying the intellectual ferment unleashed by the early New Left.

Whilst the *New Reasoner* was more confident in its desire to reconstruct a radical national past, some of the *ULR*'s leading participants were more troubled by Englishness. Behind both *ULR*'s and the early *New Left Review*'s interest in the question of race in British politics, as well as their obvious enthusiasm for 'third world' politics and the non-aligned movement, lay a disquiet with traditional representations of national traditions and identity. This was evident too in the more theoretical work of Williams and Hall. Their elaboration of the themes of pluralism and community emerged in part from their rejection of the parochialism and chauvinism of the Labour tradition; the inevitable consequence of these ideas was to perceive the nation too as an ideological terrain rather than an uncontroversial 'given' of political life. In these years though, this subterranean intellectual shift was only beginning.

These subtle and often 'invisible' differences between *ULR* and the *New Reasoner*, which were never clear-cut or neat, were partly the result of the generational experiences which had been brought into the New Left. For *ULR* and the New Left currents which emerged after 1962, formations untouched by the 'popular élan of the 1940s' (especially the experiences of the 'people's war' and the 1945 election victory), the confidence of figures like Thompson in the notion of reclaiming a radical version of nationalism was alien.[35] Significantly, a number of key figures within the London New Left milieu were of non-English origins. As Hall recalls, the group of 'independents' in the Oxford Labour Club who constituted the original milieu for *ULR* in the mid-1950s:

> attracted more than its fair share of exiles and migrants, which reinforced its cosmopolitanism. 'Chuck' Taylor was a French-Canadian Rhodes scholar (as well as that even more perplexing phenomenon, a sort of Catholic Marxist); Dodd Alleyne was Trinidadian; I was Jamaican; Sadiq al Mahdi was later to play a significant role in the Sudan; Clovis Maksoud was a founder member of the Syrian Ba'ath Party. Some, like Alan Lovell, a Welsh pacifist and conscientious objector, Alan Hall, a Scots classicist from Aberdeen, and Raphael Samuel, Gabriel Pearson, Stanley Mitchell and Robert Cassen, who were all Jewish, were what one might call 'internal emigres'.[36]

More generally, the 'colder' international climate fostered by the 'realpolitik' of the 1950s, as well as the unfavourable political circumstances facing the left in this decade, engendered scepticism about the political effectiveness of reappropriating radical traditions from the past. In this milieu, internationalism was tied to an unspoken unease about nationalism, a position which foreshadowed the more explicit anti-nationalism pursued by *New Left Review* after 1962. During the first New Left's lifetime, these differences were seldom aired, yet underlay the movement's praxis. Whilst exploration of the movement's international agenda progressed rapidly therefore, scant attention was paid to related developments nearer home, partly because of an unthinking conflation of English and British identity, but also because these touched upon sensitive and unresolved questions within this movement. Scotland and Wales were occasionally cited in articles about politics and culture, yet the burgeoning nationalist movements in both countries were ignored.[37] So, too, was Northern Ireland, which received negligible comment although the IRA was beginning its cross-border campaign in this period.[38]

## THE COMMON MARKET

These tensions were evident too within the movement's response to West European integration, an issue which touched on the questions of national sovereignty and identity. The issue of British membership of the Common Market, raised by Macmillan's overtures in 1961, cut across orthodox ideological alignments: both 'pro' and 'anti' camps included strange and unlikely bedfellows across the spectrum of left opinion. In the New Left too, no neat or simple division of opinion on this question was visible. The Common Market was regarded with distaste by many as an environment alien to the left, in which European capitalism would provide a colossal enemy and would seriously restrict the prospects of redistribution, intervention and regulation by the sovereign nation state. This perspective often relied on a traditional understanding of Britain's political and economic role in the world, and tended to take for granted the nature of the British state. These assumptions were called into question within the New Left. In a joint essay, Anderson and Hall argued that:

> The worst construction which could be placed upon this call for an alternative is that we should rest on our splendid isolation and depend

upon our traditional Empire ties, our 'Empire mission', unreconstructed and untouched, to float us through... This is the call of the past – and no less so because the Left is as susceptible to it as the Right.[39]

They were equally critical of the enthusiasm for integration displayed by sections of the right in the Labour Party, pouring scorn on the idea that Britain's future lay in an American dominated bloc in Western Europe.[40] Critical views of integration were common within the movement,[41] yet some New Left thinkers contributed a distinctive voice and tone to this debate. The idea of orchestrating opposition to the Common Market on the basis of a 'settled' English identity was implicitly challenged by writers in both *ULR* and the early *New Left Review*.

The isolationist postures of Labour's Common Market critics were often rejected, even by those opposed to integration. In the words of the economist Mike Artis, 'debating points aside, the exclusion of all mention of the Common Market from the economic policy programme set out in the Labour Party's latest manifesto – Signposts for the Sixties – is a weakness, not a source of strength'.[42] Writers in this milieu typically scorned the absence of a credible and popular alternative to the integrationist case.[43] This perspective allowed minority strands of opinion to articulate strongly pro-European sentiments: Alasdair MacIntyre, in a debate on this issue sponsored by the journal *Encounter*, was especially positive: 'I do not understand those socialists who are against Franco-German capitalism but somehow prefer British capitalism. I detest the anti-German chauvinism of the anti-Common marketeers... I can see nothing but good in an enforced dialogue with the exciting movements on the Italian left'.[44] The New Left revived an older aspiration through its belief that socialism did not have to surrender to the national context, a view which inspired *New Left Review* from 1962 onwards. Nairn's critique of the unquestioning defence of national sovereignty among large sections of the British left, in the context of the Common Market referendum of 1972, was therefore anticipated by some of the pro-European (though rarely pro-Common Market) sentiment within this movement.[45] By 1961-2, sections of this movement were beginning to sense the anxieties about Britain's identity and future which were to play such a key role in the nation's political life over subsequent decades.

## THOMPSON'S 'PATRIOTISM'

Whilst the New Left's contribution to debates about international affairs has been recognised by later commentators, the subterranean connections between positive neutralism and the issue of national identity have rarely been explored. The single influential exception here is Anderson's assessment of Thompson's 'patriotism' in *Arguments Within English Marxism* (1980). Anderson points to the Popular Front of the 1930s and the Second World War as important influences upon Thompson's conception of the junction between national and international struggle, a belief compatible with the emphasis on national roads to socialism prevalent in the Communist International in the 1950s: 'nothing is more striking in Thompson's development than the coherence and continuity of his thought, across his Communist and non-Communist phases'.[46] According to Anderson, Thompson's interpretation of socialist internationalism was applied to the popular uprisings against Communist rule in Hungary and Poland in the mid-1950s and encouraged him to view CND as 'a mass movement which simultaneously insisted on Britain's capacity to "lead the world"... and, at the same time, emphasised the universalist goals of international peace and solidarity with colonial peoples'.[47]

Anderson's argument is misleading on several accounts, however. He is, firstly, guilty of conflating Thompson's ideas with mainstream thinking within CND. Thompson was always critical of the national chauvinist assumptions of the argument that Britain should provide moral leadership for other nations. Anderson also underestimates the complex impact of British communist traditions and culture upon Thompson as a political and intellectual figure. Thompson's notion of 'the English people' was influenced by the earlier Popular Front politics of anti-fascism, and the intellectual work of the party's History Group which attempted to write 'people's history'. But this 'people' were always theorised as challenging the establishment. They were not part of the dominant national tradition. The Historians' Group were also trying to challenge the view that communism was an alien, un-English importation. The notion of rediscovering indigenous traditions of radicalism, was, in part, an attempt to circumvent such an accusation. Undoubtedly this sometimes encouraged an uncritical attitude towards these traditions and a rhetorical exaggeration of their significance; yet this perspective did not necessarily involve an uncritical attitude to nationalism itself. Other members of the group, most notably Eric Hobsbawm, took a completely different approach, and subsequently provided some influential critical reflections on nationalism as an historical phenomenon.[48] The question of the relationship between Thompson's conception of indigenous radicalism and English nationalism is, thus, more complex than Anderson suggests. Finally, Anderson assumes that Thompson spoke for the early New Left as a whole on these questions. But Thompson's intellectual and political development was extremely singular; he cannot even be cited as typical or representative of the *New Reasoner* milieu with which he was most closely associated, let alone this diverse and heterogeneous movement. As we have seen, the question of national identity in an English context was less consensual within the early New Left than Anderson assumes.

The 'militant' internationalism pursued within *New Left Review* after 1962 – involving an uncompromising assault upon English traditions and culture – was premised on this view of the early New Left: this earlier wave, according to Anderson, was seriously restricted by its commitment to older traditions of national radicalism and insufficiently intellectually rigorous in its engagement with international questions. Neither accusation stands up to close scrutiny. Some within the early New Left began to sense the problems associated with national identity in a British context in this period. Moreover, innovative and influential ideas were generated by the enthusiasm of some of the movement's intellectuals for developments in the 'third world'. The dichotomy Anderson poses between the early movement's ideas and those of the later New Left is overdrawn; aspects of the 'internationalist' projects pursued by currents within *New Left Review* after 1962 were anticipated by some of these earlier developments. Perhaps most significantly of all, he neglects the extent to which the early New Left retained – though it struggled to carry it out – a commitment to forging a connection between intellectual development and radical political practice. Its pursuit of an intellectual breakthrough in these areas was also expressed, therefore, in its involvement within the peace movement, the most important contemporary agency capable of effecting a break in the Cold War stalemate in Britain.

## 'LET BRITAIN LEAD': THE PEACE MOVEMENT, 1957-62

The fortunes of the first New Left became closely intertwined with the peace movement of the late 1950s. Whilst the New Left was always a small, intellectually orientated formation, the Campaign for Nuclear Disarmament

(CND) became a popular and broadly based movement which, at its peak, could mobilise thousands of sympathisers. Like the New Left, however, its contemporary influence was short-lived; it receded quickly after 1962, becoming a small and marginal grouping until its reappearance as a mass force in the early 1980s. The peace movement of the late 1950s grew up around a resolute commitment to the unilateral renunciation of nuclear weapons by Britain. This provided the central focus for the movement's disparate supporters and attracted many in a period of international tension and widespread fear about the capacities of nuclear weapons. A variety of tactics was employed by the movement during these years to highlight the immorality of nuclear weapons and develop a politics of resistance to the presence of this weaponry. The peace movement thus transcended older patterns of interest group politics in Britain, combining more conventional lobbying strategies with radical direct action beyond the confines of Westminster.

Whilst the formation of the mass anti-nuclear movement of the late 1950s and early 1960s was prepared by earlier pacifist and anti-nuclear actions, the later movement differed both in size and political impact. The campaign against nuclear weapons of the late 1950s drew support from different social strata and developed an effective populist appeal. Shortly after the Suez crisis had mobilised opinion hostile to the government's action in a way that had not been seen in British politics since the 1930s, the first significant wave of anti-nuclear protest occurred. In March 1956 the Direct Action Committee was formed to raise money for the disruption of nuclear testing at Christmas Island in the Pacific Ocean. This was followed, in July 1957, by the formation of the National Campaign Against Nuclear Weapons Testing, a fusion of several groupings working in this area. Two months previously, two thousand women, sporting black sashes and flags, had marched to Trafalgar Square. Among their number were Peggy Duff, Pat Arrowsmith and April Carter, who all became high-profile, public exponents of the anti-nuclear cause.

Throughout 1957 pressure for the unilateral renunciation of nuclear weapons by Britain increased. Following Bevan's condemnation of this policy at the Labour Conference of 1957, the call for unilateralism was increasingly associated with the development of an autonomous peace movement. In the following year, CND emerged – with a self-appointed executive committee, Canon Collins as Chair and the philosopher Bertrand Russell as President. CND was driven by the belief that nuclear weaponry was obscene and immoral and should be renounced unilaterally. In many ways, this was a strength: the moral clarity of its politics enabled it to attract a degree of commitment and loyalty which other political groups struggled to match. On the other hand, this moral argument did not always provide guidance on political and strategic questions, a limitation to which the New Left was especially sensitive.

CND made its mark on British political life through its highly successful annual marches to the Aldermaston missile base. Organised in opposition to a culture of perceived orthodoxy and consensus within British political life:

> the colour and the mime, the discomfort and physical exhilaration, the informality and sense of purpose, the intense political discussions and the sentimental moralising songs, all contributed to Aldermaston becoming the central unifying experience of the new peace movement.[49]

The Campaign employed a range of tactics, which many of its activists found innovative and exciting. These included sit-down protests at missile bases as well as local meetings, fund-raising events and political lobbies. In terms of the symbolic protests at missile sites which were a regular feature of its life, the movement was heavily influenced by the developing civil rights struggle in the United States, learning much about the tactical and moral aspects of non-violent direct action.[50] Older indigenous traditions were also important, especially the pacifist ideas expounded in the pages of *Peace News*. In December 1958 the methods of peaceful direct action came to public attention at two high-profile demonstrations at American rocket bases at Swaffham and North Pickenham. The impetus behind these actions was intensified by the failure of several summit meetings to produce any significant agreement on multilateral disarmament. The march to Aldermaston at Easter 1960 was especially effective, attracting the highest number of participants until that date.

Indeed, the Campaign appeared to be making some headway during 1960. First, the United States cancelled the Blue Streak missile system, the only contemporary opportunity for Britain to possess its own nuclear deterrent. In the same year, following a period of successful lobbying within several trade unions, Labour's Scarborough Conference passed a resolution supporting unilateralism as party policy.[51] These apparent victories were misleading though: the disappearance of the option of a 'go-it-alone' policy for Britain on nuclear weapons did not signal a change of heart towards them within the political establishment; leading figures on the Labour right had for a long time opposed the idea of an independent nuclear force on the grounds that this would damage relations between Britain and the United States; and whilst the growth of support for CND was evident within the Labour Party, it is not clear that the Conference vote of 1960 represented a profound shift within the party's thought: the majority of constituency party delegate opinion actually backed Gaitskell's opposition to unilateralism.[52] In the end, the motion was carried by a probably unrepresentative section of party opinion. If unilateralism was to be maintained as party policy against the hostility of Gaitskell and the Campaign for Democratic Socialism, a pressure group formed within the party after the Scarborough conference, a strategy of ideological mobilisation was needed throughout the labour movement. Yet, none was forthcoming from the left of the Labour Party. In 1961 this decision was duly overturned; thereafter, it subsided as an issue within Labour's ranks. To many in the peace movement, it seemed as if unilateralism had provided a convenient stick for the Labour left to beat the party's leadership, rather than becoming a deeply held conviction. CND, it seemed to many activists, had gained little from its extensive efforts within the Labour Party.

Within the peace movement, a shift away from parliamentary lobbying was increasingly evident, though other forms of protest had been part of the movement's tactical repertoire from the beginning. A new grouping, the Committee of 100, played a leading role in presenting direct action philosophy as a real political alternative to more conventional lobbying.[53] The hybrid of civil disobedience and confrontationalist ideas espoused by the Committee sustained an innovative culture of protest, generating a critical perspective on conventional political life.[54] By 1961, the Committee of 100 was the fulcrum of the peace movement (though membership of local Committee groups and CND frequently overlapped), organising numerous initiatives both nationally and locally. These culminated in a well-attended demonstration in Trafalgar Square on 17 September 1961. The tense atmosphere fostered by these actions reached their apogee in the summer of 1961 when the Berlin crisis revealed the instability of the superpower relationship. From September onwards, direct action philosophy inspired a series of local actions across the country. Simultaneously, the authorities began to abandon the low-profile approach which had informed their previous treatment of such demonstrations. The coercive dimension of the state was increasingly evident in the guise of police (mis)behaviour and harsher judicial sentences for protesters. As the atmosphere of crisis in international affairs deepened (the Berlin and Cuban missile crises ensured this throughout 1961 and 1962), radicals within the movement called for independent action against the whole political system. This took two forms: the birth of the Independent Nuclear Deterrent Election Committee (INDEC) and the salience of the Committee's militant approach to direct action. This shift to independent action was accelerated by the detachment of much of the Labour left from the Campaign, following the rise of Wilson, who seemed more sympathetic on foreign policy questions.

After 1962 the movement's activities began to decline as the national and international situation changed. Hall was commissioned by CND to produce a new political statement of the direction of peace politics after the defeat of the unilateralist resolution at the 1961 Labour Party Conference and in the wake of the Cuban crisis. The result, *Steps Towards Peace* (1962), was downbeat about the movement's immediate prospects, a sentiment reinforced by the recognition of Britain's apparent insignificance in world affairs, highlighted during the Cuban missile crisis.

## THE NEW LEFT AND THE PEACE MOVEMENT

CND presented the New Left with challenges and opportunities. With hindsight, some commentators have regarded its involvement in CND as a diversion from its main tasks.[55] Others have argued that it remained too aloof from a movement which might have provided a powerful vehicle for its ideas.[56] From an early stage, New Left activists were enthusiastically involved in CND. The movement's intellectuals viewed the peace movement as a radical and innovative political movement outside the deadweight orthodoxies of left politics. While New Left assistance was uneven in terms of resources and numbers throughout CND's growth, it was the most successful of all the political groupings working within the Campaign. According to Richard Taylor, 'the New Left's perspective offered a qualitatively superior strategy and ideological framework which might have formed the basis of a successful extra-parliamentary mobilisation...'[57] The New Left possessed two advantages over its political rivals, especially the Trotskyist Socialist Labour League and the Communist Party. First, the New Left was shaped by the same political crises which produced the peace movement. Second, both developed in comparable ways: neither opted for the organisational hierarchies of the Labour or Communist parties, preferring a more fluid structure and grassroots-orientated culture. But in choosing this course, they faced a range of problems which have since become familiar to extra-parliamentary social and political movements in Britain: both the New Left's and the early peace movement's encounters with these obstacles prefigured the experiences of these later currents. These problems included the tensions generated between provincial regions and the metropolitan centre – a recurrent problem for British political movements; the difficulties of sustaining such movements without a sound institutional base; the lack of space afforded by the British party system to non-party movements; and the magnet-like quality of the 'parliamentary state' in Britain, which makes a foothold within the country's highly centralised political and party institutions a necessary condition of survival for such movements. These difficulties merely added to the strains placed upon the New Left by participation in the peace movement. Throughout its life, the New Left looked to the Labour Party as the key political agency on the left. At several points this brought it into conflict with those parts of the peace movement which had, by 1961, become irredeemably hostile to Labour. As these views became entrenched in the Committee of 100 and direct action took precedence within peace circles, these differences were widened.

The tension was largely the result of the New Left's confusions about its own identity and role, which were exacerbated by the rise of CND. For the most part it empathised greatly with the countercultural, libertarian and non-party format which the peace movement adopted. This empathy led, in the early months of 1962, to a more concerted attempt to fuse New Left themes with radical pacifist ideas. This process was evident both in the centrality of figures such as Alan Lovell and Nicholas Walter, who straddled both camps, and the willingness of *Peace News* to open its pages to New Left ideas. The downturn in the New Left's fortunes by 1962 made the peace movement a relatively attractive alternative for activists disillusioned with the conflict and in-fighting prevalent in the former.

Simultaneously though, the New Left was sometimes critical of the peace movement and its activists. This attitude stemmed both from the scepticism of more experienced political activists towards a new generation (a tendency which was also evident within the New Left itself), and the development of a quasi-vanguardist aspiration (though this was far less pronounced than its Trotskyist counterparts) which encouraged some in the New Left to view themselves as a potential political-intellectual leadership for the peace movement. These emphases encouraged a continuing critique of aspects of the peace movement's politics which, at different points, were perceived by the New Left as overly naive, moralistic and unthinkingly nationalistic.

The New Left was, for example, sometimes at odds with the enthusiasts of direct action, critical of the fetish of action of any sort, as long as it was dramatic and non-violent, and of the dangers of creating a self-absorbed and non-engaged political culture within the peace movement. Thus, leading New Left figures sometimes viewed the peace movement with suspicion. In an article intended to reconcile the peace movement and the New Left (on the latter's terms), Thompson could not help remarking that 'the young marchers of Aldermaston, despite all immaturities and individualistic attitudes' were moving towards more mature political ideas.[58] The assumption here was that the moralistic nature of peace movement thinking lacked a sufficiently grounded political foundation. John Rex and Peter Worsley reiterated the importance of developing an alternative to the strategic thinking of the major political parties, arguing that 'the Campaign cannot base itself upon a self-righteous desire to absolve Britain from individual national responsibility for nuclear arms'.[59] The refusal of some in the peace movement to think beyond the policy of unilateralism grated against the New Left's approach to questions of political strategy: 'Those who support unilateral disarmament are required to formulate an alternative policy for Britain, to turn a protest *against* the Bomb into a policy that can lead to pressure on the world as a whole, and it is particularly urgent that we should do this when the Campaign is under such heavy attack.'[60] The New Left continually strove to provide the outlines of this 'alternative policy'.

New Left critics also pointed to the elements of national chauvinism and nostalgia embedded in some presentations of the call for unilateral nuclear disarmament, a criticism repeated beyond these circles.[61] Anxieties about national identity were connected to CND's appeal in the late 1950s as it sought to capture the soul of the nation, frequently relying on the assumption that Britain was still capable of providing moral leadership within the world.[62] For some New Left critics, the admixture of moral principle and little Englandism failed to provide a sufficiently combative alternative to the dominant notions of national security and military necessity. The idea that nuclear weapons should be renounced 'because they are totally evil' bound opponents of the bomb in an emotional communion but provided little strategic guidance.[63] Some activists in the peace movement were sensitive to the dangers of this approach and the peculiarly British foreign policy tradition it mobilised.

To some degree, these criticisms stemmed from the New Left's failure to appreciate the nature of peace movement activism and the moral appeal of unilateralism, as well as its lack of awareness of the difficulties involved in sustaining a protest movement on a day-to-day basis. Its response to the peace movement was, in one sense, old-fashioned: New Left intellectuals sometimes found the lack of immediate influence they exerted on this heterogenous and spontaneous movement frustrating. The New Left was not alone in wanting to 'politicise' CND: the Communist Party and Trotskyist groups also aimed to do this, but all found the culture of the peace movement resistant to external influence. This undoubtedly generated tensions in its relations with the peace movement, encouraging accusations that the New Left was aloof and, despite appearances, constrained by the orthodoxies of conventional political life.

Despite these tensions, the New Left did make an important contribution to the politics of the peace movement because its vanguardist aspirations were counterbalanced and usually subsumed by its enthusiasm for this current, and its willingness to work alongside political groups with different views and aspirations to its own. New Left clubs were run alongside the burgeoning peace movement in a creative and non-sectarian way. As Hall has since noted, this was not true of other political organisations which regarded CND as a 'soft' recruiting ground.[64] For the New Left, more generally, banning the bomb was part of a wider strategy of constructing an international order based on positive neutralism, a perspective which tallied with the ideas of CND. The *ULR* wing of the New Left was most enthusiastic in its presentation of CND as a new kind of political organisation, prefiguring the creation of a more democratic political culture. The relationship between parts of the New Left and CND therefore remained close. Hall recalls that 'the London New Left Club pioneered in central London the propaganda and leafleting for the first CND Aldermaston March, which the Club membership supported *en masse*'.[65] Finally, the early New Left provided a welter of strategic ideas and political commentary which frequently surfaced in the Campaign's literature.[66]

Ultimately though, the peace movement, like the New Left, failed in its immediate political ambitions. The New Left was undoubtedly affected by the downturn in fortunes which the peace movement experienced, rendering the idea of meaningful political initiatives outside the party system harder to justify. The problems which both movements faced were overwhelming. To a great extent, both were the victims of circumstances over which they had little control: for the peace movement, the warmer climate of international affairs in the early 1960s and the increase in superpower co-operation relaxed public anxieties about the imminence of nuclear warfare. The increasing likelihood of a Labour election victory under the auspices of a leader who emerged with a reasonably radical pedigree on foreign policy issues contributed also to the marginalisation of the Campaign at this time.

The complexity of the New Left's involvement with CND – oscillating between tremendous enthusiasm and more critical support – was replaced amongst the later New Left by a more hostile attitude. Anderson's full-scale attack in 1980 upon the peace movement's moralism, bourgeois origins and political naivety ended with an unfavourable comparison with the Vietnam Solidarity Campaign (VSC) of the late 1960s. The difference between the stance towards CND adopted by the early and later New Lefts is telling. For the early New Left, CND opened up possibilities for independent action beyond the party system and the binary logic of the Cold War, and symbolised its commitment to returning political and moral agency to the centre of British politics. The peace movement, it seemed, was the first crack in the frozen political landscape of the 1950s. It was thus received with genuine enthusiasm, as well as some muted criticism. Its later New Left counterparts, especially Anderson, were less enthusiastic about this kind of movement: CND appeared middle class, moralistic and tentative in its political commitments (features which, it is worth noting, were not altogether absent from the VSC, especially since much of the latter's membership had also been involved in CND). This reading of the peace movement resulted in wholesale rejection rather than political solidarity and engagement.

## CONCLUSIONS

The emergence of the peace movement was, in some ways, symptomatic of the slow disintegration of the dominant modes of political representation in Britain after the war; it prefigured the appearance of a range of political and social movements outside the political mainstream. James Hinton suggests that 'as a point of reference for a new rebellious youth culture – itself a product of the very affluence that seemed to be undermining traditional Labour politics – the Aldermaston marchers came to embody a new kind of politics: a forerunner of 1968'.[67] Undoubtedly, the particularity of this kind of politics – developed outside the main parties, across traditional social divisions and against the 'grain' of political life – was little understood.

Indeed, within the peace movement, the ideological dimensions of this politics were particularly confused. Many activists proved reluctant to abandon older traditions of thought and action even whilst celebrating the apparent novelty of their activities. The early New Left, meanwhile, groped towards an understanding of the implications of these new forms of political expression and organisation.[68] The attempt to explain how and why 'the Campaign eludes all the fixed categories of "politics"' was instinctively perceived as central by this movement, unlike its political successors.[69]

NOTES

1   See B.Parekh, 'Discourses on National Identity', *Political Studies*, 42, 1994, pp492-504, p493.
2   See A.Gamble, *The Conservative Nation, op cit*, pp159-201.
3   See P.Weiler, 'British Labour and the Cold War. The Foreign Policy of the Labour Governments 1945-1951', *Journal of British Studies*, 26, 1, 1987, pp54-82.
4   For a polemical account of the relationship between Labour and nationalism, see T.Nairn, 'The Left Against Europe', *New Left Review*, 75, 1972, pp5-102.
5   J.Callaghan, 'In Search of Eldorado: Labour's Colonial Economic Policy', in J.Fyrth (ed), *Labour's High Noon: the Government and the Economy 1945-51*, Lawrence and Wishart, London 1993, pp115-34.
6   N.Harding, *Lenin's Political Thought: Vol.1, Theory and Practice in the Democratic Revolution*, Macmillan, London 1977.
7   See, for instance, J.Callaghan, *Rajani Palme Dutt*, Lawrence and Wishart, London 1993.
8   Davies, *op cit*, p173.
9   P.Worsley, 'Non-alignment and the New Left', in Archer *et al, op cit*, pp88-93, p90.
10  Anderson, *Arguments Within English Marxism, op cit*, p119.
11  M.MacEwen, 'The Two Camps', *New Reasoner*, 4, 1958, pp11-19, p11.
12  Thompson, 'The Segregation of Dissent', *New University*, 6, 1961, pp13-16, p14; see also his 'NATO, neutralism and survival', *ULR*, 4, 1958, pp49-51.
13  See, for instance, G.D.H.Cole, 'Next Steps in British Foreign Policy', *New Reasoner*, 5, 1958, pp8-11.
14  Editorial, 'Hungary, H-bomb, Germany', *ULR*, 2, 1957, pp3-4.
15  Barratt Brown, 'Positive Neutralism: Then and Now', *op cit*, pp81-7.
16  *Ibid*, p86.
17  Thompson, 'The Ends of the Cold War: A Rejoinder', in R.Blackburn (ed), *After the Fall: The Failure of Communism and the Future of Socialism*, Verso, London 1991, pp100-9, p102.
18  Fred Halliday, 'A Reply to Edward Thompson', in Blackburn (ed), *After the Fall, op cit*, pp110-4, p114.
19  Thompson, 'The Ends of the Cold War', *op cit*, p103.
20  P.Worsley, 'Albert Schweitzer and the Liberal Conscience', *New Reasoner*, 3, 1957-8, pp39-54.
21  See the special feature on Algeria in *ULR*, 2, 1957, pp4-8.
22  See Hall's discussion of Rex's ideas in 'Race, articulation and societies structured in dominance', in UNESCO, *Sociological theories: race and colonisation*, UNESCO, Paris 1980, pp305-45.

23 Editorial, *ULR*, 1, 1957, p2.
24 P.Worsley, *The Third World*, Weidenfeld and Nicholson, London 1964, p242.
25 *Ibid*, pvii.
26 Rex, 'Africa's National Congresses and the British Left', *New Reasoner*, 2, 1957, pp56-64.
27 *Ibid*, p60.
28 See, for instance, Rex, *Race, Colonisation and the City*, Routledge and Kegan Paul, London 1973.
29 For an appreciation of Basil Davidson's intellectual and political careers, see T.Hodgkin, 'Where the Paths Began', in C.Fyfe (ed), *African Studies Since 1945: A Tribute to Basil Davidson*, Longman, Edinburgh 1976, pp6-16. Davidson reviewed Hodgkin's book *Nationalism in Colonial Africa* in *ULR*, 1, 1957, pp71-2.
30 Hall, 'Race, articulation and societies structured in dominance', *op cit*.
31 S.Hall and N.Fruchter, 'Notes on the Cuban Dilemma', *New Left Review*, 9, 1961, pp2-11; editorial, 'The Siege of Cuba', *New Left Review*, 7, 1961, pp2-3; P.Anderson and R.Blackburn, 'Cuba, Free Territory of America', *New University*, 4, 1960, pp17-23; R.Blackburn, 'Prologue to the Cuban Revolution', *New Left Review*, 21, 1963, pp52-91.
32 Anderson and Blackburn, 'Cuba, Free Territory of America', *op cit*, p23.
33 Hall and Fruchter, 'Notes on the Cuban Dilemma', *op cit*, p10.
34 Anderson and Blackburn, 'Cuba, Free Territory of America', *op cit*, p23.
35 Anderson, *Arguments Within English Marxism*, *op cit*, p147.
36 Hall, 'The "First" New Left', *op cit*, pp19-20.
37 See, for instance, G.Illtyd Lewis, 'Candy Flossing the Celtic Fringe', *ULR*, 2, 1957, pp34, 39-40.
38 This silence compares unfavourably with the frequent treatment of Northern Ireland in the peace movement newspaper *Peace News* in this period; see Rev.G.McConnell, 'Towards Reconciliation', *Peace News*, 17 October 1958.
39 Anderson and Hall, 'The Politics of the Common Market', *New Left Review*, 4, 1960, pp1-14, p13.
40 *Ibid*, p2.
41 See especially Barratt Brown's scathing review of arguments in favour of the Common Market, 'Neutralism and the Common Market', *New Left Review*, 12, 1961, pp26-7.
42 Mike Artis, 'England: the left and the Common Market', *New University*, 10, 1962, pp23-4, p23.
43 Barratt Brown, 'Neutralism and the Common Market', *op cit*, p26.
44 A.MacIntyre, 'Going into Europe: Symposium III', *Encounter*, February 1963, pp64-74, p65.
45 Nairn, 'The Left Against Europe', *New Left Review*, 75, 1972, pp5-120.
46 Anderson, *Arguments Within English Marxism*, *op cit*, pp145-6.
47 *Ibid*, p147.
48 See E.Hobsbawm, *Nations and Nationalism Since 1780: Image, Myth, Reality*, Cambridge University Press, Cambridge 1990.
49 Hinton, *Protests and Visions*, *op cit*, p162.
50 M.Randle, 'Non-violent direct action in the 1950s and 1960s', in R.Taylor and N.Young (eds), *Campaigns for Peace, British Peace Movements in the Twentieth Century*, Manchester University Press, Manchester 1987, pp131-61.
51 For an account of the change in policy within four key unions, see Howell, *op cit*, pp224-7.
52 For a more detailed account of the unilateralist vote in 1960, see Minkin, *op cit*,

pp107, 109-10, 167, 188-91, 273, 279-80, 283.

53  R.Taylor and C.Pritchard, *The Protest Makers: The British Nuclear Disarmament Movement of 1958- 1965, Twenty Years On*, Pergamon, Oxford 1980, pp80-91, p179.

54  See P.Whannel and S.Hall, 'Direct Action? (interview with Alan Lovell)', *New Left Review*, 8, 1961, pp16-27, p17.

55  P.Duff, *Left, Left, Left,: a personal account of six protest campaigns, 1945-1960*, Allison and Busby, London, 1971, p128.

56  P.Sedgwick, 'Damned Fools in Utopia', *New Left Review*, 13-14, 1962, pp119-28; 'Farewell Grosvenor Square', *New Statesman*, 13 September 1974.

57  R.Taylor, 'The British Nuclear Disarmament Movement of 1958 to 1965 and its legacy to the Left', PhD, University of Leeds, 1983, p454.

58  Thompson, 'The New Left', *Peace News*, 18 September 1959.

59  Rex and Worsley, 'Campaign for a Foreign Policy', *New Left Review*, 4, 1960, pp49-53, p50.

60  Editorial, *New University*, 3, 1960, pp1-3, p1.

61  D.Marquand, 'England, the Bomb, the Marches', *Commentary*, 29, May 1960, p384; 'The Decline of CND', *Socialist Commentary*, 1965, pp25-6.

62  J.B.Priesley, *New Statesman*, 2 November 1957.

63  *Six reasons why Britain must give up the Bomb*, CND pamphlet, 1962, p1.

64  Hall, 'The "First" New Left', *op cit*, p32.

65  Hall, *ibid*, p29.

66  M. Veldman, *Fantasy, the Bomb, and the Greening of Britain: Romantic Protest, 1945-1980*, Cambridge University Press, Cambridge 1994, pp180-203.

67  Hinton, *Protests and Visions, op cit*, p165.

68  See, for instance, R.Williams, 'The New Politics', *New Left Aldermaston Portfolio 1962*, 22 March 1962.

69  Editorial, *New Left Review*, 8, 1961, front cover and pp2-3; the quotation is from the front cover.

# CHAPTER SEVEN

# Conclusions:
# 'Damned Fools in Utopia'?

Having considered the different aspects of the first New Left's intellectual and political practice, this chapter offers an assessment of the movement's significance, as well as a consideration of the weaknesses of much of its historiography. It begins with a brief discussion of the problems raised by comparative examinations of the New Left, and moves on to a consideration of the importance of specifically British factors in considering its fortunes. I then examine the legacy of the movement, charting its ideological influence on the currents involved in '1968', and connections with the later New Left; I also attempt to assess three less explored parallels which reveal much about its significance. Finally, I offer some observations on trends in the historiography of the New Left, and highlight the question of the relationship between intellectuals and political life in Britain in understanding a movement such as this.

## COMPARATIVE ISSUES

The rise of the British New Left was paralleled throughout Western Europe and in North America in the late 1950s and early 1960s. Indeed, it was the example of the French *nouvelle gauche* which inspired the initial efforts of some in Britain. Moreover, some of the theoretical innovations described above can be traced to the influence of New Left thinkers from other countries. All were the product of the changing international context of the post-war period, especially the intensification of the Cold War, the discrediting of 'official' communism and the proliferation of the 'arms race'. Equally significant were the profound social and economic changes common to these different societies, which can be grouped under the headings of affluence, consumerism and classlessness. Not surprisingly, therefore, commentators have noticed the interchange and similarity of ideas between these various movements.[1] Wini Breines, in a recent account of the first wave of the New Left in the United States, describes its eclectic ideological outlook as encompassing 'a critique of bureaucracy, the centrality of everyday life and ... the thought of Lukacs, Korsch, Gramsci, Luxemburg, the Frankfurt School and the council communists'.[2] In her account, this movement's political interests were strikingly similar to those of the first New Left in Britain.

In Britain, as elsewhere, the impact of these changes was mediated by national conditions and traditions. The movement in Britain drew substantially upon national experiences and lineages, devoting a large part of its political and intellectual energy to understanding the nature of British society and politics. Whilst it can be argued that the New Left developed a body of ideas which, despite an indigenous idiom, can be compared with the insights of existentialist Marxists in France, the early work of the Frankfurt School, the ideas of Lukacs and Gramsci, and the writings of Eastern European Marxist humanists, the nature of these parallels remains underresearched; in particular, the degree to which this movement's thinking was shaped by its national context in comparison with other New Left currents.

The party system in which it emerged, the particular history of Labour politics in Britain, the pre-modern nature of the country's political institutions, and the anti-intellectualism of British political culture all exerted a singular impact upon the New Left in this context. These conditions of existence encouraged an ambiguous political identity within the movement. Much of its energy was expended as a lobbying group, conscience and critic of Labour. Despite its proximity to the world of conventional politics, through its involvement in the Labour Party, most participants remained ambivalent about the political system. The New Left undoubtedly broke from the logic of party politics, charting the terrain for later radical movements and celebrating the importance of local and individual experience against the directive and regulatory tendencies of the party elite, corporate interests and the state. This ambiguous identity – involved in, yet opposed to, party politics – generated a series of paradoxes which characterised this movement: it wished to provide a new political identity for those disillusioned with the orthodoxies of socialism, yet it remained closely engaged with developments in the Labour Party; it set out to rethink orthodox socialist ideas but never abandoned socialism as a creed;

and it developed an instinctive sympathy for the popular dimension of political and ideological struggle, yet was fascinated by the avant-garde and modernistic elements of British society and culture.

Overall, the first wave of the New left in Britain lacked a settled political identity. In some ways, the history of the New Left, especially its inability to put down roots outside the political parties, is indicative of the resilience of the party system. The complex history of British labourism, which successive radical and intellectual currents have struggled to displace or reform, is especially important. The story of the New Left's relationship with the Labour Party is an important supplement to accounts of the bids for ideological hegemony within the party which intellectuals from the social democratic tradition have made; these were not the only intellectuals who sought to reshape Labour's traditions and identity.[3] Whilst it is clear that the Labour leadership was opposed to nearly all of the early New Left's ideas and policy proposals, the relationship between the two is more complex than is usually imagined. Indeed this is an especially pertinent issue given the recent accession of Tony Blair to the party's leadership and his relative openness to ideas which have emerged from outside Labour's familiar intellectual universe. Commentators have rarely considered the role of intellectuals beyond or on the fringes of the party in legitimising policy shifts among wider sections of the intelligentsia, either by empathising with the need for 'modernisation' espoused by a figure like Wilson, or by discrediting the ideas of Labour's left. A parallel may be drawn here between the Labour leadership in the 1980s and the ideas associated with the journal *Marxism Today*; this is discussed in greater detail below.

## THE LEGACY OF THE FIRST NEW LEFT

### *New Left Review*, '68 and after

Consideration of this movement also illuminates the larger history of New Left politics in Britain since the 1960s, despite the apparent displacement of the earlier movement by a later generation. The most overlooked connection between this formation and subsequent New Left politics concerns the immediate legacy bequeathed by the first New Left – *New Left Review*, the only surviving institutional manifestation of the movement which began in 1956. The *New Left Review*, albeit in a radically different form, has continued until the present day, and has been both a forum for many crucial debates, and an important vehicle for bringing a British readership into communication with a wide range of key international writers and philosophers. In terms of the subsequent development of *New Left Review*, it is important to appreciate the particular history of the journal's foundation and the organisational and political tensions which seriously affected it from the start. Anderson is right to place events after 1962 in the context of the political weakness which had gripped the journal and the wider movement.

In addition, the question of the ownership of *New Left Review*, which became a central issue as the first New Left fell apart, has remained controversial. The journal has, by and large, maintained the same structure until recently: a core editorial team concerned with the practical administration of the journal's production has worked alongside a diverse, talented and unwieldy board which has struggled to maintain a strong input into the journal's agenda. In the minds of critics, this structure, together with the continuing pattern of ownership of the journal, has allowed a small group to reassert its control over *New Left Review*'s direction and content.[4]

Whilst there are good reasons for maintaining a clear separation between the first and later New Lefts, this division has been drawn far too neatly. A number of points of continuity exist, though the main protagonists in the dispute between them have obscured these connections. The hostile reaction of some former participants in the first wave to the key New Left 'moment' of 1968 has served as a convenient dramatisation of these differences. In fact, a number of figures from this earlier wave of activity played prominent roles in the student protests of 1968 (for example Hall, Saville and Worsley). In thematic terms, the ideas of the first New Left generation largely shaped the political arguments which emerged out of this later conjuncture. This was perhaps ironic given the enthusiasm for '1968' which the group associated with the later *New Left Review* articulated during a period in which the different strands gathered around the journal were more concerned with the rediscovery of older Marxist traditions, and found it hard to carve out a meaningful political role, given their abandonment of practical politics after 1962. This left a space in which these earlier New Left ideas reappeared.[5] The first New Left's challenge to conventional definitions of politics foreshadowed the argument of feminists that the 'personal is political'; its celebration of political activity from below anticipated the explosion of small-scale enterprise and radical initiative in the wake of 1968; and the democratic commitments of this movement encouraged the rejection of orthodox models of political behaviour on the left. The struggles over democracy in the Labour Party from the late 1970s may, for instance, constitute one indirect legacy of the New Left's agenda. Clearly, this earlier movement was not the sole source of these later emphases; as we have seen, its politics and ideas were too contradictory for this to be the case. But it played a critical role in disseminating and legitimating these ideas among the constituencies of future waves of radicalism. As Sheila Rowbotham suggests:

> Strands of the New Left ... could be traced within the Labour Party, Anarchist groups, in Solidarity, International Socialist groups, and trade unions in the mid sixties. From the late sixties they could be seen helping to create 'History Workshops', becoming involved in the women's movement, in left cultural movements and in radical intellectual work.[6]

Moreover, the movement's emphasis upon the political space between everyday life and orthodox party politics – the realm of civil society – has been indirectly influential among later radicals. The New Left extended a longstanding tradition of hostility to statist concepts of socialism, offering to later generations an alternative set of ideas about how the left ought to conduct its political struggles and where it needed to find allies for these.[7]

The movement's impact has, therefore, been more diffuse and interesting than most of its critics allow. The prevailing emphasis upon its *a priori* failure has distracted critical attention from its legacy and potential influence. In fact, rendering a judgement of its success or failure is a more complex matter than is usually assumed. Undoubtedly, the New Left failed – if judged by its publicly stated ambitions. In addition, it expired quickly as a political movement and produced no direct immediate successor. But success can be judged according to different criteria. Commentators have rarely evaluated the balance of possibilities and constraints which affected the movement. It might be plausibly argued, for instance, that the New Left was both the product and victim of circumstances beyond its control. Like the peace movement, its fortunes were profoundly affected by the change in national and international political contexts of the early 1960s, which simultaneously made independent political initiatives harder to justify, and increased the faith of radicals in the Labour Party. These changing circumstances were particularly influential in a party system which militated against independent political movements. The significance of such external factors needs to be weighed against the internal characteristics of the movement.

Furthermore, the politics espoused by the New Left challenged many of the conventional assumptions about British politics which underpin most definitions of political success and failure. The early New Left's 'mission' was to connect politics with culture, ideology and intellectual life more generally; in these different projects it may well have enjoyed some longer term 'success'. To most historians of the movement, though, these do not constitute achievements to be ranked alongside the gaining of influence over Labour Party policy or winning support within trade unions. Judgement of its success or failure depends, therefore, on prior assumptions about the nature of political power and the role of ideas in political life.

## FURTHER CONNECTIONS

Equally, the question of the legacy of the movement is more ambiguous than is sometimes presented. To illustrate this, three possible legacies, which have been underplayed by commentators on the New Left, are briefly explored below, though further research is needed to establish these connections more fully.

### The New Right

The emergence of the New Right as an ideological current in the late 1970s, and governmental force thereafter, has led some critics and participants to speculate upon a possible parallel with this earlier formation and the New Left more generally: did the first New Left provide the first coherent and systematic critique of the weaknesses of the post-war settlement in Britain and undermine the confidence of key sections of the intelligentsia in this social and political system?

The New Right's later critique of the political settlement enshrined in the post-war consensus carried a resonance with the ideas of this earlier group. Both currents rejected statist and corporatist approaches to economic and social management, opposing the increasing regulation of civil and social life, as well as the compromises built into the mixed economy. Clearly, these ideas were articulated with very different political projects, yet the comparison is still uncomfortable for many British radicals, though well established in the literature on the New Left in the United States.[8] According to Leonard Williams:

> The ideologies of the New Left and New Right thus express similar
> attitudes toward the social problems of bureaucracy, alienation, and class

stratification. To remedy these problems, both advocate decentralisation ... Both ideological movements have emerged in the context of an advanced industrial society that has certain characteristic features – state intervention in the economy, an ideology of technical rationality producing a depoliticised public, and a class structure rooted in the development of postindustrialism.[9]

Hilary Wainwright provides a more extensive theoretical account of the relationship between the New Left and New Right. She suggests that Hayek's strictures on the irreducible complexity of individual knowledge allowed the New Right to hijack some of the central features of New Left politics, especially the celebration of the diverse and specific features of social knowledge and identity in opposition to the 'tyranny' of the all-knowing central state.[10] Certainly, the first New Left emphasised the many points in society where initiative, spontaneity and autonomy were increasingly subjected to the regulation and bureaucracy of the post-war state. This perspective led to a celebration of the unrealised capacities and potential of the individual in the modern world: the strong ethical language which this movement deployed shaped its commitment to establish the social and political conditions in which meaningful individuality might be realised. A parallel can be drawn with the New Right's outlook, especially its rejection of the limitations of the mixed economy. This comparison may suggest that some of the tensions within the post-war settlement, which were systematically explored by neo-liberal critics in the 1970s, were sensed by the early New Left, though included within a very different political project. This earlier period may, therefore, constitute an important moment in the history of the British left when a rudimentary alternative, or counter-hegemony, to the post-war consensus was floated, anticipating some features of the project which subsequently uprooted this political settlement. Indeed, one commentator has gone so far as to assert that the New Left aided the New Right by undermining the intellectual basis of welfare policies in this period.[11] The ideological project pursued by this movement may, consequently, illuminate some important questions about the nature of post-war politics in Britain.

## Marxism Today

The re-emergence on the left in the 1980s of a comparable revisionist milieu around the journal *Marxism Today*, which also sought to challenge existing orthodoxies and explore the space between orthodox communism and social democracy, throws the question of this movement's legacy into relief. Central to the latter's politics was an attempt to understand the directions and implications of contemporary social and political changes.[12] As we have seen, a similar emphasis characterised the first New Left, though its perspective was less theoretically coherent. *Marxism Today* echoed the commitment of this earlier movement to confront the left's imagination with the 'realities' of the contemporary world, lambasting the persistence of socialist orthodoxies which prevented a more flexible, popular and hegemonic counter-politics from emerging. These emphases ensured that *Marxism Today* moved into the same territory as the early New Left. The development of Hall's ideas is especially pertinent in providing continuity between these projects although Eric Hobsbawm's role in the journal suggests another line of dissent – the critical communists of 1956. This comparison highlights the recurrent attempt by dissident intellectuals to shift Labour Party thinking and break the historic mould of socialist politics in Britain. In both cases, an attractive and populist journal provided the intellectual space within which unorthodox and challenging ideas could be developed on the fringes of both the academic and political communities. Interestingly, the history of the importation and deployment of Gramscian ideas by British radicals was affected by both of these currents. The similarity extends also to the difficulties which both projects experienced in developing a meaningful and successful political strategy on the basis of these ideas.

There are limitations to this comparison though. The historical contexts which spawned these ventures differed greatly, as did the milieux which sustained them. Despite superficial similarities – a lengthy period of Conservative electoral dominance and crisis in the Labour Party, these conjunctures were markedly dissimilar. In the case of the first New Left, no single project or perspective ever drove this formation, making it far less cohesive than *Marxism Today*. It remained a political movement of sorts, until 1962, whilst *Marxism Today* is more accurately characterised as a milieu with a particular history stretching back to the the internal struggles of the Communist Party in the 1970s. The idea that *Marxism Today* constituted the direct successor of this earlier group is particularly problematic in that the first New Left's legacy was both complex and plural. Its political ideas unravelled in a number of directions, with the result that its mantle has been claimed by individuals who remain steadfastly opposed to the reassessment of the socialist tradition, as well as by more 'revisionist' thinkers. The journal

*Socialist Register*, founded by Saville and Miliband, which has been committed to the continuation of older socialist traditions, is equally heir to the politics of this movement.

## New Social Movements in Britain

The history of the first New Left is revealing about the problems facing independent political currents in the British context. Its inability to survive on the fringes of the conventional party system should be interpreted not only as an *a priori* sign of weakness but also as indicative of the gravitational pull exerted by the Labour Party for such movements, as well as the hostility with which Labour has often responded to them. Equally important is the centralised pattern of British political life more generally. Rather than dismissing the New Left as naive or incompetent therefore, more is to be gained from retracing the intellectual and political efforts this movement made to define a position on the margins of the conventional political system. The New Left was thoughtful in its attempt to interpret its political and social contexts, yet politically immobile in response to both. The movement's most important legacy may well lie, therefore, in its exploration of this terrain – between the orthodox political world and the social experience of individuals and communities – which later movements and campaigns have, likewise, sought to occupy.

The implications of its ambivalent relationship to the conventional political system have been obscured by the two predominant interpretations of the left's extra-parliamentary traditions. For example, commentators such as Thompson have observed:

> how very large has been the left presence in Britain in the past 50 years...
> a presence which is not to be identified with official party-political
> expressions. It has been there in the Left Book Club, in Aid for Spain, in
> the Common Wealth Party, in the New Left, in CND, in movements of
> social reform and cultural expression, all of them more vigorous and
> (perhaps) more effective than anything the politicians could offer.[13]

In this perspective, the New Left kept alive a radical, non-party tradition which has proved as enduring as the achievements of the Labour Party. Hilary Wainwright makes a similar case, pointing to the importance of the tradition of non-state forms of public action which the New Left developed in numerous ways and which the new social movements continue. She sees this praxis as pertinent, given popular disenchantment with statist forms of social provision throughout Europe. Her concern is to re-establish a historical link between contemporary social movements and New Left politics: 'the experiments towards a participative, anti-paternalist view of socialism of fifteen, ten, even five years ago, have been forgotten'.[14] The weakness of such arguments is that they can serve to encourage a teleological approach to these currents, yoking them together into an unfolding tradition and assuming that they constitute a coherent political alternative. Sometimes this perspective relies on 'heroic' celebration rather than hard analysis in its approach to these movements.

## NEW LEFT HISTORIOGRAPHY AND THE ROLE OF INTELLECTURALS

The ideas of Thompson and Hilary Wainwright have emerged as responses to the dominant school of left historiography outlined in the Introduction to this book. This school has too often written extra-parliamentary currents out of the story of socialism in Britain. This 'realist' approach reproduces the dominant values of the British political system, emphasising immediate access to policy, the influence of political elites and the centrifugal nature of the British parliamentary system. It can result in small and unorthodox political currents being left out of accounts of the labour movement or Labour Party. This 'realist' perspective has failed to capture the diversity and vitality of extra-parliamentary politics in Britain and forecloses some interesting and important questions about the process by which currents such as the first New Left are marginalised. Commentators imbued with this perspective point, sometimes gleefully, to the tradition of 'heroic failure' which seems to characterise the New Left in Britain.[15] This approach is not confined to Britain, however: Wini Breines' study of the New Left in the United States is motivated by a similar objection to the methodological assumptions of the bulk of this movement's interpreters:

> With only a few exceptions, commentators from the political right, left and centre, from conservative social scientists to Leninists, have been almost uniformly critical of the new left. Whilst their political standpoints diverge, most studies share the view that the new left was a utopian, anti-organisational, even anti-political movement which, for these reasons, was bound to fail. That it appeared to fail is taken as proof of the arguments.[16]

Neither overly optimistic nor 'realist' interpretations provide a wholly convincing picture of a movement such as the first wave of the New Left in Britain. A more flexible and appropriate methodology would point to historical antecedents, analyse the political space which such currents seek to occupy, and simultaneously address the relationship between these and the major political parties. Commentators who have combined these emphases have produced some perceptive analyses of the impact of new social movements and small parties in West European countries.[17] A similar approach may well throw new light upon New Left movements. This kind of analysis tends to incorporate the specificity of different political contexts, exploring what one commentator terms the 'political opportunity structures' of each national situation.[18]

What is absent from nearly all interpretations of the New Left phenomenon is an adequate characterisation of the role of intellectuals and their complex relationship to political movements and parties. This reproduces a more general characteristic within the historiography of British socialism: the impact of intellectuals and currents of thought which sit uneasily within more conventional political frameworks have been neglected. Consequently, the question of the relationship between mainstream political life and innovative intellectual practice has featured all too rarely in historical writing on the British left.[19] Thus, little attention has been paid to the possibility that marginal and unconventional forces, such as the New Left, are sometimes free to develop the most imaginative assessments of the direction and nature of contemporary social change. As Jack Newfield argues, 'there is a sense in which it is always the untypical few who have the verve and energy to first articulate what is typical of their times'.[20]

It follows from this observation that the first wave of the New Left can be placed in an entirely different context from those hitherto explored by its critics. It can be seen as providing a snapshot, in a particular historical setting, of the troubled relationship between political and intellectual practice in Britain. It is significant that the most important and resonant antecedents of the movement were also overwhelmingly intellectual in their composition and predilections, in particular the guild socialist movement of the 1920s and the Left Book Club of the 1930s. These currents, despite their differing contexts, manifested a recurrent commitment to a wider definition of the left's constituency, usually envisaging a more diverse social coalition, and a more broadly conceived political project, intertwining cultural, moral and social analysis with more orthodox political and economic concerns.

Without overstressing their similarities or devising a teleology of dissident intellectual currents on the British left, the continuity of this perspective is striking. To some degree, this can be traced to the troubled relationship between intellectuals and the Labour Party, especially the anti-intellectualism which has often characterised Labour's political culture. For 'progressive intellectuals', the Labour Party has proved a difficult, inhospitable location. The project of organising and sustaining an independent space, where more intellectually orientated and theoretically innovative work might be linked to political practice, has proved appealing on different occasions throughout this century, especially as new social strata have emerged from fundamental changes in the technical division of labour in British society. In Rustin's view, this movement, and its emphasis on culture:

> reflects the enhanced importance of cultural work and cultural workers in a society in which the service, information and people-processing industries, and the new occupations they generate, have become central. As a rising class fraction in the 1960s, these groupings were radical and optimistic in their sentiments and aspirations. Thus the New Left found some real resonance and social roots.[21]

In political terms, the apparent imperviousness of Britain's elites to political change, and the resistance to intellectual and ideological novelty within its political culture, have often combined to leave intellectuals without a clear role. These factors have, on occasions, resulted in independent political-cultural initiatives, outside or alongside the orthodox political world, with the ultimate goal of reforming or refounding the party system. A host of radical campaigns, from CND to the Anti-Nazi League of the 1970s, have arisen, in part, as responses to these conditions. This aspiration has taken different ideological and political forms: the formation of the Social Democratic Party in 1981 constitutes a recent manifestation of this process, though it was influenced by a particular set of intellectual and political antecedents.[22] These different attempts to 'break the mould' of the party system have been repeatedly stymied by the capacity of the Labour Party to resist – and occasionally co-opt – novel ideas, as well as the tendency of the political system in Britain to hive off ideological innovation. This has generated a recurrent paradox for radical members of the intelligentsia in Britain. It also provides a challenging and novel context for interpreting the politics of the first New Left.

The problem of relating intellectual life to politics was especially acute in the late 1950s when the Cold War polarised ideology and culture so deeply. The first wave of the New Left played a key role in clearing a makeshift space between the poles of Cold War orthodoxy, in which critical ideas about both Western and Eastern European societies could be aired. As a number of former participants have noted, the turn to virulent anti-communism was largely absent in Britain;[23] for a small number of ex-communists, the early New Left provided an environment where a critique of communism could be developed in a socialist atmosphere.

The early New Left also coincided with an important moment in the history of the British intelligentsia, parts of which had become detached from the accepted political positions of the day and had begun to protest against the constraints and limitations of post-war society. The virulence of the resulting critique (by, among others, John Osborne, Shelagh Delaney, Lindsay Anderson, Alan Sillitoe and Dennis Potter), as well as the range of questions this unleashed about culture and politics, appealed strongly to the New Left, as we have seen. Simultaneously, these writers, artists and critics articulated a libertarian ethos which played a key role in the political ideas of both the left and right in subsequent years.

The New Left marks an important stage in the intellectual development of these and other intellectual figures. Increasingly impatient with the inability of Labour to comprehend the changing basis of society and politics, dissident intellectuals have, since the late 1960s, turned to theoretical sources outside Britain to challenge existing orthodoxies. The importance of Gramscian thought in this process is now well documented: as Forgacs shows, this has provided a fertile source of concepts and methodological insights, as well as a flexibility and malleability which have allowed for very different political interpretations.[24] The first wave of the New Left should be inserted into the story of the importation of Gramscian ideas into Britain, not due to its familiarity with this body of thought but because some of the theoretical and methodological shifts registered by this formation paved the way for the popularity of concepts such as hegemony, organic intellectuals and the war of position. Indeed, this process goes beyond Forgacs' suggestion that it was the New Left's 'work on culture... [which] provided a framework, an intellectual space, within which Gramsci, or at least a certain side of Gramsci, could be made visible and readable'.[25] In a striking, but since neglected, contemporary article, Gwyn Williams explored this parallel more fully:

This particular consonance between many of the concepts of Gramsci and those of the current British left is not the freakish coincidence it appears. English concern with the 'Establishment', with a suspected oligarchical tendency within modern parliamentary democracy, is but one manifestation of the sustained process of critical re-examination to which Socialist thinkers are subjecting their basic doctrines. This 're-thinking' is the product of a particular constellation of political and cultural forces. The exhaustion of the Labour Movement's ethic and its electoral defeats coincide with the apparent establishment in Britain of a new form of 'managerial' and 'affluent society' based on active consent and clearly entering its 'moment of hegemony'. Confronted with this bleak prospect, increasing numbers of British Socialists are abandoning the apparently bankrupt orthodoxy of Fabian empiricism and seeking enlightenment in a reinterpretation, in modern terms, of their older and more fundamental traditions.[26]

This comparison was overstated and has since been questioned by Gwyn Williams himself,[27] yet it does articulate the possibility that larger theoretical shifts were effected at this time, though expressed in an inherited, largely empirical idiom. Undoubtedly, the New Left's exploration of the interrelations between moral, political and cultural questions was often rudimentary, yet this and other intellectual innovations have been obscured by the predominant image of the populism and romanticism with which it was supposedly afflicted.

Obviously, there are dangers in re-assembling a particular moment in the political past of these figures: the temptation to bathe the period in nostalgia or to exaggerate its significance is strong. The kind of intellectual and political ferment which is described here is lacking in the contemporary context, making it all the easier to romanticise the early New Left. Sympathetic historians are sometimes guilty of simplistic extrapolation from earlier periods and contexts, as if these untried ideas might provide the answers to contemporary problems. Yet it is clear that some of the first New Left's intellectual and political achievements have been substantially underestimated. The New Left was particularly effective when it challenged the orthodoxies of conventional socialist thought and sensed the long-term significance of social and political developments which have fundamentally altered the landscape of modern Britain. At its sharpest, New Left praxis followed Williams' intonation: 'only connect'. His emphasis upon the totality of the social process enabled these writers to establish important connections between the difficulties facing contemporary socialists and the emergence of new political and social questions. If aspects of this project have survived in British politics, they are enshrined in those individuals and groups committed to open discussion and innovative thought, unmoved by the lure of orthodoxy, and embattled against the dominant ideas of the day.

## NOTES

1   Young, *An Infantile Disorder, op cit*, p20; Jack Newfield, *A Prophetic Minority: The American New Left*, Anthony Blond, London 1967, p21.
2   W.Breines, *Community and Organisation in the New Left, op cit*, p16.
3   See R.Desai, *Intellectuals and Socialism: 'Social Democrats' and the Labour Party*, Lawrence and Wishart, London 1994.
4   See Willie Thompson, 'Tom Nairn and the Crisis of the State', *op cit*, p311; J.Ezard, 'Claims of coup as mass resignations from 17-strong editorial group assist small socialist magazine in search of £25,000 savings', *The Guardian*, 5 March 1992.
5   Chun, *The British New Left, op cit*.
6   S.Rowbotham, 'The Women's Movement and Organising for Socialism', *op cit*, p34.
7   Wainright, *Arguments for a New Left, op cit*.
8   See A.Arblaster, 'Review of Arguments for a New Left: Answering the Free Market Right by Hilary Wainwright', *The Guardian*, 25 January 1994.
9   L.Williams, 'Ideological Parallels between the New Left and the New Right', *Social Science Journal*, 24, 3, 1987, pp317-27, p321, p326.
10  Wainwright, *Arguments for a New Left, op cit*.
11  M.Rustin, 'The New Left and the Present Crisis', *op cit*, p71.
12  See Hall, 'The Great Moving Right Show', in *The Hard Road to Renewal, op cit*, pp9-56.
13  Thompson, 'Preface', in MacEwen, *The Greening of a Red, op cit*, pxii.
14  Wainwright, *Arguments for a New Left, op cit*, pxvi.
15  Paul Anderson, 'Togetherness', *New Statesman and Society*, 4 February 1994, p45; though glee is absent in this case.
16  Breines, *Community and Organisation in the New Left*, p1.
17  See, for instance, C.Rootes, 'Student radicalism: the politics of moral protest and legitimation problems in the modern capitalist state', *Theory and Society*, 9, 3, 1980, pp473-502; G.Ross and J.Jenson, 'French Rainbows. Towards a New "New Left" in France?', *Socialist Review*, 18, 1, pp98-104; F.Müller-Rommel, 'New Politics Movements and "New Politics" Parties in Western Europe', in R.J.Dalton and M.Kuechler (eds), *Challenging the Political Order: New Social and Political Movements in Western Democracies*, Polity, Cambridge 1980, pp209-31; A.Scott, *Ideology and the New Social Movements*, Unwin Hyman, London 1990.
18  H.Kitschelt, 'Political opportunity structures and political protest: anti-nuclear movements in four democracies', *British Journal of Political Science*, 16, 1986, pp57-85.
19  There are of course important exceptions here; see, for instance, Stuart MacIntyre, *A Proletarian Science, op cit*.
20  Newfield, *A Prophetic Minority, op cit*, p14.

21  M.Rustin, 'The New Left as a Social Movement', in Archer, *et al*, *op cit*, pp117-128, p116.
22  See H.Stephenson, *Claret and Chips: the rise of the SDP*, Michael Joseph, London 1982.
23  Thompson, *Open Letter to Kolakowski*, *op cit*, p305.
24  Forgacs, 'Gramsci and Marxism in Britain', *op cit*.
25  *Ibid*, p74.
26  G.Williams, 'The concept of 'egemonia' in the thought of Antonio Gramsci: some notes on interpretation', *Journal of the History of Ideas*, 21, 1960, pp586-99, p596.
27  Forgacs, 'Gramsci and Marxism in Britain', *op cit*, p74.

# Index